Laughing
Matters

OTHER TITLES IN THE LONGMAN TOPICS READER SERIES

Laughing Matters

MARVIN DIOGENES
Stanford University

New York   San Francisco   Boston
London   Toronto   Sydney   Tokyo   Singapore   Madrid
Mexico City   Munich   Paris   Cape Town   Hong Kong   Montreal

Senior Sponsoring Editor: Virginia L. Blanford
Senior Marketing Manager: Sandra McGuire
Project Coordination, Text Design, and Electronic Page Makeup:
    GGS Book Services PMG
Cover Design Manager: Wendy Ann Fredericks
Cover Photo: © Purestock/SuperStock
Senior Manufacturing Buyer: Roy L. Pickering, Jr.
Printer and Binder: Courier Corporation—Westford
Cover Printer: Coral Graphics Services, Inc.

For permission to use copyrighted material, grateful acknowledgment
is made to the copyright holders on pp. 272–274, which are hereby
made part of this copyright page.

Library of Congress Cataloging-in-Publication Data
Laughing matters / [compiled by] Marvin Diogenes.
        p. cm.—(A longman topics reader)
    Includes bibliographical references.
    ISBN-13: 978-0-321-43490-6
    ISBN-10: 0-321-43490-0
    1. Humorous stories.   2. Wit and humor--History and criticism.
I. Diogenes, Marvin.

PN6071.H795L38 2009
813'.4--dc22   2008031135

Please visit us at www.pearsonhighered.com

ISBN-13: 978-0-321-43490-6
ISBN-10: 0-321-43490-0

3 4 5 6 7 8 9 10—CW—12 11

CHAPTER 7 Imitation Is the Sincerest Form of Comedy 237

Many cultural commentators have noted, not always with approval, that we live in an age dominated by forms of comedy, particularly satire and parody. Comic rhetoric—featuring irony, sarcasm, and various forms of lampoon and caricature—has become a dominant form of public discourse readily available through traditional print forms as well as through the electronic media—think YouTube and blogs—that drive popular culture. While some predicted or called for an "end to irony" after the trauma of September 11, it's clear that political satire and other comic genres remain resonant and powerful. From the comic writing of Molly Ivins, Dave Barry, and a host of others to the headlines of *The Daily Show, The Onion,* and *Saturday Night Live*'s "Weekend Update," contemporary comedy plays a prominent role in defining and delivering critical perspectives on public issues, handing down judgments on the morality and effectiveness of policy decisions, and mocking the mistakes of elected leaders and other policymakers.

Given this cultural moment, I found it timely and appropriate to move toward a more systematic rendering of the principles that propel comic rhetoric. While I've found that people in general and thus students as well resist thinking too rigorously about humor, I nonetheless decided that taking an analytical approach was worth the risk. I'm arguing in this book that humor is fundamentally rhetorical (i.e., aimed at persuasion). To help me develop this argument, I'll depend on a long-dead theorist whom I've come to think of as a friend, Henri Bergson, whose book-length essay *Laughter*, published in 1900, provides a starting point for developing a method for understanding the workings of comic rhetoric.

Though Bergson doesn't use the word "rhetoric," he argues that laughter is society's means of correcting behavior that is less than fully human. Bergson had a sunny view of human potential—he believed we're capable of acting rightly from moment to moment, taking the needs of others into account and responding well. For him, humor brings the errant individual back into line by illuminating antisocial behavior. Since his time, we're more likely to turn his argument about the purpose of laughter upside-down: the individual—the stand-up comic, the ironic columnist working in the tradition of Jonathan Swift, the host of a satirical news show—corrects a society that has become all too inhuman in its operations. I'll rely on the key premise from Bergson, though: Comedy argues about fundamental issues and should thus be considered central rather than peripheral to our lives as citizens. This book, then, will serve as a guide to analyzing how comic arguments are made and also to crafting effective arguments using the rhetorical strategies particular to comedy. In compiling the selections, I was reminded that the tradition of comic critique has had a long life, so I've included pieces from the 18th century on; though the diction of the older readings may seem archaic at times, the irreverent tone will be familiar.

While many books featuring comic writing have come out in recent years—Jon Stewart's *America: The Book*; Al Franken's diatribes railing against the right; the *Mirth of a Nation* biannual anthologies edited by Michael Rosen; *The Onion* anthologies of their online newspaper stories; a slew of books from comics including Margaret Cho, Ellen DeGeneres, Jerry Seinfeld, et al.—there is not yet a reader that takes a rhetorical view of the comedy that surrounds us. That's the reader you're holding in your hands.

I owe many thanks to my colleagues in the Program in Writing and Rhetoric at Stanford for their support during the creation of this book: Andrea Lunsford, Clyde Moneyhun, Claude Reichard, Corinne Arraez, Alyssa O'Brien, Mark Feldman, Helle Rytkonen, Nancy Buffington, Christine Alfano, Kevin DiPirro, Wendy Goldberg, Jonathan Hunt, Jonah Willihnganz, Donna Hunter, Ambassador Jerry White, and many others. They have generously shared their wisdom and, most importantly, their laughter. I am also grateful to Lynn Huddon and Ginny Blanford, my editors at Longman, assistant editor Rebecca Gilpin, and the reviewers who gave useful suggestions during the development of this book: Bev Hogue, Marietta College; Deborah A. Mael, Newbury College; Janice McIntire-Strasburg, St. Louis University; Richard Nordquist, Armstrong Atlantic State University; and Steve Sherwood, Texas Christian University.

MARVIN DIOGENES

INTRODUCTION TO
LAUGHING MATTERS

Let's agree at the start that comedy works in mysterious ways. Laughter and its dour denial, "That's not funny," are not easily explained, as our responses to jokes depend on a complex slew of individual, interpersonal, and cultural variables. This book will not attempt to resolve the mystery or to pronounce any kind of last word on the subject, though I will try to add something to the long, earnest conversation about comedy's methods and purposes, as well as provide a range of examples of comic writing. We will look at several theories of comedy, considering both its fundamental strategies and social uses, and especially at how writers use humor to make arguments to change the people and culture around them. Thus, the intended audience for this collection consists of students in writing classes focused on persuasion and argument as well as those studying contemporary culture and the role of comedy in public life. *Laughing Matters* will offer students models and ideas for three kinds of projects: analytical essays showing how comic texts make us laugh while persuading us; research-based essays exploring a particular kind of comedy, a particular comic, or the role of comedy in relation to a specific issue; and comic arguments that use humor to persuade.

THEORIES OF COMEDY

The writer E. B. White, well known for children's classics like *Stuart Little* and *Charlotte's Web* and the venerable writing guide *The Elements of Style* (growing out of the durable lessons of his teacher William Strunk), warns in his short essay "Some Remarks on Humor" that humor is a delicate thing, and that analysis runs the risk of killing the subject: "Humor can be dissected, as a frog can, but the thing dies in the process and the innards are discouraging to any but the pure scientific mind." He has a point, perhaps, but I'm proposing that knowing more about how comedy works might add to the richness of our emotional and intellectual experience of comic works. While I'm not recommending that analysis replace appreciation and pleasure, I'm suggesting that a critical awareness of comic principles can co-exist peacefully and productively with the immediate jolt of laughter. I certainly hope the readings in the book will provoke laughter—and then further thought about what the laughter means. In relation to humor's larger social purpose, a guiding premise of *Laughing Matters* is that laughter signals agreement with the writer's argument or worldview. In other words, the audience's laughter is a mark of successful persuasion or at least successful connection.

While theories of comedy abound (many are referenced in the bibliography), I will depend on French philosopher Henri Bergson to elucidate the social role of comedy. He argues that laughter spotlights antisocial behavior, "the mechanical encrusted on the living." First, then, laughter is a form of critique of how humans fall into predictable patterns of behavior. Bergson then offers a more specific rhetorical purpose—laughter is a corrective, moving the audience and perhaps the target of the laughter to action that will make them better citizens and better people. He states, "What life and society require of each of us is a constantly alert attention that discerns the outlines of the present situation, together with a certain elasticity of mind and body to enable us to adapt ourselves in consequence." We're required to respond *in the moment*, not depending on formulas and platitudes that may have served us well enough in the past. Laughter exposes us when we don't live up to that high standard of human conduct. When we laugh at the posturings of politicians, for instance, as presented in a skit on *Saturday Night Live* or skewered in Jon Stewart's opening monologue on *The Daily Show*, we're in a sense voting with our laughter, letting the politicians know that the targeted behavior must change if they want to remain in office.

Other theories of comedy focus more on structure and the intellectual and psychological moves that audiences must make to get the joke. Murray Davis, a 20th-century theorist, lays out how laughter stems from our recognition of disparate realities or systems of meaning brought into unexpected conjunction with each other. Puns illustrate this structure at its most basic, as a single word is made to function in two different ways, evoking two different though simultaneously occurring realities. Davis argues that the more complex and ingeniously crafted the relationship of the two systems brought into comic play, the bigger the comic payoff. He concerns himself less with humor as argument than with humor as a kind of intellectual puzzle; considering Bergson's and Davis's ideas together allows us to consider both rhetorical purpose and comic structure.

COMIC RHETORIC

While the first two chapters of the book offer a theoretical frame for comedy (courtesy of Bergson, Davis, and several other writers) and a set of essays analyzing particular cultural uses of comedy (providing models for one kind of essay students might be assigned to write), I'll use another philosopher, Aristotle, to help organize the comic readings in Chapters 3–7. How does comedy connect to classical thinking about rhetoric? Developing his view of rhetoric from the teachings of his teacher Plato, who had serious doubts about rhetoric's allegiance to truth, Aristotle asserted that rhetoric helps us discuss and debate questions that cannot ultimately be decided once and for all. The immediate circumstances and the history of the issue at hand commingle and intertwine with the character of the speaker and the nature of the audience, giving us options for creating effective appeals. Comedy, too, can be understood in this way, as contingent on the specifics in play at the moment. What's funny (and persuasive) can't be fixed permanently, though, as with rhetoric, we can develop principles and practices to guide us in the quest to use humor well.

Aristotle, who tended to put things into categories, divided the art of persuasion into three major forms: the deliberative, or political, focusing on decision-making in government assemblies; the judicial, or forensic, focusing on questions of right and wrong, justice and punishment; and the ceremonial, or epideictic, focusing on what's admirable in human character and behavior. In each of these contexts, we can apply Bergson's premise that automatic responses pose a threat to the ethical and humane operation of society and Davis's insight that humor grows out of disparate systems being brought into a single frame.

Chapter 3, focused on deliberative, decision-making rhetoric, ranges from weighty political issues and marriage proposals to how best to give advice and how decisions are made in business settings. In all of these selections, drawn from Irish, English, and American writers of the last three centuries, the writers use comic appeals to guide us toward proper behavior. Aristotle notes that deliberative rhetorical situations often generate a tension between self-serving, expedient policies and more altruistic, moral courses of actions, and you'll see this conflict in many of the selections in this chapter, particularly Jonathan Swift's "A Modest Proposal," perhaps the most celebrated piece of ironic argument in English. Chapter 4, focused on judicial rhetoric, shows how legal thinking and discourse conventions can be brought into fruitful comic dialogue with a range of other contexts, providing strong examples of Davis's theory of how comic structure works (we'll see cartoon characters engaged in a lawsuit and Supreme Court justices playing basketball). While legal proceedings generally aim to determine guilt and innocence in courtrooms and through formal documents, several of the readings in this chapter focus on the laws of family relations, setting out to preempt criminal domestic behavior by laying down the law clearly in advance.

Chapters 5 and 6 are devoted to the capacious category of ceremonial rhetoric, which assesses who or what should be praised and who criticized. This form of rhetoric, while linked to public events like graduation ceremonies and funerals (we'll hear a toast at a military celebration and a eulogy), also surrounds us in everyday life, from casual conversations to talk shows, and in literary forms such as essays and memoirs reflecting on past experience and pointing out what's admirable and despicable in how people choose to live (and, in one case, how to punctuate). Chapter 6 focuses more narrowly on gendered behavior and relations between the genders, a nod to the many comic renderings of the battle between the sexes, from situation comedies to the plays of Shakespeare and the novels of Jane Austen. Chapter 7, which presents a selection of parodies, from scholarly and scientific essays to grammar guides, can also be considered to operate in the ceremonial mode, in many cases simultaneously praising through imitation and critiquing through illuminating the mechanical moves that writers may fall prey to when following the formal conventions of a genre or indulging a strong style of their own.

Again, the guiding idea of this book is that comedy asks more of us than laughter—comedy also guides us to reflection and ultimately to judgment and action. Comedy aims to change us and society, first by exposing what needs to be corrected, and then by pointing us toward a better way, demanding that we act with full awareness of how our choices in each moment shape the world around us.

How Comedy Works

Introduction

How do we know what's funny? Let's return to the premise about society in Henri Bergson's *Laughter*: "What life and society require of each of us is a constantly alert attention that discerns the outlines of the present situation, together with a certain elasticity of mind and body to enable us to adapt ourselves in consequence."

Perhaps the elasticity of mind Bergson expects from us connects to how we know when to laugh; when we laugh, we confirm our superiority to the target of the laughter, affirming our agreement with the comic who has exposed the mechanical, absentminded, antisocial behavior. Bergson further connects elasticity to a strong moral sense of the obligations we have to each other as members of a community—focusing on individual needs leads us to self-serving and predictable behavior, while putting the needs of others first ideally leads to a kind of suppleness and flexibility in our actions.

Other theorists in this chapter, primarily Davis, emphasize incongruity, disruption, dissonance, and the upending of logical systems as the core of comedy. Comics don't let things go along as planned—that leads to sleepwalking and absentmindedness, droning herds of people on mental and spiritual autopilot. The audience capable of receiving comic persuasion must be active, knowing the systems called into play and recognizing the incongruous elements, the "funny," and how this initial dissonance can give way to a new order, a new system that helps us to see the world in a different way.

Jimmy Carr and Lucy Greeves address the way comedy serves the individual, and how laughter can contribute to psychological well-being along with supporting congenial social relationships. Robin Hemley moves us from theory toward the realm of comic

1

practice, making the abstruse theories presented earlier in the chapter more accessible by leavening Bergson's dictates with the comic stylings of his young daughter.

Excerpt from *Laughter*

The Comic in General—the Comic Element in Forms and Movement— Expansive Force of the Comic

HENRI BERGSON

Headnotes/Things to Look For

French philosopher Henri Bergson (1859–1941) published Le Rire (Laughter) *in 1900, offering a theory of comedy that draws on literary examples as well as astute observation of the dynamics of social life. Bergson's other major works include* Time and Free Will *and* Creative Evolution. *He was awarded the Nobel Prize in Literature in 1927.*

Note how Bergson characterizes society as requiring constant attention and adjustment from each individual member, a version of the concept of kairos, *or timely attention to the immediate situation. Bergson sees the greatest danger not from social demands for conformity, which can be resisted, but rather from the sleeping souls of the absentminded living on autopilot.*

◆

. . . [W]e shall not aim at imprisoning the comic spirit within a definition. We regard it, above all, as a living thing. However trivial it may be, we shall treat it with the respect due to life. We shall confine ourselves to watching it grow and expand. Passing by imperceptible gradations from one form to another, it will be seen to achieve the strangest metamorphoses. We shall disdain nothing we have seen. Maybe we may gain from this prolonged contact, for the matter of that, something more flexible than an abstract definition,—a practical, intimate acquaintance, such as springs from a long companionship. And maybe we may also find that, unintentionally we have made an acquaintance that is useful. For the comic spirit has a logic of its own, even in its wildest eccentricities. It has a method in its madness. It dreams, I admit, but it conjures up in its dreams visions that are at once accepted and understood by the whole of a social group. Can it then fail to throw light for us on the way that human imagination works, and more particularly social, collective, and popular imagination? Begotten of real life and akin to art, should it not also have something of its own to tell us about art and life?

At the outset we shall put forward three observations which we look upon as fundamental. They have less bearing on the actually comic than on the field within which it must be sought.

I

The first point to which attention should be called is that the comic does not exist outside the pale of what is strictly *human*. A landscape may be beautiful, charming and sublime, or insignificant and ugly; it will never be laughable. You may laugh at an animal, but only because you have detected in it some human attitude or expression. You may laugh at a hat, but what you are making fun of, in this case, is not the piece of felt or straw, but the shape that men have given it,—the human caprice whose mould it has assumed. It is strange that so important a fact, and such a simple one too, has not attracted to a greater degree the attention of philosophers. Several have defined man as "an animal which laughs." They might equally well have defined him as an animal which is laughed at; for if any other animal, or some lifeless object, produces the same effect, it is always because of some resemblance to man, of the stamp he gives it or the use he puts it to.

Here I would point out, as a symptom equally worthy of notice, the *absence of feeling* which usually accompanies laughter. It seems as though the comic could not produce its disturbing effect unless it fell, so to say, on the surface of a soul that is thoroughly calm and unruffled. Indifference is its natural environment, for laughter has no greater foe than emotion. I do not mean that we could not laugh at a person who inspires us with pity, for instance, or even with affection, but in such a case we must, for the moment, put our affection out of court and impose silence upon our pity. In a society composed of pure intelligences there would probably be no more tears, though perhaps there would still be laughter; whereas highly emotional souls, in tune and unison with life, in whom every event would be sentimentally prolonged and re-echoed, would neither know nor understand laughter. Try, for a moment, to become interested in everything that is being said and done; act, in imagination, with those who act, and feel with those who feel; in a word, give your sympathy its widest expansion: as though at the touch of a fairy wand you will see the flimsiest of objects assume importance, and a gloomy hue spread over everything. Now step aside, look upon life as a disinterested spectator: many a drama will turn into a comedy. It is enough for us to stop our ears to the sound of music in a room, where dancing is going on, for the dancers at once to appear ridiculous. How many human actions would stand a similar test? Should we not see many of them suddenly pass from grave to gay, on isolating them from the accompanying music of sentiment? To produce the whole of its effect, then, the comic demands something like a momentary anesthesia of the heart. Its appeal is to intelligence, pure and simple.

This intelligence, however, must always remain in touch with other intelligences. And here is the third fact to which attention should be drawn. You would hardly appreciate the comic if you felt yourself isolated from others. Laughter appears to stand in need of an echo. Listen to it carefully: it is not an articulate, clear, well-defined sound; it is something which would fain be prolonged by reverberating from one to another, something beginning with a crash, to continue in successive rumblings, like thunder in a mountain. Still, this reverberation cannot go on forever. It can travel within as wide a circle as you please; the circle remains, nonetheless, a closed one. Our laughter is always the laughter of a group. It may, perchance, have happened to you, when seated in a railway carriage or at *table d'hôte*, to hear travellers relating to one another stories which must have been comic to them, for they laughed heartily. Had you been one of their company, you would have laughed like them, but, as you were not, you had no desire whatever to do so. A man who was once asked why he did not weep at a sermon when everybody else was shedding tears replied: "I don't belong to the parish!" What that man thought of tears would be still more true of laughter. However spontaneous it seems, laughter always implies a kind of secret freemasonry, or even complicity, with other laughers, real or imaginary. How often has it been said that the fuller the theatre, the more uncontrolled the laughter of the audience! On the other hand, how often has the remark been made that many comic effects are incapable of translation from one language to another, because they refer to the customs and ideas of a particular social group! It is through not understanding the importance of this double fact that the comic has been looked upon as a mere curiosity in which the mind finds amusement, and laughter itself as a strange, isolated phenomenon, without any bearing on the rest of human activity. Hence those definitions which tend to make the comic into an abstract relation between ideas: "an intellectual contrast," "a patent absurdity," etc., definitions which, even were they really suitable to every form of the comic, would not in the least explain why the comic makes us laugh. How, indeed, should it come about that this particular logical relation, as soon as it is perceived, contracts, expands and shakes our limbs, whilst all other relations leave the body unaffected? It is not from this point of view that we shall approach the problem. To understand laughter, we must put it back into its natural environment, which is society, and above all must we determine the utility of its function, which is a social one. Such, let us say at once, will be the leading idea of all our investigations. Laughter must answer to certain requirements of life in common. It must have a *social* signification.

Let us clearly mark the point towards which our three preliminary observations are converging. The comic will come into being, it appears, whenever a group of men concentrate their attention on one of their number, imposing silence on their emotions and calling into play nothing but their intelligence. What, now, is the particular point on which their attention will have to be concentrated, and what will here be the function of intelligence? To reply to these questions will be at once to come to closer grips with the problem. But here a few examples have become indispensable.

II

A man, running along the street, stumbles and falls; the passers-by burst out laughing. They would not laugh at him, I imagine, could they suppose that the whim had suddenly seized him to sit down on the ground. They laugh because his sitting down is involuntary. Consequently, it is not his sudden change of attitude that raises a laugh, but rather the involuntary element in this change,—his clumsiness, in fact. Perhaps there was a stone on the road. He should have altered his pace or avoided the obstacle. Instead of that, through lack of elasticity, through absentmindedness and a kind of physical obstinacy, *as a result, in fact, of rigidity or of momentum*, the muscles continued to perform the same movement when the circumstances of the case called for something else. That is the reason of the man's fall, and also of the people's laughter.

Now, take the case of a person who attends to the petty occupations of his everyday life with mathematical precision. The objects around him, however, have all been tampered with by a mischievous wag, the result being that when he dips his pen into the inkstand he draws it out all covered with mud, when he fancies he is sitting down on a solid chair he finds himself sprawling on the floor, in a word his actions are all topsy-turvy or mere beating the air, while in every case the effect is invariably one of momentum. Habit has given the impulse: what was wanted was to check the movement or deflect it. He did nothing of the sort, but continued like a machine in the same straight line. The victim, then, of a practical joke is in a position similar to that of a runner who falls,—he is comic for the same reason. The laughable element in both cases consists of a certain *mechanical inelasticity*, just where one would expect to find the wide awake adaptability and the living pliableness of a human being. The only difference in the two cases is that the former happened of itself, whilst the latter was obtained artificially. In the first instance, the passer-by does nothing but look on, but in the second the mischievous wag intervenes.

All the same, in both cases the result has been brought about by an external circumstance. The comic is therefore accidental: it remains, so to speak, in superficial contact with the person. How is it to penetrate within? The necessary conditions will be fulfilled when mechanical rigidity no longer requires for its manifestation a stumbling-block which either the hazard of circumstance or human knavery has set in its way, but extracts by natural processes, from its own store, an inexhaustible series of opportunities for externally revealing its presence. Suppose, then, we imagine a mind always thinking of what it has just done and never of what it is doing, like a song which lags behind its accompaniment. Let us try to picture to ourselves a certain inborn lack of elasticity of both senses and intelligence, which brings it to pass that we continue to see what is no longer visible, to hear what is no longer audible, to say what is no longer to the point: in short, to adapt ourselves to a past and therefore imaginary situation, when we ought to be shaping our conduct in accordance with the reality which is present. This time the comic will take up its abode in the person himself; it is the person who will supply it with everything—matter and form, cause and opportunity. Is it then surprising that the absent-minded individual—for this is the character we have just been describing—has usually fired the imagination of comic authors? . . . Absentmindedness, indeed, is not perhaps the actual fountain-head of the comic, but surely it is contiguous to a certain stream of facts and fancies which flows straight from the fountain-head. It is situated, so to say, on one of the great natural watersheds of laughter. Now, the effect of absentmindedness may gather strength in its turn. There is a general law, the first example of which we have just encountered, and which we will formulate in the following terms: when a certain comic effect has its origin in a certain cause, the more natural we regard the cause to be, the more comic shall we find the effect. Even now we laugh at absentmindedness when presented to us as a simple fact. Still more laughable will be the absentmindedness we have seen springing up and growing before our very eyes, with whose origin we are acquainted and whose life-history we can reconstruct. To choose a definite example: suppose a man has taken to reading nothing but romances of love and chivalry. Attracted and fascinated by his heroes, his thoughts and intentions gradually turn more and more towards them, till one fine day we find him walking among us like a somnambulist. His actions are distractions. But then his distractions can be traced back to a definite, positive cause. They are no longer cases of *absence* of mind, pure and simple; they find their explanation in the *presence* of the individual in quite definite, though imaginary, surroundings. Doubtless a fall is always a fall, but it is one thing to tumble into a well because you were looking anywhere but in front of you, it is quite another thing to fall into it because you were intent upon a star. It was certainly a star at which Don Quixote was gazing. How profound is the comic element in the over-romantic, Utopian bent of mind! And yet, if you reintroduce the idea of absentmindedness, which acts as a go-between, you will see this profound comic element uniting with the most superficial type. Yes, indeed, these whimsical wild enthusiasts, these madmen who are yet so strangely reasonable, excite us to laughter by playing on the same chords within ourselves, by setting in motion the same inner mechanism, as does the victim of a practical joke or the passer-by who slips down in the street. They, too, are runners who fall and simple souls who are being hoaxed—runners after the ideal who stumble over realities, child-like dreamers for whom life delights to lie in wait. But, above all, they are past-masters in absentmindedness, with this superiority over their fellows that their absentmindedness is systematic and organised around one central idea, and that their mishaps are also quite coherent, thanks to the inexorable logic which reality applies to the correction of dreams, so that they kindle in those around them, by a series of cumulative effects, a hilarity capable of unlimited expansion.

Now, let us go a little further. Might not certain vices have the same relation to character that the rigidity of a fixed idea has to intellect? Whether as a moral kink or a crooked twist given to the will, vice has often the appearance of a curvature of the soul. Doubtless there are vices into which the soul plunges deeply with all its pregnant potency, which it rejuvenates and drags along with it into a moving circle of reincarnations. Those are tragic vices. But the vice capable of making us comic is, on the contrary, that which is brought from without, like a ready-made frame into which we are to step. It lends us its own rigidity instead of borrowing from us our flexibility. We do not render it more complicated: on the contrary, it simplifies us. . . .

What life and society require of each of us is a constantly alert attention that discerns the outlines of the present situation, together with a certain elasticity of mind and body to enable us to adapt ourselves in consequence. *Tension* and *elasticity* are two forces, mutually complementary, which life brings into play. If these two forces are lacking in the body to any considerable extent, we have sickness and infirmity and accidents of every kind. If they are lacking in the mind, we find every degree of mental deficiency, every variety of insanity. Finally, if they are lacking in the character, we have cases of the gravest inadaptability to social life, which are the sources of misery and at times the causes of crime. Once these elements of inferiority that affect the serious side of existence are removed—and they tend to eliminate themselves in what has been called the struggle for life—the person can live, and that in common with other persons. But society asks for something more; it is not satisfied with simply living, it insists on living well. What it now has to dread is that each one of us, content with paying attention to what affects the essentials of life, will, so far as the rest is concerned, give way to the easy automatism of acquired habits. Another thing it must fear is that the members of whom it is made up, instead of aiming after an increasingly delicate adjustment of wills which will fit more and more perfectly into one another, will confine themselves to respecting simply the fundamental conditions of this adjustment: a cut-and-dried agreement among the persons will not satisfy it, it insists on a constant striving after reciprocal adaptation. Society will therefore be suspicious of all *inelasticity* of character, of mind and even of body, because it is the possible sign of a slumbering activity as well as of an activity with separatist tendencies, that inclines to swerve from the common centre round which society gravitates: in short, because it is the sign of an eccentricity. And yet, society cannot intervene at this stage by material repression, since it is not affected in a material fashion. It is confronted with something that makes it uneasy, but only as a symptom—scarcely a threat, at the very most a gesture. A gesture, therefore, will be its reply. Laughter must be something of this kind, a sort of *social gesture*. By the fear which it inspires, it restrains eccentricity, keeps constantly awake and in mutual contact certain activities of a secondary order which might retire into their shell and go to sleep, and in short, softens down whatever the surface of the social body may retain of mechanical inelasticity. Laughter, then, does not belong to the province of esthetics alone, since unconsciously (and even immorally in many particular instances) it pursues a utilitarian aim of general improvement. And yet there is something esthetic about it, since the comic comes into being just when society and the individual, freed from the worry of self-preservation, begin to regard themselves as works of art. In a word, if a circle be drawn round those actions and dispositions—implied in individual or social life—to which their natural consequences bring their own penalties, there remains outside this sphere of emotion and struggle—and within a neutral zone in which man simply exposes himself to man's curiosity—a certain rigidity of body, mind and character that society would still like to get rid of in order to obtain from its members the greatest possible degree of elasticity and sociability. This rigidity is the comic, and laughter is its corrective.

• • •

To sum up, whatever be the doctrine to which our reason assents, our imagination has a very clear-cut philosophy of its own: in every human form it sees the effort of a soul which is shaping matter, a soul which is infinitely supple and perpetually in motion, subject to no law of gravitation, for it is not the earth that attracts it. This soul imparts a portion of its winged lightness to the body it animates: the immateriality which thus passes into matter is what is called gracefulness. Matter, however, is obstinate and resists. It draws to itself the ever-alert activity of this higher principle, would fain convert it to its own inertia and cause it to revert to mere automatism. It would fain immobilise the intelligently varied movements of the body in stupidly contracted grooves, stereotype in permanent grimaces the fleeting expressions of the face, in short imprint on the whole person such an attitude as to make it appear immersed and absorbed in the materiality of some mechanical occupation instead of ceaselessly renewing its vitality by keeping in touch with a living ideal. Where matter thus succeeds in dulling the outward life of the soul, in petrifying its movements and thwarting its gracefulness, it achieves, at the expense of a body, an effect that is comic. If, then, at this point we wish to define the comic by comparing it with its contrary, we should have to contrast it with gracefulness even more than with beauty. It partakes rather of the unsprightly than of the unsightly, of *rigidness* rather than of *ugliness*.

• • •

V

Before going further, let us halt a moment and glance around. As we hinted at the outset of this study, it would be idle to attempt to derive every comic effect from one simple formula. The formula exists well enough in a certain sense, but its development does not follow a straightforward course. What I mean is that the process of deduction ought from time to time to stop and study certain culminating effects. . . . Now, we have just reached one of these mental crossways. *Something mechanical encrusted on the living* will represent a cross at which we must halt, a central image from which the imagination branches off in different directions. What are these directions? There appear to be three main ones. We will follow them one after the other, and then continue our onward course.

1. In the first place, this view of the mechanical and the living dovetailed into each other makes us incline towards the vaguer image of *some rigidity or other* applied to the mobility of life, in an awkward attempt to follow its lines and counterfeit its suppleness. Here we perceive how easy it is for a garment to become ridiculous. It might almost be said that every fashion is laughable in some respect. Only, when we are dealing with the fashion of the day, we are so accustomed to it that the garment seems, in our mind, to form one with the individual wearing it. We do not separate them in imagination. The idea no longer occurs to us to contrast the inert rigidity of the covering with the living suppleness of the object covered: consequently, the comic here remains in a latent condition. It will only succeed in emerging when the natural incompatibility is so deep-seated between the covering and the covered that even an immemorial association fails to cement this union: a case in point is our head and top hat. Suppose, however, some eccentric individual dresses himself in the fashion of former times, our attention is immediately drawn to the clothes themselves; we absolutely distinguish them from the individual, we say that the latter *is*

disguising himself,—as though every article of clothing were not a disguise—and the laughable aspect of fashion comes out of the shadow into the light.

Let us go on to society. As we are both in and of it, we cannot help treating it as a living being. Any image, then, suggestive of the notion of a society disguising itself, or of a social masquerade, so to speak, will be laughable. Now, such a notion is formed when we perceive anything inert or stereotyped, or simply ready-made, on the surface of living society. There we have rigidity over again, clashing with the inner suppleness of life. The ceremonial side of social life must, therefore, always include a latent comic element, which is only waiting for an opportunity to burst into full view. It might be said that ceremonies are to the social body what clothing is to the individual body: they owe their seriousness to the fact that they are identified, in our minds, with the serious object with which custom associates them, and when we isolate them in imagination, they forthwith lose their seriousness. For any ceremony, then, to become comic, it is enough that our attention be fixed on the ceremonial element in it, and that we neglect its matter, as philosophers say, and think only of its form. Everyone knows how easily the comic spirit exercises its ingenuity on social actions of a stereotyped nature, from an ordinary prize-distribution to the solemn sitting of a court of justice. Any form or formula is a ready-made frame into which the comic element may be fitted.

2. Our starting-point is again "something mechanical encrusted upon the living." Where did the comic come from in this case? It came from the fact that the living body became rigid, like a machine. Accordingly, it seemed to us that the living body ought to be the perfection of suppleness, the ever-alert activity of a principle always at work. But this activity would really belong to the soul rather than to the body. It would be the very flame of life, kindled within us by a higher principle and perceived through the body, as though through a glass. When we see only gracefulness and suppleness in the living body, it is because we disregard in it the elements of weight, of resistance, and, in a word, of matter; we forget its materiality and think only of its vitality, a vitality which we regard as derived from the very principle of intellectual and moral life. Let us suppose, however, that our attention is drawn to this material side of the body; that, so far from sharing in the lightness and subtlety of the principle with which it is animated, the body is no more in our eyes than a heavy and cumbersome vesture, a kind of irksome ballast which holds down to earth a soul

eager to rise aloft. Then the body will become to the soul what, as we have just seen, the garment was to the body itself—inert matter dumped down upon living energy. The impression of the comic will be produced as soon as we have a clear apprehension of this putting the one on the other. And we shall experience it most strongly when we are shown the soul *tantalised* by the needs of the body: on the one hand, the moral personality with its intelligently varied energy, and, on the other, the stupidly monotonous body, perpetually obstructing everything with its machine-like obstinacy. The more paltry and uniformly repeated these claims of the body, the more striking will be the result. But that is only a matter of degree, and the general law of these phenomena may be formulated as follows: *Any incident is comic that calls our attention to the physical in a person, when it is the moral side that is concerned.*

3. Let us then return, for the last time, to our central image— something mechanical encrusted on something living. Here, the living being under discussion was a human being, a person. A mechanical arrangement, on the other hand, is a thing. What, therefore, incited laughter, was the momentary transformation of a person into a thing, if one considers the image from this standpoint. Let us then pass from the exact idea of a machine to the vaguer one of a thing in general. We shall have a fresh series of laughable images which will be obtained by taking a blurred impression, so to speak, of the outlines of the former and will bring us to this new law: *We laugh every time a person gives us the impression of being a thing.*

Discussion Questions

1. Bergson offers as an axiom that laughter can occur only when there's an "absence of feeling," advancing the position that comedy appeals to the intellect. Do you agree with Bergson that "laughter has no greater foe than emotion"?

2. Bergson's central claim is that laughter serves the social function of correcting individual member's or group's mechanical or absentminded behavior. Does this match your sense of comedy's role in your society? Consider your favorite comic characters. Are they absentminded sleepwalkers who need to wake up, held up to ridicule as cautionary examples, or are they critics of sleepwalkers, demanding that we, and their targets, wake up?

3. What does Bergson mean when he states that "The ceremonial side of life must . . . always contain a latent comic element"? What ceremonies do you

regularly participate in or observe? What latent comic elements can you describe?

4. Bergson notes the perennial clash between the moral personality (soul) and the "stupidly monotonous body." What examples of this clash can you describe?

Writing Activities

1. Write two accounts of the same event, one "objective" and one "emotional," to test Bergson's assertion about emotion being the enemy of laughter. You might think of the objective account as emphasizing the body, the emotional, the soul or spirit.

2. Write an account of an everyday mechanical or repeated behavior with the intent of persuading your audience to laugh. Choose an activity that generally is not considered comic.

3. Write an account of an everyday ceremonial event, aiming to bring to the surface the latent comic elements Bergson claims are present in all ceremonies.

Excerpt from *What's So Funny*

Wit's Weapons: Incongruity and Ambiguity

MURRAY DAVIS

Headnotes/Things to Look For

Murray S. Davis, a sociologist, lives in Berkeley, California. His books include Intimate Relations, SMUT: Erotic Reality/Obscene Ideology, *and* Aphoristics: How "Interesting Ideas" Turn the World Inside Out.

Along with the previous piece by Bergson, this selection includes some challenging theoretical language and many scholarly references, but Davis also gives us a steady flow of accessible examples. Note that Davis doesn't explain the jokes, simply integrating them into his account of comic principles.

--- ✦ ---

Near the beginning of the nineteenth century, the ascendance of a new basic conceptual paradigm—initiated in philosophy and aesthetics mainly by Immanuel Kant—motivated the major thinkers of the time to shift their focus from the objective to the subjective world. The objective world could not be understood in itself, they now felt, because it was determined as much—if not more—by the subject. This Copernican revolution in the history of ideas influenced comic theorists to begin to look for the source of laughter not in the comic object but in the comic subject, shifting their attention from the funny something to the person who finds something funny. The new subjectivist view of comedy was succinctly summed up by Baudelaire: "The comic, the power of laughter, is in the laugher, not at all in the object of laughter" (1972:148). Even today most comic theorists no longer regard the objective world as intrinsically funny but as somehow made funny by its human observers.

In an ancillary section of *Critique of Judgement* in 1793, Kant himself felt the need to extend his humorless philosophy to laughter, whose source he located in the subject's temporal *expectation:* "Laughter is an affection arising from the sudden transformation of a strained expectation into nothing" (1951:177). From the kernel of this brief definition evolved "incongruity theory," the most influential theory of humor in cognitive psychology today, and the psychological underpinnings for the sociological analysis of humor I will develop here.[1]

In 1819 William Hazlitt elaborated Kant's conception of the comic by contrasting it with its opposite: "To understand or define the ludicrous, we must first know what the serious is." Hazlitt proceeded to identify the serious with the *expected:* "Now the serious is the habitual stress which the mind lays upon the expectation of a given order of events, following one another with a certain regularity and weight of interest attached to them." And the comic with the *unexpected:* "The ludicrous, or comic, is the unexpected loosening or relaxing this stress [on the expected] below its usual pitch of intensity, by such an abrupt transposition of the order of our ideas, as taking the mind unawares, throws it off its guard, startles it into a lively sense of pleasure, and leaves no time nor inclination for painful reflections" (1930; 6:7).

Since the unexpected is an essential feature of humor, comics continually try to undercut their audience's expectations; for instance, by refusing to follow commonplace sentiments:

My job is simply bringing joy to the wealthy.

MARTIN MULL

emotional presumptions:

> My wife comes home and says, "Pack your bags. I just
> won $20 million in the California lottery." "Where are we
> going Hawaii, Europe?" I ask jubilantly. "I don't know
> where you're going, Doug, as long as it's out of here."
>
> DOUG FERRARI

or political platitudes:

> When [Reagan] came into office in 1981, he took an idle
> nation and restored it to its former glory. Unfortunately,
> the idle nation was Japan.
>
> JOHNNY STEELE

SYSTEM AND INCONGRUITY

For us to be able to expect that "a given order of events follow[s] one
another with a certain regularity," the set of events must be arranged
according to an orderly plan or *system* in which each element is
related to all the others. Systems may be subjective (exist in the
mind) or objective (exist in the world). Subjective systems whose
interrelated elements cluster coherently have been termed "universes" (Monro 1951:45–46), "frames" (Bateson 1972:177–93;
Goffman 1974), "meaning structures" (Zijderveld 1968:290), "associative contexts" (Koestler 1974:6), "scripts" (Raskin 1985:81), as well
as "gestalts," "realms," "planes," "grounds," or "schema." (I will usually use all these terms interchangeably though sometimes employing *system* to emphasize the internal elements' interconnection and
frame to emphasize their disconnection from external elements.)

If we know the state of one element in a system and the inter-
relation between all of them, we can anticipate the state of any
other element in the system. All the elements of a system, therefore,
are potentially predictable.

But the success of our prediction depends on the correlation
between our subjective "expectation system" and the objective
"real system."[2] For the particular systems I will examine in this
book this correlation is far from perfect. The earthquake of humor
makes us suddenly conscious of the chasm between them.

"The essence of the laughable," concludes Hazlitt, one of the
first to apply the term to humor, "is the *incongruous*" (1930; 6:7).
An "incongruity" is supposed to be an element of a system but turns

out to be unrelated to all the other interrelated elements of the system.[3] (Thus incongruity is a relational concept: Nothing can be incongruous in itself but only by standing out phenomenologically from an otherwise congruous system.) A real incongruity that deviates from prediction will collapse an orderly expectation system, causing those who had viewed the objective world through this particular subjective frame to laugh.[4]

The mental gestalt of an expectation system is usually delicate. For the system to continue to exist the gestalt must remain whole. Those whose expectation system gestalt becomes incomplete or partial may break up into laughter, as Ralph Waldo Emerson tried to say in the prepsychological vocabulary of the nineteenth century: "It is in comparing fractions with essential integers or wholes that laughter begins. . . . The essence of all jokes, of all comedy, seems to be an honest or well-intended halfness. . . . The balking of the intellect, the frustrated expectation, the break of continuity in the intellect, is comedy; and it announces itself physically in the pleasant spasms we call laughter" (1946:205). By replacing only one congruous element with an incongruous element, humor can disintegrate an expectation system. The humorous incongruity disorders what had been ordered, breaking open the frame and scattering its elements. Erving Goffman calls this loss of frame "negative experience" (1974:378–438), for it takes its character from what it is not—that is, ordered, and therefore expected, experience.

Several characteristics of incongruities and systems *intensify* humor's negative experience. The more incongruities that explode a given expectation system, the funnier. Ethnic jokes, for instance, have been perennially popular in part because they are multi-incongruous, simultaneously undermining egalitarian ideology ("they are as good as us") *and* either cognitive rationality:

> Did you hear about the Pole who locked his family in the car? He had to find a coat hanger to get them out.

or normative mores:

> A Pole walks into a local bar and goes straight up to the bartender, who turns away in disgust at the handful of horeshit the Pole is holding. "Hey, Harry," says the Pole, "look what I almost stepped in."

The correlation between number of incongruities and degree of funniness, however, holds only up to a point. Beyond that point, the audience will no longer be able to figure out what system all these incongruities are supposed to be incongruous to. Psychologist Paul McGhee, a leading expert on children's humor, agrees that too many incongruities spoil the joke:

> Up to a point, the greater the number of characteristics of the object violated, the more incongruous it is (it is not yet clear whether funniness increases directly as a function of the number of incongruous elements).
>
> Beyond this unspecified point, so many elements have been distorted or changed that the child has difficulty recognizing the object; rather than becoming an incongruous depiction of a familiar object, the extremely discrepant depiction of the object is simply perceived as a totally novel and unfamiliar object. This eliminates the funniness. [1979:73]

Not just any incongruous element will detonate a system into laughter. We distinguish "quality humor," in which incongruous elements clash with a system's core characteristics, from "mere silliness," in which they clash with its peripheral aspects. More precisely, rather than being either essential or inessential, a system's elements have *degrees* of essentiality; consequently, the various incongruities that annihilate them produce *degrees* of funniness. Conversely, the larger the laugh, the more essential the system's aspect that must have been annihilated. Mort Sahl, for instance, cuts to the (bleeding) heart of one ideological system:

> A liberal newspaper is one that would report a nuclear exchange between the United States and the Soviet Union with a headline reading, "WORLD ENDS: WOMEN AND MINORITIES HARDEST HIT."

The better-known the system an incongruity makes strange, the more our amusement. Consequently, humor often deforms proverbs and clichés:

> What we do practice extensively in our age is the twisting of proverbs to suit new purposes. . . . As Jacobs recognizes, "a proverb, being a highly conventionalized, fixed formulation, lends itself to distortion.". . . Jacobs quotes as an example, "Many are called but few get the right number." He adds that "the literal significance of a common phrase or proverb can also be evoked by placing it in an unexpected context; as Hamlet's 'O that this too, too solid flesh should melt' sometimes found on weighing scales." [Redfern 1986:150]

How funny we find an incongruity also depends on how firmly we are attached to the expectation system it attacks. If we find incongruities that temporarily annihilate our *cognitive* expectation system to be funny, we may find those that temporarily annihilate our *moral* expectation system even funnier. Before the recent liberalization, the emigre Andrei Siniavski reported, Russians valued humor so greatly because Soviet society prohibited so much:

> Perhaps nowhere in the history of letters has the theme of prohibition been so fundamental and forceful as in the Soviet joke. . . . There are taboos on obscenity, political subversion, truth, the state of affairs in general, government secrets. . . . Numerous jokes are structured like taboos, which are then subjected to unceremonious transgression. . . . The joke . . . simply does not exist without crossing into forbidden territory. [1984:356–60]

Normative prohibitions, however, can be too strong for humor just as they can be too weak. We do not find funny an incongruity that breaks up an expectation system to which we are morally committed either very much or very little. Christopher Wilson puts this proposition more technically: "[Social Psychological experiments indicate] an inverted-U shaped relationship of funniness and degree of incongruity. Jokes are moderately incongruous; minimal or extremely high levels of incongruity are unfunny" (1979:150–52).

In short, how funny we find an attempt at humor depends in part on the quantity and quality of its incongruities as well as on our familiarity with and commitment to the expectation system to which they are incongruent.

SYSTEMS AND AMBIGUITY

We have located humor's epicenter in the *incongruous* element that shatters an expectation system into nothing. This model of humor focuses on a single system. But many jokes are based on two systems. Since every congruous element can be incongruous somewhere else, humorists also ply their trade by interpolating an element congruous with the other elements of one system into another system where it is *less* congruous or even incongruous. For instance, a humorist may imagine Evelyn Wood expanding her "speed reading" techniques from their original literary home into the realms of art and music:

> Try to grasp the essence of a picture or a piece of music
> as fast as you can; forget the irrelevant derails. You should

be able to view an average size museum in fifteen minutes, or hear a Beethoven symphony in ten.

Although it may be appropriate to approach literature (especially non-fiction and light fiction) in such a hasty instrumental way, approaching art or music in this way is ludicrously incongruous with the leisurely aesthetic contemplation usually associated with these quasi-sacred activities.

We can also locate humor's epicenter, then, in the *congruous* element that connects two opposing expectation systems or frames. In this second model, humorists proceed first by showing an element to be congruous with other elements in one system, and then by suddenly showing it to be congruous or even *more* congruous with those in another system:

> A man comes home from work early and takes the elevator up to his seventh-floor apartment. When he gets off the elevator, he notices a smiling man with a big cigar getting on. When he goes into his apartment, he smells smoke and sees some ashes in an ashtray. Since neither he nor his wife smoke, he becomes very suspicious. His suspicions are confirmed when he goes to the bedroom and sees both his bed and his wife in disarray. He runs to the balcony, and sees the smiling man with the big cigar walking out of the building below. Blinded by rage, he picks up a refrigerator (for he is a very strong man) and throws it down on the man with the big cigar, flattening him. His wife runs out of the bedroom and over to the balcony, looks down, sees the dead man, and cries to her husband, "What have you done? I've never seen that man before in my life!" Consumed with remorse for killing an innocent man, the jealous husband jumps over the balcony to his death.
>
> *Next scene:* the entrance to heaven. Three men encounter St. Peter, who asks them to describe the moment of their death.
>
> *First man*: I was walking along smoking my favorite cigar, thinking of how good my life is when—bang!—out of the blue something hits me on the head and I'm dead.
>
> *Second man:* I had just killed a man who I thought had been sleeping with my wife, but discovering I was wrong made me so upset that I killed myself in remorse.
>
> *Third man:* I don't know what happened. I was hiding in this refrigerator. . . .

In the "single system" model, humor shifts its audience's attention from one system into no system via an *incongruity*; in the "double system" model, humor shifts its audience's attention from one system into another system via an *ambiguity*, an element congruous with both systems—their "overlap point" (Davis 1983:57–58): the refrigerator in the above joke, for example.

Since every *thing* is a nexus of attributes, *everything* is potentially ambiguous, and therefore potentially humorous. For a joke can rotate its audience's attention around an ambiguous object from one attribute (and the entire system associated with it) to another attribute (and the different system associated with it). In the above joke, the second use of "refrigerator" suddenly shifts its audience's focus from its heaviness to its hollowness (and between the systems associated with each). And the following joke hinges on the ambiguity of a grocery store's attributes:

> My grandfather was into nostalgia: "I remember when I could go to the corner store and pick up a bag of potato chips and a can of beer and a *Jet Magazine* for 5 cents."
> "Can't do that now, Grampa, they've got those video surveillance cameras."
>
> AL CLETHEN

As the joke's specification of the store's attributes rotates from its merchandise to its monitors, the frame in which we locate them suddenly shifts from sentimental to larcenous.

Frequently, a joke's attribute rotation will convert a seemingly irrelevant detail into a crucial one:

> A Pole who finds himself in Moscow (in the mid-1980s) wants to know the time. He sees a man approaching him carrying two heavy suitcases and asks the fellow if he knows the correct time.
> "Certainly," says the Russian, setting down the two bags and looking at his wrist. "It is 11:43 and 17 seconds. The date is Feb. 13, the moon is nearing its full phase and the atmospheric pressure stands at 992 hectopascals and is rising."
> The Polish visitor is dumbfounded but manages to ask if the watch that provides all this information is Japanese. No, he is told, it is "our own, a product of Soviet technology."

"Well," says the Pole, "that is wonderful, you are to be congratulated."
"Yes," the Russian answers, straining to pick up the suitcases, "but these batteries are still a little heavy."

Here, the transformation of the suitcases from implied travel accessories to revealed watch batteries suddenly shifts our interpretive frame of the society that produced them from hypercompetent to incompetent.

In brief: *from an expected continuation within one system, the comic mind pivots around an ambiguity to branch off into another system.* In the next chapter, we will see that many ambiguous pivots are merely phonetic:

How many Californians does it take to screw in a light bulb? None. They screw in hot tubs.

The subtler ones, however, are more semantic:

Well, it's hard to find a good relationship. Recently, I took this one girl home and put on "We Are the World," hoping it would put her in a giving mood. Instead, she got hungry.

GARRY SHANDLING

Arthur Koestler was the best-known modern exponent of the view that humor is produced by the intersection of systems or frames,[5] which he called "associative contexts":

It is the sudden clash between these two mutually exclusive codes of rules—or associative contexts—that produces the comic effect. It compels the listener to perceive the situation in two self-consistent but incompatible frames of reference at the same time; his mind has to operate simultaneously on two different wavelengths. While this unusual condition lasts, the event is not only, as is normally the case, associated with a single frame of reference, but "bisociated" with two. The term bisociation was coined by the present writer to make a distinction between the routines of disciplined thinking within a single universe of discourse—on a single plane, as it were—and the creative types of mental activity that always operate on more than one plane. In humor, both the *creation* of a subtle joke and the *re-creative* act of perceiving the joke involve the delightful mental jolt of a sudden leap from one plane or associative context to another. [1974:5–6]

Sociologists have tried to sociologize the humorous shift between frames of reference. William Cameron provided an example of a humorous shift between the frames of urban and rural reference groups:

> A fundamental concept in social psychology is that of the frame of reference, and related to it, the reference group. These twin notions are highly useful in examining jokes. Many jokes derive their effect by contrasting two different frames of reference in which something would be appropriate to one is mistaken and inappropriate to the other. . . .
>
> > There was a young man from the city,
> > Who saw what he thought was a kitty,
> > He gave it a pat, but it wasn't a cat,
> > And we buried his clothes out of pity.
>
> The man from the city, with an urban frame of reference, wrongly defined the real situation involving the skunk, with disastrous results. . . . Perhaps the reader identifies with the rural population and exults when vaunted urban superiority takes a fall. [1963:85–86][6]

A few years later, Anton Zijderveld provided an example of a humorous shift between the frames of adult and child social categories (although his example shifts them not within the joke itself but between its tellers):

> Joking is defined as the conscious or unconscious transition from one institutionalized meaning structure to another, without changing much of the original role behavior and logic. . . .
>
> A *zote* is a risqué, sexual joke. . . . An old and stale *zote* told by somebody who obviously tries to be funny . . . is nothing to laugh about. Such a stale joke is common property, whereas a joke, on the contrary, draws its power from being new and rare. If, however, this stale *zote* is all of a sudden told by a child of five or six, who obviously does not know what he is talking about, but tells it in order to look like an adult, the entire situation changes completely. . . . the stale joke is transported by the child from one frame of reference to another and gains by that new substance and meaning. The old *zote* has become a joke again. It is funny not because of the original substance and meaning, but because the narrator is still a child. [1968:290–91]

Unfortunately, neither Cameron nor Zijderveld were able to convince other social scientists to examine the social implications of humorous shifts between systems or frames.

The linguist Victor Raskin recently translated Koestler's gestalt-based psychological theory of humor into a "script-based semantic theory" of humor, which has been far more influential: "first, in order to be a joke, any text should be partially or fully compatible with two different scripts and secondly, a special relation of script oppositeness should obtain between the two scripts" (1985:xiii).[7] Raskin analyzes jokes into the paired opposing scripts whose conjunction produces them; for instance finding a Doctor [instrumental] script and a Lover [erotic] script in the following example:

"Is the doctor at home?" the patient asked in his
bronchial whisper: "No," the doctor's young and pretty
wife whispered in reply: "Come right in."

The semantic "trigger" for switching scripts is the joke's *ambiguity* (or negatively its *contradiction*) (1985:114ff.). Raskin applies his theory specifically to sexual, ethnic, and political humor to "disambiguate" them into their various paired opposite scripts.[8]

I will contribute to this tradition by distinguishing more abstract oppositional entities than Raskin does when he analyzes humor into the opposing scripts whose conjunction creates it.

Several characteristics of ambiguities and systems *intensify* humor's dislocatory experience. Compared to more contemplative activities like art or science, comedy pivots its audience's attention between systems *quickly*. Wit, in particular, is the ability to rapidly discover and articulate the common ambiguous element in seemingly different systems. In 1690, John Locke (following Hobbes) compared synthetic "wit" to analytic "judgement" (which he clearly preferred) in a definition which would be influential, if not fully accepted (see Martin 1974), for two hundred years:

[Wit lies] most in the assemblage of ideas, and putting those together with quickness and variety wherein can be found any resemblance or congruity, thereby to make up pleasant pictures and agreeable visions in the fancy; judgement, on the contrary, lies quite on the other side, in separating carefully one from another ideas wherein can be found the least difference, thereby to avoid being misled by similitude and by affinity to take one thing for another. [1939:280][9]

In 1711, Addison in *The Spectator* (no. 62) supplemented Locke's definition of wit by stressing that the resemblance must be unexpected: "It is necessary that the Ideas should not lie too near one another in the Nature of things, for where the Likeness is obvious, it gives no Surprize" (1965:264). An article in the *British Quarterly Review* a century later reverses perspective on wit's perspective reversal, from what wit combines to what had kept them apart. The anonymous author finds exactly the right image for the "shock of agreeable surprise" produced by wit's "original and striking comparison": "It is as if a partition-wall in our intellect was suddenly blown out; two things formerly strange to one another have flashed together" (quoted in Martin 1974:43).[10]

Comics need find only one element that ambiguously connects two seemingly different systems to raise a laugh. For instance, those who use the term *nail* metaphorically as sexual slang to describe an erotic coupling in terms of a mechanical one may provoke a slight smirk (at least among adolescent boys preoccupied with both kinds of couplings, however contradictory the mind-set each requires). But those who attempt to extend the comparison between the two systems over more than one element may prolong a larger laugh.[11] One comic connected two types of intimated relations with two types of metallic fasteners:

> Girls used to get *pinned* in high school, now they get *nailed.*

> BILL MAHER

And this apocryphal newspaper headline managed to connect an escaped mental patient who raped a woman with three types of metallic fasteners: Nut Bolts and Screws (Redfern 1986:120). Koestler observed that the archetypical, if not the longest, sustained humorous comparison between two incompatible realms—fantasy and reality—is *Don Quixote*:

> Jokes and anecdotes have a single point of culmination. The literary forms of *sustained humor*, such as the picaresque novel, do not rely on a single effect but on a series of minor climaxes. The narrative moves along a line of intersection of contrasted planes—e.g., the fantasy world of Don Quixote and the cunning horse-sense of Sancho Panza—or is made to oscillate between them; as a result tension is continuously generated and discharged in mild amusement. [1974:81]

Jack Mingo (1983) provides a more contemporary example of sustained humorous comparison in *The Official Couch Potato*

Handbook by pointing out the isomorphism between the category of human TV watchers and the category of "potatoes." Mingo equates various types of potatoes with various types of TV viewers: "M*A*S*H Potatoes" are those addicted to that TV sitcom and other sophisticated comedy shows, "Red-Eyed Potatoes" are those addicted to late night TV viewing, etc. The comic form that transposes elements between the styles of individuals or social realms in the most sustained manner is parody. The best parodies suggest a secret similarity between realms presumed to be very different, such as religion and computers:

> [Jeffrey Armstrong] is rewriting the Bible and recasting famous prayers. Dubbing himself St. Silicon, savior of data, he represents CHIP [Church of Heuristic Information Processing]. . . .
> Armstrong has redone the psalms, turned the commandments into commands. . . . He said that his Eastern religion helpmates have designed the perfect new mantra for meditators too. It goes: "OEM, RAM. ROM, EPROM.". . .
> He plans to market a set of binary rosary beads, too. "There's a zero on one bead and a one on the other," he said. . . .
> One of his favorite prayers is Hail Memory:
>
> Hail Memory.
> Full of space.
> The motherboard is with thee.
> Blessed art thou amongst micros.
> And blessed is the fruit of thy processor: data.
> Holy memory.
> Motherboard of ROM.
> Pray for us beginners.
> Now and at the hour of our sign-off.
> Enter.
>
> All of his prayers end with "Enter" or "Return." His favorite saying is the golden rule of St. Silicon: Do unto your data that you were able to undo.
>
> JOHN DVORAK, *SAN FRANCISCO EXAMINER*, 9 MAR, 1986. D3

Sex is so multifarious an activity that it is relatively easy to sustain the correspondence between its elements and those of other realms. In HBO's "This Was Burlesque" (Nov. 1983), some bell-boys, listening at the door of the hotel room of a married couple, mistake the couple's conversation about trying to close a suitcase with conversation about sex:

> "You get on top."
> "No, you get on top."
> "Let's both get on top!"

Only the last line makes the bellboys realize, after momentarily trying to stretch its application, that their sexual interpretation must be inappropriate. Since Freud, in fact, it has become so common to interpret jokes sexually (more technically, to map their ambiguous elements isomorphically onto a sexual plane) that it now comes as an amusing surprise when the connection between a series of seemingly sexual elements turns out to be more innocent:

> QUESTION: "What is it that Gorbachev has a long one, Bush has a short one, the Pope has one but doesn't use it, and Madonna doesn't have one?"
> ANSWER: "A last name."
>
> LESLIE GIBBON

Amateur comedians usually joke about a variety of topics; professionals who have their act together often restrict their humor to variations on a single theme. Those unable to sustain the systematic comparison between two realms (as above) may maintain the easier comparison between a single realm and various other realms—sandblasting the base realm with elements derived from the secondary realms. By using these external elements to bring out ambiguities, the comic can chisel away at a topic from various directions like a sculptor. But unlike the sculptor who begins with a formless matter and gradually clarifies its edges, the comedian begins with what his audience believed to be a clear subject matter and proceeds to blur its edges, making ambiguous what his audience thought they clearly understood. With this defocusing comic technique in mind, listen to Lenny Bruce destabilize his early 1960s audience's already precarious puritanical views even further:

> That's why they don't like Americans anywhere . . . —
> because [in World War II] we fucked all of their mothers
> for chocolate bars. . . .

If this society was the least little bit correct, if religion helped it out a little bit, and that act was the least bit the antithesis of what is perverse, and you felt that it was a true Christian act of procreation, if it was sweet hugging and kissing—watch. The fellow comes off the plane:

British voice: Is that the fellow who fucked Mother? Oh, yes! How are you? *Damn,* I haven't seen you in so long, and you're such a *wonderful* person. You certainly made Mother feel *good.* I certainly would like to *thank* you—that certainly was a nice thing to do. And I understand you gave her some candy besides.

But we don't agree that it's a nice act. It's a filthy, dirty act. In fact, that's what any eighteen-year-old chick or thirty-year-old chick will tell you when you take her out:

"You don't *love* me, you just want to *ball* me."

BOY!: Listen to that:

GIRL: He was a *nice* guy—he didn't try to fool around with me. But *you* don't love me, you just want to ball me.

GUY: *What?* Of course I love you—I wouldn't want to sleep with you if I didn't love you.

GIRL: No, no. If you loved me you'd drive me to Wisconsin; punch me in the mouth; read the Bible to me all night; you'd borrow money from me. You wouldn't want to ball me. You don't do that to someone you love—you do that to somebody you hate. Really *hate*.

In fact, when you *really* hate them, what's the vernacular we use?
   "*Screw you,* mister!"
   If you were taught it was a sweet Christian act of procreation, it was the nicest thing we can do for each other, you'd use the term correctly, and say
   "*Unscrew you,* mister!"

LENNY BRUCE

The audience's response to the monologist's humor mirrors the children's response to the psychologist's humor encountered in the previous section. The psychologist presented the children with many incongruities simultaneously, *before* they were able to recognize what these incongruities were supposed to be incongruous to. Unable to construct a coherent expectation system, the children didn't find funny the incongruities that undermined it. The monologist articulated many ambiguities that undermined his topic sequentially, *after* his audience had already possessed a coherent expectation system for it. By the end of his monologue, much of his audience could no longer recognize what they had been laughing at.

INCONGRUITIES AND AMBIGUITIES

The comic has been difficult to comprehend because it conflates the two models implicit in the following eighteenth-century aphorism: "Wit consists in discerning the resemblance between diverse things, and the difference between similar things" (Montesquieu [?]). *Incongruity* is related to the second part of this definition: the real difference between things that seem alike. An element of a system that is sufficiently unlike its other elements can destroy an audience's perception of the system's integrity. *Ambiguity* is related to the first part of this definition: the real resemblance between things that seem to differ. An element of one system that is sufficiently like the elements of a second system can also destroy an audience's perception of the first system's integrity. In short, incongruities, which emphasize internal differences, produce humor by fitting too poorly in a system; ambiguities, which emphasize external similarities, produce humor by fitting too well in too many systems. Most people find the combination of incongruity and ambiguity (ordinary jokes) funnier than either incongruity (nonsense humor) or ambiguity (bad puns) alone.

Some humor, then, annihilates a single system with an *incongruity*. The audience for this "annihilated single system" model of humor suddenly sees that one element in an otherwise coherent system is incongruous with it. But they never resolved the incongruity, for the system is destroyed without being replaced by another one. Consequently, the audience never restores its cognitive equilibrium.[12] Other humor transposes a double system with an *ambiguity*. The audience for this "transposed double system" model of humor also suddenly sees that one element in an otherwise coherent system is not as congruous with it as they believed, at least not uniquely so. But they resolve the incongruity by reconceiving the element from the perspective of a second system, to which the element is ambiguously related. (Most of the other elements of the second system, however, are incongruous with the first.) Consequently, the audience restores its cognitive equilibrium by switching systems.[13]

"Shaggy dog stories," by the way, are those drawn-out pointless jokes that continually imply that their tellers will soon shift the system, soon resolve the incongruity, soon restore the audience's cognitive equilibrium—but they never do. Thus shaggy dog stories transform the expected "transposed double system" humor into "annihilated single system" humor.

It is easier to distinguish these two models in theory than in practice because it is sometimes difficult to distinguish incongruities within each system from incongruities between each system. It is more productive to distinguish these two models according to whether the difference or similarity, frames or switch point, incongruity or ambiguity stands out phenomenologically in a particular instance of humor. In general, it is better to analyze humor whose *form* is more prominent (for example, linguistic humor) in terms of ambiguity, and humor whose *content* is more prominent (ethnic humor) in terms of incongruity. Consequently, I will employ both these models, pointing out incongruities or ambiguities, depending on the particular type or aspect of humor I am dealing with.

THE HUMORIZER

The general technique comics use to explode phenomena into laughter I will call the "humorizer," as in "Let's put it through the humorizer to see if we can make it funny." Humorists use the humorizer to rub various things against their topic until they find one that can scratch off its attributes into incongruities or ambiguities or preferably both, generating the spark of laughter.

The humorizer may produce humor by continually juxtaposing phenomena until a pair appears whose attributes are incongruous. For example, a computer that randomly joins objects or processes assembled the following novel pairs:

> Comic Headlines:
>> Scientists Discover New Moon Orbiting Kate Smith
>> Tornado Kills Five, Self
>
> Diseases:
>> Athlete's Brain
>> Cheese-in-Mouth Disease

New Inventions:
  Emergency Dribble Mug
  I. Q. Retardant

Gourmet Items:
  Insect Brittle
  Endangered Species Au Gratin
  Fur-Ball Shortcake

JOHN SWARTZWELDER, *PLAYBOY*, DEC. 1982, 32

Since most paired objects or processes randomly joined by a computer are irrelevant to each other, their juxtaposition produces at best nonsense humor. But I selected the above pairs from the author's selection of the computer's random output because I felt they were funnier than mere nonsense. Each pair contains subtle congruous elements that hold it together, implying an encompassing system that articulates its incongruous elements. This use of the humorizer recalls Kenneth Burke's "perspective by incongruity" (1965:71–124), which involves "the merging of categories once felt to be mutually exclusive" (69).[14]

The humorizer may also produce humor by searching out a topic's ambiguities, which relate it to other phenomena, especially those differently evaluated. In the above monologue Lenny Bruce articulated the ambiguities that connect problematic copulation to pleasurable procreation. This use of the humorizer employs what I will call "perspective by ambiguity." Sociologist Donald Levine has argued most persuasively that modern science, especially modern social science, has overlooked ambiguity's heuristic value:

> Literary ambiguity signifies the property of words or sentences of admitting more than one interpretation; experiential ambiguity signifies a property possessed by any stimuli of having two or more meanings or even simply of being unclear as to meaning. . . . Now I wish to posit a connection between the two modalities of ambiguity by asserting that the ambiguities of life are systematically underrepresented, when they are not ignored altogether, by methodologies oriented to constructing facts through strictly univocal modes of representation. [1985:8]

More than any other kind of current commentator on human existence, humorists bring out its multiple interpretations and meanings.

In the 1930s Burke analogized perspective by incongruity to "the same 'cracking' process that chemists now use in their refining of oil" (1965:119).[15] I would also analogize perspective by ambiguity to the same process, though it produces different distillates. Today we would compare both perspectives to a particle accelerator that splits apart a physical phenomenon to reveal its components. Humor, in short, can reveal the components of a nonphysical phenomenon by exploding it; the humorizer is the closest thing to an atom smasher the nonphysical sciences have.

Notes

1. Keith-Spiegel (1972:8) notes some pre-Kantian precursors of the incongruity theory of humor. So does Morreall (1987:130), who mentions Aristotle and quotes Pascal: "Nothing produces laughter more than a surprising disproportion between that which one expects and that which one sees."

2. The conception of comedy elaborated here also holds in a purely subjectivist scheme in which neither system nor incongruity exist in the world, but only in the mind. In this purely subjectivist scheme, the comic contradiction is not between the subjective expectation system and the objective real system, but between two sides of the subjective expectation system: not between what we *expect* to be going on in the objective world and what is *really* going on there, but between what we *expect* to be going on in the objective world and what we *believe* is really going on there.

3. Joyce Hertzler lists the various synonyms for "incongruity" that have appeared in the literature on humor: "Human beings tend to respond with laughter when they are confronted with the incongruous, the contradictory, the inharmonious, the unfitting, the inappropriate, the imperfect or crude; the accidental, the disorderly, or unusual; the unexpected, unaccustomed, or unconventional; the startling, the mischievous, the awkward; the ironical, the ludicrous, the ridiculous, or absurd; the pretentious, inflated, humbug, or masquerading; the eccentric or queer; the clever and exceptional; the exaggerated, the miscarried, or misshaped; the logically incoherent or implausible; the irrational, the nonsensical, the stupid, or idiotic; the monstrous, the indecent, the deformed, the deviate, the grotesque" (1970:13–14). I will explore the nuances that distinguish some of these terms in the text.

4. This statement needs two qualifications. First, not every incongruity is funny. Incongruities that collapse expectation systems

cause laughter *only under the extrasystem conditions* I hope to specify elsewhere. Second, some congruities are funny, especially hypercongruities. Summarizing previous humor theorists, Joyce Hertzler concludes that "much laughter is a response to some breach of the usual or regular or expected order of events," but he goes on to note that "we also laugh occasionally because of the surprise or satisfaction afforded, not by the unexpected but rather by the expected, as when some person suspected of cockiness or stupidity does perform in a cocky or stupid manner" (1970:13–14). Freud explained the laughter that results from this "rediscovery of what is familiar" in terms of the "economy of psychic expenditure" it creates (1960:120–21). But if we laugh whenever something confirms rather than denies our expectation, our psychic savings account would grow so large that we would be laughing almost all the time. A better explanation is that we sometimes expect human variability but encounter inhuman invariance instead.

5. We should not forget D. H. Monro's *Argument of Laughter*, the first modern synthesis of the history of humor theories (written mostly during World War II—a not irrelevant circumstance). Before Koestler, Monro described the production of humor by the intersection of systems or frames, which he called "universes":

> In discussing the stories of Kimmins' schoolchildren, we have seen that they often depend on the intrusion into one sphere of an incident or attitude of mind which is appropriate only to an utterly different sphere. The Indian rajah spreads his costly silks before the king with all the courtly ceremony that accompanies Oriental gifts. And the king, instead of responding with similar courtliness, is represented as exclaiming: "Ow much for the lot?" . . .
>
> But the story of the rajah does not depend merely on contrast. There is here the mental shock of being jolted out of a whole frame of mind, a whole universe of discourse, with all sorts of rich associations, all sorts of stock responses leaping to the forefront of consciousness. . . . We put kings in one mental compartment, and costers [cart sellers of fruits or vegetables] in another. We surround each of them with different associations, and we respond to each with a particular attitude. . . .
>
> The point is merely that a particular atmosphere has been built up, an atmosphere that does depend largely on stock responses. And this atmosphere is suddenly destroyed by a single inappropriate remark. It is this which gives the sensation of being suddenly hurled from one universe into another. . . .

Universe-changing is a very important element in humour; we may even find it is the key to all humour. [1951:45–46; see also 62–67].

6. Cameron also notes that some jokes emphasize the reality of the new frame by deemphasizing the reality of the old frame: "The shift of frame of reference in which what we thought was true is suddenly shown to be false is a basic element in jokes, at least in our culture. Many jokes end on a tag line in which one of the characters says to the other, 'Oh, thank Heaven, I thought you said. . . .' . . . An example is the man who hears a speaker predict the end of the world and says in fright: 'When did you say?' 'One hundred million years.' 'Oh, thank heaven, I thought you said a million!' . . . "We have many jokes about deafness, in which the deficiency confuses frames of reference" (Cameron 1963:89).

7. Raskin also gives a more technical formulation of his theory: "The *Main Hypothesis* on which this approach is based can be formulated as: *A text can be characterized as a single-joke-carrying text if both of the [following] conditions are satisfied: (1) The text is compatible, fully or in part, with two different scripts [and] (2) The two scripts with which the text is compatible are opposite. . . . The two scripts with which some text is compatible* are said to *overlap fully or in part on this text*" (1985:99).

8. It is surprising that Raskin, at least in his main work (1985), does not acknowledge the influence of Koestler. Some contributors to Raskin's journal *Humor*, however, have pointed out the connection. Salvatore Attardo (1988:358ff.) finds commonalities between European humor research derived from Koestler's "bisociation" theory and Raskin's semantic "script overlap" theory. Neal Norrick (1989:119) compares Raskin's "opposition between semantic scripts" with Koestler's "bisociation" and with his own "schema conflict." The Workshop on Humor and Cognition, held at Indiana University in February 1989 and synopsized in *Humor* (1989:417–40), also compares Raskin's semantic "script opposition" theory of humor with Douglas Hofstadter's cognitive psychological "frame blend" theory.

9. Hazlitt criticized Locke's definition of wit for being too broad because other mental functions that reveal unexpected similarities are not funny: "On this definition Harris . . . has very well observed that demonstrating the equality of the three angles of a right-angled triangle to two right ones, would, upon the principle here stated, be a piece of wit instead of an act of the judgment, or understanding, and Euclid's *Elements* a collection of epigrams" (1930; 6:19).

10. Humor theorists have often described wit's ability to find simi-
    larities between apparently opposing frames in terms of those
    paradigms of the union of opposites—sex: "Wit, you know, is the
    expected copulation of ideas, the discovery of some occult rela-
    tion between images in appearance remote from each other"
    (Johnson 1969:251); and marriage: "A favorite definition of
    joking has long been the ability to find similarity between dissim-
    ilar things—that is, hidden similarities. Jean Paul [Richter] has
    expressed this thought itself in a joking form: 'Joking is the dis-
    guised priest who weds every couple.' Vischer carries this further:
    'He likes to wed couples whose union their relatives frown upon'"
    (Freud 1963:11).
11. Although humor increases as the comic begins to sustain a com-
    parison between seemingly different realms, beyond a certain
    point the humor changes to absurdity as the comparison
    becomes more farfetched (see Davis 1971). For instance, a comic
    may point out that advocacy groups have shifted from "human
    rights" to "animal rights," and then proceed to reduce their views
    to amusing absurdity by imagining them shifting still further to
    "fish rights," "insect rights," and even "vegetable rights."
12. Thus comics can amuse their audience merely by pointing out
    that ordinary things do not make sense (that is, cannot be located
    in any coherent system):

    > "In a nutshell, I would say that I spot absurdities," [Jim
    > Samuels] said after [winning the 1982 San Francisco Comedy
    > Competition]. "The world makes no sense, and we don't have
    > to take it."
    >   He would joke about Jack-in-the-Box serving croissants
    > ("Whenever I'm in the mood for French food, I head for Le
    > Box") and describe his cure for San Francisco's parking prob-
    > lems ("Drive a forklift"). [obituary for San Francisco comedian
    > Jim Samuels]

    Of course, not everything that does not make sense is amusing.
    Few find funny such extraordinary existential absurdities as a
    comic's premature death: Samuels died of AIDS at age 41.
13. The main psychological tradition of humor research—see Deckers
    and Buttram (1990) and McGhee, Ruch, and Hehl (1990) for
    references—has distinguished an "incongruity" model of humor
    from an "incongruity-resolution" model of humor, which parallels
    my own distinction between an "annihilated single system" model
    of humor that centers on "incongruity," and the "transposed double

system" model of humor that centers on "ambiguity." The psychological models of humor focus on its audience's cognitive equilibrium whereas my system models of humor focus on the abstract properties of systems that create it. This psychological tradition of humor research (see especially McGhee 1990) has expended much effort to confirm that most people find "incongruity-resolution" humor funnier than pure "incongruity" (nonsense) humor, and that appreciation for "incongruity" humor decreases with age whereas appreciation for "incongruity-resolution" humor increases with age.

14. Burke derives this concept from the writings of Nietzsche and his followers, which accounts in part for their witty style:

> These are historical perspectives, which Spengler acquires by taking a word usually applied to one setting and transferring its use to another setting. It is a "perspective by incongruity," since he established it by violating the "properties" of the work in its previous linkages. The device as used by Spengler is, in a blunter way, precisely the same as it is used in Nietzsche. . . . Nietzsche establishes his perspectives by a constant juxtaposition of incongruous words, attaching to some name a qualifying epithet which had heretofore gone with a different order of names. He writes by the same constant reordering of categories that we find in the Shakespearean metaphor. . . . Nietzsche knew that probably every linkage was open to destruction by the perspectives of a planned incongruity. Throughout his life he "undermined," carefully qualifying his nouns by the juxtaposition of modifying matter that had the "wrong" moral inclination. The humorists, the satirists, the writers of the grotesque, all contributed to this work with varying degrees of systematization, giving us new insights by such deliberate misfits. [1965:90–91]

His "perspective by incongruity" is especially appropriate for describing linguistic oxymorons like Veblen's term *trained incapacity:* "Our notions of what goes with training naturally suggest capacity rather than incapacity" (91). Rather unsystematically, Burke lists seven ways to apply his perspective by incongruity, which (I will add) humorists also employ: (1) see the large in the small, (2) see the small in the large, (3) see the good in the bad and vice versa, (4) omit the background knowledge customarily used to interpret a phenomenon, (5) adopt a false premise, (6) apply the jargon of one field to another, (7) see what is usually distant from close and what is usually close *sub specie aeternitatis* (119–24).

15. Comics need not crack human creations deliberately. Sometimes they crack on their own:

> There constantly exists, for a certain sort of person or high emotional content, at work creatively, the danger of coming to a point where something cracks within himself or within the paragraph under construction—cracks and turns into a snicker. Here, then, is the very nub of the conflict: the careful form of art, and the careless shape of life itself. What a man does with this uninvited snicker (which may closely resemble a sob, at that) decides his destiny. If he resists it, conceals it, destroys it, he may keep his architectural scheme intact and save his building, and the world will never know. If he gives in to it, he becomes a humorist, and the sharp brim of the fool's cap leaves a mark forever on his brow. [White 1941:xix]

Discussion Questions

1. Davis's starting point is expectation: comedy disrupts the sets and systems we've come to understand by introducing incongruous elements, the *unexpected*. Do you accept this as the wellspring of comedy? Why or why not?

2. What's your response to Davis's point that too many incongruities can spoil a joke? To what degree are you attracted to humor that's so incongruous that it approaches surrealism or absurdity?

3. Davis argues that jokes are funnier if the incongruous elements are "essential" to the system being disrupted, suggesting that jokes about moral values will be more successful than jokes about less essential aspects. Think of some of your favorite jokes—does Davis's conjecture fit those jokes? How does this idea connect to Bergson's point about the moral clashing with the physical?

4. Davis claims that the best jokes move between two systems, setting up a complex relationship of the two systems and a dynamic of disruption. Again, think of some of your favorite jokes—can you discern whether two systems are in play?

Writing Activities

1. Write a description of a system functioning as designed, then slowly introduce unexpected or disruptive elements from another system.

2. Revise or continue the description above to the point of absurdity, or a surreal degree of incongruity. Note the point at which the description becomes more strange than comic.

3. Write a joke or a comic story in which the body and morality or spirituality are in conflict with each other.

Tickling the Naked Ape:
The Science of Laughter

JIMMY CARR AND LUCY GREEVES

Headnotes/Things to Look For

Jimmy Carr is a stand-up comedian, actor, and writer working in England. Before turning to comedy, he was a marketing executive for Shell Oil. Currently he hosts game shows on British television and releases comedy DVDs. Carr and his co-writer Lucy Greeves, who works in advertising as a copywriter, published their book Only Joking *(The Naked Jape in England) in 2006.*

While assessing the scientific dimensions of laughter and joking, Carr and Greeves adopt a more casual tone than Bergson and Davis in the preceding selections, drawing also on a range of popular culture references. One thing to be attentive to is how many of their expressions and examples are distinctively British, making a U.S. reader stretch to get the meaning or the joke.

──────────── ✦ ────────────

Why do human beings tell jokes? Well, why did the chicken cross the road? In keeping with the willfully literal punch line to that particular riddle, we answer thus: to make each other laugh. And to understand why provoking laughter is something that so many citizens of the world aspire to, we need to start by looking at the nature of laughter itself.

We're assuming that everyone reading this book agrees, to some extent, with Darwin's notion that human beings evolved from ape-like ancestors through a process of natural selection, characterized by the "survival of the fittest."[1] That means agreeing that most, if not all, of our fundamental characteristics—our large brains, opposable thumbs, capacity to form pair-bonds—have a role in furthering the success of our species. Evolutionary theory suggests that a near-universal behavior like laughing must

───────────

[1]Not necessarily a safe assumption these days. Creationists, for example, believe that everything Genesis says is literally true. We don't even think Phil Collins is a very good drummer.

serve some purpose; otherwise all the funny people would have died out a very long time ago. Man is arguably the planet's most successful species, barring the cockroach. We're top dogs, kings of the jungle, mammalian overlords. So does our ability to laugh make humans fitter to survive, and has it helped us to become the number one ape?

From Aristotle onward, and probably long before him too, mankind has arrogantly assumed that he's the only animal that laughs. More recent research suggests that may not be true; what the scientific literature calls "repetitive vocalizations in response to pleasure stimuli" have been observed in several other creatures. Both Dian Fossey and Jane Goodall describe how gorillas chuckle when tickled (although the alternative theory that the gorillas' "chuckles" actually signified "crazy lady go now never touch Bobo again" remains untested). More recently, animal behaviorists at the University of Plymouth observed smiling and laughter in baby chimps as young as one month old. The apes responded to their human handlers' smiles and laughed out loud when tickled, just as human babies would. A chimp's "laugh" is not quite the same as a human's, however. The ape makes its characteristic "play face"—mouth open, lower teeth exposed, upper teeth covered—and makes a panting sound on both inward and outward breaths.[2] When students of neuropsychologist Robert Provine were played a recording of chimp "laughter" and asked to guess what it was, their answers included a dog panting, sanding wood and masturbating.

Actually, perhaps that should read, "a person sanding wood, a person masturbating *or* a dog panting." It's anyone's guess what an out-of-breath, horny canine carpenter would sound like.

Meanwhile, in a lab somewhere in Boston, grown men and women have been tickling rats in the name of science, and making them laugh—or at least chirrup happily. Surely that's the kind of animal testing we can all approve of. Above and beyond the response to tickling, it seems that some more sophisticated beasts may have a rudimentary sense of humor that allows them to appreciate simple practical jokes. Researcher Roger Fouts claimed that one of his subjects, a chimpanzee name Washoe, once urinated down his neck while riding on his shoulders, then made the sign for "funny."

---

[2] If you're reading this on the bus, we recommend you wait until you get home to experiment with your "play face."

In the face of this evidence, we'll grudgingly relinquish the notion that laughter is ours alone. But even if we allow the great apes a sense of humor, the verbal complexity of jokes like the ones in this book would put them beyond the reach of even the most intensively trained signing chimp. The ability to *make jokes* in order to make each other laugh is surely safe to claim as exclusively human property. Deriving amusement from a story or riddle that depicts an external situation or event—a concept, not a practical joke—*is* a uniquely human habit. More than that, it's a fundamental element of the mystery of consciousness. If gorillas were better at telling jokes, they might not get such a raw deal with the zoos and the poachers and the shrinking natural habitat. Maybe it's not the opposable thumb thing holding them back, after all. No one's denying that apes are funny: making faces, throwing poo—you can tell they're making an effort. What they lack is a really good script editor.

• • •

Laughter has always been part of our repertoire of noises. Like crying, whimpering and moaning, it's an instinctive and universal mode of human expression. These noises mean the same in all cultures and we develop them in our very early life, long before language gets a look-in. For example, rhythmic crying is a communication tool available to us from birth. Few babies need much incentive to pick it up and run with it. The smile appears a long and weary five weeks later, on average, with laughter and tantrums following at three to four months. Note that these two strike simultaneously, like thunder and lightning; we learn both to be furious and to laugh it off at around the same stage of our development. With all of these signals, the infant is broadcasting its emotional state. Adults are no different: when we laugh, we are telling each other something whether we are conscious of communicating or not.

The generally accepted evolutionary explanation for the development of laughter argues that it evolved from a threat response or warning. To paraphrase slightly: Early man, the theory goes, thought he saw a woolly mammoth charging across the tundra. He bared his teeth, narrowed his eyes and prepared to scream the alarm to the rest of his tribe. Suddenly the woolly mammoth slipped[3] and fell down, out cold. Early man's grimace

---

[3]This sort of accident was, sadly, all too common during the Ice Age.

of fear softened into a wide smile and his scream of alarm became a hearty laugh as he ran to fetch his mammoth-disemboweling hook and his brothers.

In other words, laughter is a release of tension on discovering that a perceived threat is not, in fact, a threat at all. Think of a child's first experiences of laughter, which generally occur at around the same time as it learns to distinguish its parents by sight from other adults, and develops a fear of strangers. Imagine the dilemma: Large hairy adult looms threateningly over me. Will it attack? No, thank goodness. It is merely running its fingers lightly over my tummy. Most of us experience our first laugh through being tickled.

Experiments in neuroscience appear to support the "threat diffused" theory of laughter too. Neuroscientist V. S. Ramachandran used his work with brain-damaged patients to identify a "laughter circuit" in the brain: a network deep in the limbic system, the seat of our emotions, which fires up when we find something funny. Or, in the case of some of Dr. Ramachandran's patients, when we are in pain. Patients with damage to a particular region of the insular cortex suffer from pain asymbolia: instead of feeling fear and agony when the good doctor repeatedly pricks a pin into their fingers, they find it excruciatingly funny. (We only have his word for that, but he is quite a distinguished scientist.) What we can take this to mean is that the neural pathways for pain, fear and laughter are intimately interconnected. It makes neurological sense that an aborted fear response would end up as a laugh, and perhaps also helps to explain why the spectacle of somebody falling, hard, upon their arse is probably the single funniest thing in the world. We empathize with the pain, but in the end it's someone else's arse. Phew!

The notion that laughter is a response to a conceptual shift, a change in our perception of the state of the world around us, is closely mirrored by the classic joke structure. First, the setup: we are presented with a universe of facts and characters. This universe can be surreal, but it has internal logic.

A traffic policeman stops a speeding car, and is surprised to discover six live penguins in the trunk.

"Yes, Officer—I'm in a terrible state. I won these penguins in a raffle and I don't know what to do with them."

Replies the policeman, "If I were you, I'd take them to the zoo."

The following day, the policeman notices the same car, and flags it down again. The six penguins are still huddled in the trunk, but now they're wearing sunglasses. "I thought I told you to take them to the zoo," says the policeman.

"Yes, you did—and they enjoyed it so much I'm taking them to the seaside today."

The setup of the joke creates a vivid word picture which, for all its absurdity, nevertheless conforms to certain expectations. We identify with the baffled traffic policeman, who is somewhat surprised to find live penguins in a man's car and instructs him to do the sensible thing and take them to the zoo. So far, it's just a zany story in the *National Enquirer:* "PENGUIN FREAK IN HIGHWAY ARREST." And then, with the punch line, comes a paradigm shift. That one line forces you to reinterpret all the facts that went before, presenting an entirely different picture of events, with a different internal logic. Suddenly you're in a world where penguins are two-foot-tall tourists with communication skills and aesthetic judgment, where they treat humans as their chauffeurs. And they *wear sunglasses.* The setup isn't a threat of the order of, say, a charging mammoth, but any story generates a certain amount of suspense until it reaches its conclusion. The fact that you know how a joke works and expect a funny punch line increases this feeling of pleasant tension. The punch line works by resolving the suspense of the story in an unexpected way. Your brain responds to this tiny paradigm shift by making a conceptual leap that mirrors the jump from perceived threat to no threat, with the same result—laughter.

• • •

If it's true that laughter originated as an expression of relief in response to a fearful situation that turned out to be harmless, it follows that the sensation of laughter is closely associated with pleasure—it's a release of tension. In fact, laughing is so pleasurable that we go to great lengths to recreate that sensation of release in completely artificial circumstances, by telling jokes. And it's still fun. There's no real threat in a joke, but we enjoy that slightly giddy shift of expectation nonetheless. Why is it so enjoyable to laugh? Especially considering that the best kind of laughter is the kind that starts to hurt; that takes our bodies over and sometimes even turns into tears. For years, scientists have been trying to determine the physical benefits of laughter. A recent study by Professor Robin Dunbar found that laughter raised people's pain thresholds. His explanation is that shared social laughter causes an endorphin rush and the release of oxytocin in the brain—the same chemical reactions that we have to human touch. Endorphins are natural opiates. They make us feel relaxed, encourage social and sexual interaction and increase our levels of trust.

Another study claimed to prove that people who laugh more have healthier immune systems. A third experiment appeared to show that the increase in heart rate produced by a good laugh had health benefits equivalent to fifteen minutes on an exercise bike. However, the doctors at the University of Maryland, whose research yielded the startling insight that people suffering from heart disease are precisely 40 percent less likely to see the funny side of life, were probably wasting their time, as well as ours.

Undaunted by the fact that not one of these studies could be said to constitute compelling medical evidence, a whole industry has grown up around the notion that laughter isn't just enjoyable, but actively good for you. Which immediately makes it sound less fun, somehow, in the same way that the implicit imperative in "Fun Fair" guarantees anything but (£4 for a toffee apple, £5 for crippling nausea and no charge for the near certainty that your fourteen-year-old daughter will be pregnant by 9 P.M.). You can go on a Laughter Cruise, do Laughter Yoga and visit humor conferences to learn about pain management through giggling. In the mid-1960s a man called Norman Cousins was almost paralyzed by an agonizing and supposedly incurable degenerative disease called ankylosing spondylitis. He was so convinced of the benefits of laughter that he refused conventional treatment and cured himself with repeated viewings of the Marx Brothers movies. He later recovered from a massive heart attack using the same techniques, and finally died, peacefully and presumably chuckling away to himself, aged seventy-five. The books he wrote about his experiences coincided with a huge upsurge of interest in holistic healing and ensured that joking and laughter had a central place in the new movement.

The current poster boy for laughter as physical therapy is Dr. Hunter "Patch" Adams, immortalized by Robin Williams in a film so saccharine that, although we tried to watch it in the name of research, we had to switch it off halfway through because all our teeth were falling out. We have no idea how the film ends, but we do know that the real-life Adams recovered from a major breakdown in his early twenties by discovering his inner clown, and went on to found the Gesundheit Institute, a sort of comedy hospital staffed by clown-doctors that, despite more than thirty years of planning and the revenues for the film rights to his life story, still exists more as an ideal than an actual healthcare institution. Patch Adams has this to say about comedy:

> Comic relief is a major way for happy folk to dissipate pain. In a healthier world, humor would be a way of life. People would be funny as a rule, not an exception. One of the best aids in the transition from a "heavy" to a "light" existence is to open up the comedian in oneself.

Patch Adams has his detractors. As the old joke has it, "Laughter is the best medicine. Unless you've got VD, in which case I recommend penicillin." Certainly some of Adams's advice is not terribly practical: he advocates brightening up a depressing day by going to the grocery store with your underpants over your trousers, which is surely only a whisker away from what the rest of society likes to call mental illness. (In fact, why not try popping down to Kmart with your underpants on your *head*. Then they'll clearly see you're nuts.) But he also has thousands of supporters who testify to the therapeutic benefits of filling their lives with laughter and joking. In his defense, he puts forward the reasonable argument that "everyone who goes to a job he doesn't like is a lot weirder than I am."

On the other hand, we would like to call nineteenth-century novelist Anthony Trollope as a witness for the prosecution. We'd like to, but he's dead. The cause? Excessive laughter occasioned by readings from F. Anstey's comic novel *Vice Versa*. One of Trollope's biographers described the final curtain thus: "For a while, Uncle Tony roared as usual, then suddenly Tilley and Edith realized that as they were laughing, he was silent." He had suffered a severe stroke; he never spoke again and died several weeks later. Doubtless it's what he would have wanted, although probably not as much as he would have wanted to *not die just yet. Vice Versa* is clearly a very dangerous book, which, incidentally, left a diabolic legacy. As the original identity-swap comedy, its many bastard progeny include *Freaky Friday* and *Big*, but as far as we know nobody has yet died laughing at either of them.

The demise of much-loved men of letters notwithstanding, it's clear that laughter can act as an intensely pleasurable physical release mechanism. It has even greater powers as a psychological pressure valve. According to anthropologist Terrence Deacon, laughter "is not just an expression of emotion. It is a public symptom of engaging in a kind of mental conflict resolution." When we first approached the question of jokes as therapy, we were, if we're honest, a little sneery about it. What changed our minds was the testimony of a depressed Welshwoman on the radio (*Woman's Hour*, BBC Radio 4—where else?). "My face didn't move for two years at first. Your face gets set, with the depression, doesn't it?" She is a member of a humor workshop led by Alice Hortop, an occupational therapist who first noticed the effects of laughter while fitting amputees with stump socks—a painful process that doesn't seem a terribly promising source of humor. But Alice found that telling jokes during the process reduced the patients' anxiety and helped them deal with the pain. Her anecdotal evidence is borne out by a number of studies (not least the recent one by Professor Dunbar, mentioned earlier) that suggest laughter raises our pain threshold. Hortop decided to apply her insights to psychological pain, with dramatic results.

The Swansea-based humor workshop group meets weekly to play games and tell jokes, under Alice Hortop's guidance. "It's not about orchestrated laughter in groups; we're trying to get genuine laughter." For many of them, even practicing a smile is a big step forward. Some weeks a participant is just too deeply depressed to even make it to the meeting. But little by little they start to take the laughter home with them. One woman talks about doing her homework—playing with her daughter, throwing M&Ms at each other and trying to catch them in their mouths. "It's nice for my daughter to see, because in the past she hasn't really seen her mum smiling or laughing."

It's rather moving. Hortop has created a very special space, a social arena where laughter and joking are celebrated. Some of us are lucky enough to live in this sort of environment all the time, taking it completely for granted, but for these people it's a rare opportunity to flex funny bones that have grown brittle through years of disuse. "We teach people how to be approachable, how to be witty, how to be confident—that's a big one. When you tell a joke and it goes flat, there's nothing worse. We teach people to find the right place to tell the joke, and we practice joke-telling in the group. Because we analyze our humor types at the workshop, people get an idea of what they're good at." For these depressed individuals, joking can unlock a childlike lightness of being that has been lost to their illness. This liberation comes first of all in the safe circle of the workshop, but with time and perseverance can spread throughout their lives. Every single person who has participated in the workshop has shown a reduction in symptoms of anxiety and depression, and a less tangible but far more important increase in general levels of happiness.

• • •

The individuals in the laughter workshop are taking tentative steps toward being able to tell one joke, one day. At the other extreme, there are some people who joke compulsively—they just can't stop. In 2004, British comedian Tim Vine entered *Guinness World Records* for telling the highest number of jokes in an hour. It's an extraordinary feat of memory, and certainly represents outstanding value for money if you measure your stand-up comedy in terms of jokes per minute (approximately 8.3167 in this case, since you ask). Vine's jokes are also mini master classes in the art of the silly pun.

"I went to the butchers the other day and I bet him 50 quid that he couldn't reach the meat off the top shelf. And he said, 'No, the steaks are too high.'"

The press dubbed Vine "the Joke Machine Gun," perhaps because if you try to tell jokes that fast, the delivery is bound to get somewhat mechanical. And in fact the pun is the most mechanical of jokes, resting as it does on a relatively small number of linguistic rules. At any rate, "Comic sets new record" sounds like a challenge to us. So we decided to go looking for a new contender for Tim's record: a worthy adversary in the gags-per-minute game. Think Kasparov versus Deep Blue. What we need is an *actual* joke machine.

In 1957, Russian biochemist, science fiction writer and self-styled humor expert Isaac Asimov wrote a short story called "Jokester." It is set in the twenty-first century. In the story, a "ten mile long" computer named Multivac is tasked with explaining where all the jokes come from. It turns out that they are an experiment played on the human race by a superior alien intelligence, and once this becomes known all the jokes vanish from the world. His inability to predict the size of twenty-first-century microprocessors notwithstanding, Asimov presents a terrifyingly convincing scenario.

Actually he doesn't; it's complete tosh. We found our joke machine much closer to home.

Ruli Manurung is indirectly responsible for writing tens of millions of jokes, but he's definitely not an extraterrestrial. Nor is he a comedian. He's a software engineer, and along with fellow academics Graeme Ritchie, Dave O'Mara and Helen Pain, he has created a computer program called STANDUP. We went to meet STANDUP at home in the Department of Informatics at Edinburgh University, and asked Ruli to put the joke machine through its paces. First of all he explained patiently that STANDUP isn't an actual machine, let alone a ten-mile-long one. It's a piece of software running on a normal PC. This was a bit of a letdown, but we did perk up considerably when we discovered that, despite his deceptively corporate laptop disguise, STANDUP can talk. In fact he does a mean impression of Professor Stephen Hawking (although it's definitely not as mean as Jimmy's).

STANDUP is based on a program developed ten years earlier by a young artificial intelligence researcher called Kim Binsted, who also happened to be an amateur improvisational comedian. As part of her Ph.D. thesis, Kim developed JAPE, the Joke Analysis and Production Engine, which was the first program capable of producing punning riddles using words from a general dictionary as its raw material. The best of the resulting riddles were blind-tested on schoolchildren alongside jokes from a standard kids' joke book. Although the computer-generated jokes fared worse, on average, than those crafted by human beings, the overall top-rated joke came from JAPE, namely:

> What's the difference between leaves and a car?
> One you brush and rake, the other you rush and brake.

JAPE also came up with this subdued gem:

> What do you call a depressed engine?
> A low-comotive.

What Binsted proved was that simple puns can be created in a laboratory. Given a sophisticated electronic dictionary, a series of rules about the relation of words, and a great deal of trial and error, the computer occasionally throws out sentences that are recognizable as jokes.

The program can replicate some of the cognitive processes that Tim Vine applies when he writes a joke. STANDUP starts with the punch line, locating a word or phrase with a double meaning. Then it constructs a setup line that makes sense of both meanings. It has thirteen different joke formats—"what's the difference between a—and a—," for example—and a dictionary of around 200,000 words with which to fill in the blanks.

While there's no denying that STANDUP is an admirable academic achievement, Tim Vine's job is quite safe for the time being.

We're still a long way off from creating a computer that knows what's funny: one that could actually entertain us on purpose. What the computer program lacks, utterly and conclusively, is a sense of humor. A computer program has no worldview, no context for its jokes. Scientists cannot yet conceive of a computer that could contain all the information it would need to predict whether someone will find a joke funny. That means that STANDUP pours out its jokes in astonishing quantity—over ten million of the "brush and rake" type alone—but it does so completely indiscriminately. It is funny by accident, and one combs through screeds of nonsense to find something that even approximates a joke, like this:

> What do you call a hip-hop tortilla?
> A rap wrap.

STANDUP is funniest when it's rude. (That's a useful rule of thumb, but in this context we mean STANDUP the computer program, not stand-up comedy in general.) Our very favorite computer-generated joke is this one:

> What's the difference between a man beard and a sexual excitement?
> One is a buck fuzz, the other is a fuck buzz.

There's a sort of charming naïveté about STANDUP. Hearing these jokes, you could find yourself agreeing with Asimov, just for a moment, that jokes are written by aliens. Mind you, Ruli's going to have to remove some words from STANDUP's dictionary before it gets into the hands of its end-users. At this point we should reassure you that research funding isn't just allocated to projects like this in the interests of keeping academics amused with inadvertent double entendres—this project has a serious purpose. STANDUP stands for System To Augment Non-speakers' Dialogue Using Puns. The software is being developed so that speech-impaired children can tell jokes. The sort of language play that leads to puns is thought to serve an important function in the development of a child's language and communication skills. A child who suffers from, for example, cerebral palsy, may have very limited powers of speech and be unable to communicate except through a communication aid. These speech computers may give you a cool robot voice, but they don't offer much scope for creative use of language. The STANDUP program is intended to allow the child to experiment with language and try out humorous ideas by helping him or her to construct, evaluate and tell simple riddles.

Watching some of these children try out a prototype of the program, what's striking is how effortlessly they perform the one vital task that the computer can't. They distinguish instantly between jokes and not-jokes, and they are equally sure which jokes are funny and which aren't. What's more, their pleasure at hearing a successful joke—one that they find funny—seems to come from two distinct sources. They can appreciate the joke for itself and judge that one little word game is more satisfying than another; a particular pun or alliteration tickles them. But the greater source of pleasure seems to be the interaction with the carer or researcher—the actual telling of the joke. Jokes have this wonderful potential to create moments of social informality, a sort of leveling out of the teller's and hearer's sometimes very unequal roles. In this case, "telling" the joke through the voice synthesizer seems to make the children feel exhilarated at their new power to amuse their adult carer.

This makes a lot of sense in the light of our earlier observation that laughter evolved as a noise to communicate emotion. For a joke to give pleasure, it needs to be shared. That's one of the reasons why human responses to particular jokes or even to humor in general are notoriously difficult to study in laboratory conditions. Robert Provine describes an abortive experiment to study laughter in individuals by playing them audio and video recordings of George Carlin, Joan Rivers, *Saturday Night Live* and so on. "Nothing seemed to work. My comic virtuosi elicited only a few grudging chuckles from the lab-bound subjects. . . . This was a humbling experience, for obtaining a sample of laughter does not qualify as what many people would consider rocket science." What this failed experiment taught Provine was fundamental. By their very inability or refusal to laugh, his subjects were telling us that laughter is social. Like misery, hilarity loves company.

Once Provine got out of the lab and into the field, examples of laughter were everywhere. Armed with little more than a pencil, a notebook and a false mustache, he and his students lurked inconspicuously on the fringes of ordinary conversations until they had collected twelve hundred "laugh episodes." They discovered that, in normal one-to-one conversations, the person who is speaking laughs 46 percent more, on average, than the person who is listening. They also found that less than 20 percent of the remarks that preceded laughter in these situations could be considered even remotely humorous. The ones that did resemble jokes or punch lines in the classic sense included "He didn't realize he was sitting in dog shit until he put his hand down to get up" (a classic slapstick premise, to be sure) and "Poor boy looks just like his father." The great majority of the laughs they recorded were in response to remarks like "It was nice meeting you too" and "What is that supposed to mean?" All the people they listened to were using laughter as part of the rhythm, the ebb and flow of conversation and communication. They didn't need a finely honed punch line—the slightest chance remark would set them off. If laughter began as a way to communicate deferred threat, it surely endured as a group bonding exercise. It fizzes around our conversations like electricity, looking for a joke to earth it.

• • •

We began this chapter with a riddle: Why do human beings tell jokes? To make each other laugh. But like most riddles, this one has a twist in the tail. A joke is a highly sophisticated verbal flourish, a product of human culture and intellect and linguistic skill, which has so far defied science's efforts to reproduce it under laboratory conditions. Animals can't do it, and machines can't do it. Telling a joke is complex higher-order communication. But the way we enjoy the joke is totally primitive. Laughter—that's a guttural, an animal noise, a physical response halfway between fear and ecstasy that we share with the apes. It flies below our intellectual radar, at the level of instinct.

A joke has special powers to bridge the gap between the tickled chimp and the academic, to short-circuit our cultural trajectory and remind us how far we haven't come. The truth, it appears, is that we only invented jokes when it became socially unacceptable for grown-ups to tickle one another in public.

Discussion Questions

1. Carr and Greeves assert that joking would have died out if it didn't serve a valuable purpose in human life. What is the purpose of laughter and the motive for provoking laughter in others?

2. While Carr and Greeves offer that animals do have some sense of humor, they argue that some aspects of comedy are uniquely human. What's your sense of the limits of an animal's capacity for understanding and practicing humor? (This question will come up again in Chapter Two, in Vicki Hearne's "Can an Ape Tell a Joke?")

3. What are some of your favorite jokes? How are they structured? In relation to Carr and Greeves's discussion of joke structure, how do your favorite jokes set up and then shift a paradigm for the audience?

4. Do you agree that people who laugh more tend to be healthier both physically and psychologically? Have you observed the positive effects of laughter in your own life or the lives of family and friends?

5. Carr and Greeves note that computer programs lack a worldview, or a full enough sense of context, to generate funny jokes consistently. What does this mean specifically? What can't computer programs understand about humor?
6. Studies show that much laughter in everyday interaction is not triggered by jokes. What is the role of this kind of social laughter?

Writing Activities

1. Write some puns that aren't funny, of the type that a computer program might generate.
2. Write several jokes that set up one context or way of understanding a situation, then come up with punchlines that force the audience to reinterpret what came before by introducing a new context or frame.

Relaxing the Rules of Reason
ROBIN HEMLEY

Headnotes/Things to Look For

Robin Hemley is the author of the short story collection The Last Studebaker, *the memoir* Nola: A Memoir of Faith, Art, and Madness, *and the writing guide* Turning Life into Fiction.

Note the strategy of Hemley's less formal approach to laying out ideas about how comedy works; this style provides a counterpoint to the more academic approaches earlier in this chapter (Hemley even singles out Bergson as particularly heavy going).

———————— ✦ ————————

Unlike tragedy, a sense of humor is determined by myriad factors: our age, our socioeconomic backgrounds, our culture. What most of us consider tragic is fairly static, though something tragic can be *made* funny by comic techniques such as repetition. In Nathanael West's *A Cool Million*, the hero keeps losing limbs and other parts of himself as he makes his way in the world until there's very little that's left of him. You lose one limb or all your limbs at once, that's tragic. But if you lose them little by little, as well as an eye, your teeth, your hair, you start defying logic, and once you've transcended logic, most people will laugh in spite of themselves, even if they find something a little horrifying at the same time.

Simply put, tragedy has serious and logical consequences. Cause and effect. Comedy usually doesn't. You throw a person off a tall building in a comedy, he bounces. You throw someone off a building in a tragedy, don't wait for the bounce. Aristotle understood this in his "Poetics" when he wrote, "The causes of laughter are errors or deformities that do not pain or injure us; the comic mask, for instance, is deformed and distorted but not painfully so."

COMIC PRINCIPLES

People have been thinking about the comic for as long as there's been laughter, and the principles of comedy have been well defined. Of course, knowing and doing are two different things, but it's useful to have some understanding of what human beings see as funny, if not why. Henri Bergson defined some of the basic forms of comedy in his famous essay "Laughter," published in 1900. Chief among these forms are the Snowball, Repetition, Inversion, the always-popular "Reciprocal Interference of Series" and Transposition. Ironically, Bergson—genius though he may be—is no laugh riot. Still, for some of the theory behind laughter, his essay is an important resource for the fledgling humorist.

FORM VS. CONTENT

My six-year-old daughter, Isabel, has been telling "knock knock" jokes for more than two years now and still doesn't quite have the hang of it.

"Knock knock," she'll say from the back seat as we're driving somewhere.

"Who is it?" I say, honoring the ritual of it.

"Tree."

"Tree who?"

"Tree, don't you know you're going the wrong way, buddy!"

She laughs hysterically at this even though it makes absolutely no sense. The funny thing is, I laugh, too. I don't know why, though I think we're laughing for different reasons. I'm not quite sure why *she's* laughing. I'm laughing because she understands the form of the knock knock joke, but not the content, and what results is something sublimely ridiculous—most of the time.

I admit there are times when Isabel's sense of humor gets a little irritating, after she's told seven of these non sequitur knock knocks in a row and the freshness has worn off. Apparently, I'm not the only one who grows tired of her jokes sometimes. Recently, she reported that a boy at her bus stop runs when he sees her "because he says he hates my jokes, Daddy." She says this proudly, not with any hint of insecurity. Personally, I love the fact that my daughter has discovered bad jokes as a source of personal empowerment. Maybe someday she'll run seminars on the subject.

Isabel, in her absurd knock knock jokes, is following Bergson's idea that "a comic meaning is invariably obtained when an absurd idea is fitted into a well-established phrase form."

Of course, Izzy loves to discuss Bergson every chance she gets. "Tell me about Reciprocal Interference of Series again, Daddy," she often begs me before bedtime.

"No more Bergson," I say. "We did Bergson last night. Don't you ever get tired of Reciprocal Interference of Series? Hey, I've got an idea! Let's talk about humor as a defense mechanism, a way of turning . . ."

She rolls her eyes. "Freud," she says.

"OK, Bergson. *A situation is invariably comic when it belongs simultaneously to two altogether independent series of events and is capable of being interpreted in two entirely different meanings at the same time.*"

"Thank you, Daddy," she says. "Now I can get to sleep."

FUNNY IS WHERE YOU FIND IT

Writing funny is a matter of perspective. How you see the world. It's not simply a matter of knowing the right formulas—it's hardly that at all. We laugh at what we find strange, unusual, illogical. When I write something funny, I generally don't set out to do so. I write, and because I see the world a little bizarrely, I suppose, it comes out funny.

What's remarkable is that in spite of the fact that humor depends on so many variables (age, era, culture), many humorous works *do* survive the ages. We still read the works of the ancient Greek playwright Aristophanes, and of course, Shakespeare's romantic comedies are produced quite often, as are works such as French playwright Molière's *The Imaginary Invalid*. And of course, our most revered author in America was essentially a humorist, Mark Twain. Humor survives the ages for many of the same reasons that great tragedies survive. The great humorists have an understanding of our common human foibles and frailties. If you want to write funny, you have to have some understanding of your own foibles first.

Start with an idea or concept or even a journal observation that you think is funny. A friend of mine once told me about a guy who murdered his first wife and put her in a freezer. He had her in a storage locker and his second wife stopped paying the bill for it, so the contents were auctioned off, and one lucky buyer purchased a freezer with a dead woman inside.

Gruesome certainly, but I could easily imagine a darkly comic story about such a situation.

What one person finds funny another person finds deranged.

I just found that idea as I was flipping through my journals. It was something that I thought was bizarre enough to take note of, regardless of whether it would ever show up in a story of mine. If you want to write, funny or otherwise, keeping a journal is a good idea. Things that are funny happen around us all the time, just about every day. The trick is being receptive to the world around you. There are some things you hear that you'll never forget and other things that are lost unless you write them down. Take, for example, the following dialogue I recorded in my journal on October 25, 1997:

I saw two women with five children ranging in age from seven to two running between, around and ahead of their mothers on a narrow walk through the grounds of a hotel where I was staying.

One woman said, "I've known parents with kids who've lost their front teeth playing a sport and then they have to go their whole lives with fake teeth."

"Oh, I know!" said the second woman.

"And isn't that just the worst look when someone's missing a front tooth and they don't replace it?"

"Oh, I know!"

I'm not sure why this amused me—it's not fall-down funny, but it's funny enough that I thought it worthy of being placed in my journal (a dubious honor, I realize). Part of what I think I find funny here is the repetition of the second woman's "I know's." There's also a kind of potential pattern here, something I'm sure I recognized more or less intuitively at the time—this kind of "dissing" is one of our more laughable and common traits as humans. One can imagine this conversation building, snowballing out of proportion. People like to have others agree with them, and that's what the second woman was doing with the first. Thus encouraged, I can imagine the first woman continuing on with "looks" that she finds awful. "And what about those children who never wipe their noses. I mean, they're just like faucets. You'd think their parents would teach them a thing or two about hygiene."

"Oh, I know!"

"That is *the* worst look, bar none."

"Oh, I know!"

"And some parents will let their kids eat anything—I mean anything, like Little Debbie donuts by the forklift, until they . . ."

Here, I could imagine an unfinished sentence, maybe a pause on the pathway as the first mother realizes too late that she's said something that might offend her friend. She *was* going to criticize parents who "allow" their children to grow chubby, but maybe one of the five children running around them is a little overweight, and now, instead of just saying "I know!" after each nasty observation, the second mother grows silent, maybe defensive. Perhaps, if the story went on from here, the situation might deteriorate into a shouting match, with each mother insulting the appearance of the other's children, down to the way they dress. Who knows? But the point is that this situation was presented to me unexpectedly as I was innocently walking from my hotel room to the hotel lobby.

FUNNY SITUATIONS

Sometimes, too, you find yourself in a situation that starts off serious but becomes absurd. When this happens, take it as a gift and write it down.

Once, I was called to serve on a jury when I lived in North Carolina. At 8:30 A.M., I found the jury lounge in the courthouse, which, according to my journal, contained about seventy-five to one hundred seats. I sat down along with about fifty other potential jurors, and I filled out the appropriate forms. The jury clerk explained the jury procedures to us at a podium with a microphone. Beside her was a Hitachi TV set on which you could see her replicated. This was my first clue that the day was going to be a bizarre one. I wondered why one would need *both* a live person explaining the proceedings *and* a TV image of them at the same time. This was not the kind of wide-screen TV that one sees at outdoor rock concerts or when the Pope comes to town so that the millionth person in the farthest corner of the venue has a chance of seeing what they came to see. This was a small TV in a small room beside a woman who could be seen and heard perfectly well without her image being projected onto the screen beside her. I decided the image must be for potential jurors who were reality-impaired.

After she was done explaining what we had already filled out, she stepped aside and a video came on the TV, a video on jury duty, of course. The video started out with a song titled "I Call North Carolina Home." I loved the lyrics, which went:

> I call North Carolina home.
> Lord, it's just like livin' in a poem.
> I like calling North Carolina home.

When the video was over, the TV switched to Regis and Kathy Lee. Then the clerk swore us in and told us to turn in our Bibles. Apparently, past jurors had taken home Bibles as souvenirs.

And on it went. The day grew increasingly bizarre, hitting its odd crescendo perhaps when I sat in the courtroom during jury selection and watched the potential juror beside me cock her thumb and index finger into a make-believe gun and blow away the defendant about whom she was supposed to feel impartial. Thankfully, she was excluded. But I wasn't, and I eventually wrote an article about my experiences for a local paper.

ANECDOTES

A story I wrote that won *Story* magazine's Humor Award began as an anecdote a friend told me once. My friend Max Childers told me that he had once had a story accepted by a magazine in Atlanta, and he waited for over a year for the magazine to publish it. This in itself isn't unusual or funny, but then he received a letter from the editor saying that the magazine was folding and that the story would appear in its last issue. Another year passed. Then the editor wrote again and he said that a terrible thing had happened—the last issue of the magazine was at press when a deranged printer, in love with a woman who was a horrendously bad poet, took out all of the real contents of the magazine and substituted his girlfriend's awful poetry. Outraged, the editor showed up on the printer's lawn, called him outside and punched him in the nose. Now he was facing assault charges.

This, I thought, was gold—one of the funniest situations I had ever heard. I asked, maybe begged Max for permission to use his anecdote, and then I wrote the story from the printer's point of view. The reason I chose the printer was because he was the one in love, driven by passion. He was the one in whom the irony of the situation resided. In other words, he didn't really think what he was doing was wrong. Or, he thought his deep love for his girlfriend excused his behavior. And furthermore, he thought his girlfriend's poetry was great.

I changed a few of the details. I made the magazine a much larger one than in the real story, a magazine like *The New Yorker*, with a formidable reputation. This situation could be believable because there are plenty of magazines that are printed hundreds of miles from their editorial offices—the printers often mail the magazines directly to subscribers and distribution centers from their printing plants. And so it wasn't beyond the realm of possibility that something like this could happen. I chose to exaggerate the situation in this way because it made the stakes higher, the consequences of the lovelorn printer's actions all the funnier.

I started the story after the damage was done, with the editor on the printer's lawn.

A man on my lawn in a white suit and a Panama hat is calling me down. He's a little chicken-headed fellow with a bow tie. He's holding a hip flask in one hand and a rolled-up copy of a magazine in another. He's one of the scrawniest fellows I've ever seen and his gray hair hangs to his shoulders.

The most pleasurable part of writing this story was the invention of the poems by the printer's girlfriend. It's a lot more difficult than one might imagine to write bad poetry, at least a poem that's earnestly bad. In other words, to be *really* funny I knew I needed to write a poem in character, a poem that I could imagine someone writing and thinking was completely profound and meaningful. After many tries, I came up with the following:

Mother Nature's Abortion

Wood nymphs and sprites are dying of pollution
So are unicorns and fairies
Oh, what is the solution?

Smokestacks belch their foul fumes
While Puck and Bacchus gag
The leprechauns and elves are doomed!

Once-mighty Zeus drinks acid rain
Hobbits hobble around on crutches
Even happy Buddha cannot hide his pain

Mother nature has had an abortion
No one even tried to stop
This ecological disaster of immense proportions.

In the course of one's life as a writer, one sees many bad examples of writing, and I have seen my share of puerile writing even worse than this. Frankly, I wrote a few such earnestly bad poems in high school. My goal wasn't to make fun of bad poets per se—too easy a target and rather mean on my part. The bad poems in my story (there's one more, titled "The Plight of the One-Legged Pony") served a larger purpose in my mind. I didn't want to make fun of anyone really. It was the main character's misguided but true love that I found so funny, and which, in a strange way, I wanted to celebrate. If I was making fun of anyone, it was the pompous editor of the magazine who showed up on the lawn of the lovelorn printer.

RELAXING THE RULES OF REASON: DAYDREAMS, DREAMS AND FANTASIES

I've always had a bit of an attention-span problem. If I find something boring, I turn away or retreat inside myself and invent something funny. As a kid, I daydreamed all the time, and while this habit had some unfunny consequences when I was a child, the daydreaming habit has served me well as a writer.

Once I dreamed that the Queen of England had a secret love-child, a Jamaican man who was a couple of years older than Charles. Who knows where this stuff comes from? I thought the dream was bizarre, even slightly embarrassing that I would dream something so ridiculous, but there's hardly anything too ridiculous to be written down and considered for a story. Don't be afraid of your ideas. If you have a strange dream or wild thought, write it down, pursue it, see where it goes.

How you pursue it, as we've seen, determines how funny the piece is. Exaggeration. Repetition. Snowballing. These are three of the comic writer's invaluable tools. But you must also allow yourself to be illogical, to make something impossible possible, if only for the time it takes to read your story. Bergson said we laugh when there is a relaxation in the rules of reason. Comic absurdity is dreamlike in this way, and it gives us the impression of playing with ideas, perhaps of relaxing the rules and conventions of society as well. That's why, in all those wonderful old Marx brothers movies, there's always a society matron or a judge or someone else who represents Reason and Order being lampooned. Comedy of this kind, the farce, is anarchic and subversive. The comedian who fools with our expectations of order, decency and logical reasoning is the well-meaning enemy of propriety. How does one "relax the rules of reason"? One might as well ask, How does one dream? In your dreams, all of your usual self-consciousness and self-censors have been turned off. In the same way, you need to relax these censors and your own fear of being a fool in order to relax rules of reason. Take a situation you know well, maybe your work situation, and turn it on its head. What if your boss issued a memo one day ordering everyone to do something ridiculous? In the film *Bananas,* Woody Allen's crazy dictator issues a directive to the people of the nation that from now on, underwear must be worn on the outside of people's clothes. And I was once told of the chair of an English department, who on having a nervous breakdown, started issuing bizarre orders to his staff such as, "Make a list!" No mention of what was supposed to be on the list. Simply, "Make a list!"

Don't be afraid to write something stupid. Undoubtedly, someone will think what you're writing is stupid. Someone else will think it's a riot.

Follow through. The bigger the limb you walk out on the better. In other words, don't be afraid to write something illogical. And if you write something illogical, don't be halfhearted about it. Push the situation for all it's worth. The dream about Queen Elizabeth's love child was one I turned into a bizarre little short story. And in another instance, I had a student at the time, blonde haired and blue eyed, who claimed to be descended from some Germanic tribe, though I can't remember which one. I thought it was somewhat amusing that this privileged kid was trying, in my opinion, to cash in a bit on identity politics. So I started daydreaming about the situation. What if some long-forgotten tribe came forward now, appearing out of the woodwork, and reclaimed its heritage? What would be the most unusual tribe, a tribe that one might not normally think of? I started with all the European and Asian tribes that I had learned of in history class—the Goths, the Visigoths—no, not so funny. The Tartars, the Vikings, the Mongols. Not funny. Then I remembered the Vandals. The Vandals. Funny. Really funny, I thought, because the Vandals had not only disappeared, they also had to be the most maligned tribe in history. They had sacked Rome, and their name was now synonymous with senseless damage to other people's property. It didn't make sense that anyone would be proud of being a Vandal, but that's exactly what made it funny. It didn't make sense.

So I wrote a story, which was eventually anthologized and read on National Public Radio, about a college student who appears in the office of a professor of classical history. The story is told from the point of view of the professor who is confronted by his Vandal student for spreading vicious lies about her people.

I decided to write the story from his point of view so we wouldn't be sure whether she was really a Vandal or just a clever student doing a snow job on her meek professor in order to get an extension on a paper and a better grade. I also decided that I would wait until about halfway through the story before I divulged what her claim was.

"I'm here to better my people," she said, looking around the office as though her people had gathered around her.

"Your people? Are you a Mormon?"

"No."

"You're not . . . I mean, you don't look. . . ."

"I'm a Vandal, Dr. Radlisch."

I put my chin in my hand. "A vandal," was all I could manage to say.

"Part Vandal," she said. "Over half."

"You deface property?" I said.

"Another lie," she said. "Another stinking Roman lie." She spat on my carpet.

"You spat on my carpet," I told her, and pointed to it.

"I'm a Vandal, Dr. Radlisch," she said. "If you only knew the truth about us."

"Amy," I said calmly. "I'm not doubting you, of course. But what you're telling me is that you're a Vandal. V-A-N-D-A-L. Vandal. Like the tribe? The one that disappeared from history in the sixth century when Belisarius defeated them and sold them into slavery?"

"Pig," she said. "Dog. Roman dung. Belisarius." And she spat again.

"Please stop spitting on my carpet," I asked her.

She nodded and folded her arms primly in her lap.

SURPRISING YOURSELF

When I was pondering writing this piece, I lay in bed one morning thinking of principles of comedy that I thought were important for other writers to know. What came to my mind, first and foremost, was *cream cheese*. There it was, floating around in my head, *Philadelphia Brand Cream Cheese*. Lying in bed, I started to formulate the *Philadelphia Brand Cream Cheese Method of Comic Writing*. It seemed plausible at the time. Maybe I could even structure an infomercial around the concept. It had something to do with the idea that cream cheese eaten in large quantities makes people hilarious. Some enzyme in the cheese. A chemical interaction with that portion of your brain that controls your ability to write comically, a portion of the brain that has been isolated in laboratory animals. And most importantly, Philadelphia Brand Cream Cheese. Maybe it had to do with W.C. Fields's famous epitaph, "I'd rather be in Philadelphia." I don't know. It was funny at the time and I went with it, mulling over the possibilities as I lay in bed in that state between waking and dreaming. To me, that's at the heart of writing funny, being open to and exploring the possibilities of an idea, no matter how odd and absurd, seeing where it takes you.

Unpredictability. We laugh at what surprises us. The humorist takes the world as it is and shows it to us upside-down. Yet, even tipped upside-down the world is somehow recognizable, and from this perspective we're often shown truths about the human condition that we're blind to when we see the world right side up (i.e., Philadelphia Brand Cream Cheese, one of the four elements that make up the world, according to the ancient Chinese: Fire, Water, Air, Philadelphia Brand Cream Cheese). Whatever the humorist's tool: exaggeration, repetition, snowballing, a comic reversal, the result is still the same—we laugh because we have been shaken out of our normal perceptions. It's as though the humorist is shaking up sleepwalkers, shouting in our ears, "Hey, wake up, don't you see this is funny?" As a writer of humor, this is what your attitude must be, but you must surprise yourself first. You must be open to seeing the world upside-down, be a bit of an anarchist, someone who doesn't mind shouting a bit, or telling anti-knock knock jokes.

Discussion Questions

1. Like Davis, Hemley emphasizes the importance of disrupting logical systems as a root source of humor. How does Hemley's looser colloquial approach to this question serve as a useful analogue to Davis's more scholarly rendering?

2. Hemley uses Bergson (who's no longer around to defend himself) as the butt of jokes involving his joke-telling daughter Isabel. In this anecdote, what is Hemley's point about the limits of theory in showing us the workings of comedy?

3. Where does Hemley find the "funny" in life? Do his examples (of the North Carolina courthouse, of an overheard conversation between two young mothers, of the deranged printer hijacking a literary magazine) seem comic, or more like everyday events? What moves an anecdote into the realm of comedy?

4. What makes the "bad poetry" Hemley offers funny?
5. Hemley's take is that humorists aim to shake up those of us who are "sleep-walkers" by "shouting in our ears," but he doesn't seem to care as much about correcting antisocial behavior as Bergson, for instance. Does Hemley locate comedy as separate from social critique? Do his examples imply any need to correct behavior?

Writing Activities

1. Write out a couple of your favorite anecdotes (the kinds of things you tell friends or that come up at family gatherings) to tease out what makes them funny and worth telling.
2. Write a "bad" poem or "bad" song lyric.
3. Write a dialogue including characters with different distinctive takes on what's funny (for example, one is young and one is old, or they come from different cultures). Have the characters observe and discuss an event that they understand in different ways.

Chapter 1: Writing Prompts

Comic Arguments

1. As several writers in this chapter mention, comedy has been the subject of many works, scholarly and popular. Write your own theory of comedy incorporating the assertions and strategies of one or more of the pieces in this chapter. You can revise or refute the ideas offered in the readings, and you can also cast your theory as a parody if you wish, if you find the theories worthy of comic critique. Include illustrative jokes and comic situations to illustrate and support your theory.
2. Write a stand-up act establishing a persona and distinctive worldview. You might prepare to do this by watching videos of several comics and reading print versions of their work.

Analysis

1. Write an analysis of a stand-up comedy routine, focusing on the effectiveness of the persona and the view of the world presented. Think about how the comic establishes and builds a relationship with the audience over the course of the set. Also consider the logical appeals, or arguments presented, and the emotional appeals, or the frame of mind the comic attempts to put the audience in.
2. Write an analysis of several everyday events you've observed or participated in, explaining the comic element. Here, Bergson's assertion about the latent

comic element in all ceremonies or repeated events can be useful, as well as his idea about costumes always suggesting something laughable.

Research

1. Research theories of comedy over time or in a particular period, illuminating trends and important areas of disagreement. You may notice that older theories focus on literary forms of comedy (plays, novels), while more contemporary theories deal with new forms like stand-up and the power of media to beam comedy to mass audiences.
2. Research women comics or comedies from a particular minority group of a particular era, exploring how they responded to the cultural attitudes of their time and the social purpose of their comedy. You may want to focus on periods of cultural upheaval or cultural repression, or a period in which progressive and conservative ideals clash.
3. Research the growth of stand-up comedy in the 1950s or 1960s or in a more recent era. What does the popularity of this comic form suggest about cultural attitudes and desires regarding comedy as entertainment and cultural commentary?

The Cultural Role
of Comedy

Introduction

Many cultural commentators have noted that we live in an age
dominated by forms of comedy, particularly satire and parody.
Staples of comic rhetoric—irony, sarcasm, and various forms of
lampoon and caricature—have become dominant forms of public
discourse readily available through traditional print forms as
well as the electronic media that drive popular culture. Garry
Trudeau's *Doonesbury* comic strip appears in hundreds of newspapers each day, sometimes on the editorial page. *Saturday Night
Live* has been on NBC without a break since 1975, and Comedy
Central's *The Daily Show* and *The Colbert Report* are among that
network's most popular shows. While some have long bemoaned
the corrosive effect of irony on the quality of civic debate (Mark
Crispin Miller labels the ironic stance the "hipness unto death"),
it's clear that political satire and other comic genres remain
culturally powerful.

The readings in this chapter point to several ways to engage
with comedy beyond the baseline level of appreciation. The
(sometimes unstated) premise of all the writers gathered here:
comedy does important cultural work, persuading us to think
about the world around us, and often to think in a focused way
about the everyday worries and concerns from which comedy
seems to provide an escape. Comedy, in these readings, is fundamentally rhetorical, formulating arguments that aim to persuade
an audience.

Elizabeth Kolbert explores how politicians attempt to short-
circuit external criticism (from sources like *Saturday Night Live*
and *The Daily Show*) by taking the initiative to mock themselves,

shifting the focus of public scrutiny from the substance of their policies to the style with which they conduct themselves in the media spotlight. J. Michael Waller locates the political use of comedy in a wider international context, proposing that the perceived threat of terrorism can be deflated with the strategic use of ridicule. Daniel Harris notes the cultural work done by a standard joke form and how such durable formulas can be adapted to serve as vehicles for topical attitudes. J. David Stevens shows the inner workings of a joke, giving the stock characters self-awareness and the desire for power and exploding the formula into a complex story. Finally, Vicki Hearne poses a challenging question regarding whether only human beings are capable of creating and appreciating comedy.

Stooping to Conquer: Why Candidates Need to Make Fun of Themselves

ELIZABETH KOLBERT

Headnotes/Things to Look For

Elizabeth Kolbert worked as a reporter for the New York Times *before joining the staff of* The New Yorker, *specializing in political subjects; this article appeared in the magazine's* Humor Issue *in 2004. Her books include* Field Notes from a Catastrophe: A Frontline Report on Climate Change *and* The Prophet of Love and Other Tales of Power and Deceit.

Kolbert describes the increasing integration of politics and entertainment, charting the rise of strategic self-mocking appearances by politicians since Richard Nixon's cameo on Rowan and Martin's Laugh-In *during the 1968 presidential campaign. Kolbert focuses on how politicians can anticipate and negate critical attacks with self-effacing humor; this relates to the rhetorical category of ethos, or ethical appeal, putting forward a likeable and electable character. While we may like to think that voters are rational beings swayed primarily by logical appeals, Kolbert reminds us that character issues and putting an audience in a receptive frame of mind (the realm of pathos, or emotional appeals) play important roles in the political process. Note how Kolbert weaves the history of politicians using humor to offset criticism and make themselves more likeable with analysis and commentary from experts in politics and popular culture. She provides historical background, and she also builds an argument using multiple sources.*

───────────── ✦ ─────────────

Three days after placing third in the Iowa caucuses and delivering the much replayed "scream," Howard Dean made a taped appearance on the "Late Show with David Letterman." His task was to deliver the Top Ten list of "ways I, Howard Dean, can turn things around":

10. Switch to decaf.
 9. Unveil new slogan: "Vote for Dean and get one dollar off your next purchase at Blimpie."
 8. Marry Rachel on the final episode of "Friends."
 7. Don't change a thing—it's going great.
 6. Show a little more skin.
 5. Go on "American Idol" and give 'em a taste of these pipes.
 4. Start working out and speaking with Austrian accent.
 3. I can't give specifics yet, but it involves Ted Danson.
 2. Fire the staffer who suggested we do this lousy Top Ten List instead of actually campaigning.
 1. Oh, I don't know—maybe fewer crazy, red-faced rants.

Dean followed up the "Letterman" appearance with an interview with Jon Stewart on Comedy Central's "The Daily Show." When the segment aired, the day before the New Hampshire primary, it consisted mostly of voice-overs of the two men's "thoughts." At one point, Dean was asked his position on gay marriage. As he held forth, his answer was drowned out by Stewart's interior monologue: "Mrs. Jon Dean . . . Mr. Howard Stewart . . . Howard and Jon Dean . . . Dr. and Mr. Jon Dean-Stewart."

Dean's performances on late-night television in no way distinguished him from his rivals. While stumping in Iowa, Representative Dick Gephardt, of Missouri, also showed up on "Letterman," in his case to enumerate the ten "signs you've been on the campaign trail too long." (No. 6: "You ask yourself, 'What would Schwarzenegger do?' " No. 2: "You agree to appear on a lame late-night talk show.") Right before officially entering the

Presidential race, last September, Senator John Edwards, of North Carolina, "announced" his candidacy on "The Daily Show." And, the day after the Missouri primary, Edwards duly recited his list of ten "things never before said by a Presidential candidate." (No. 7: "I'd give you my plan for economic recovery if I wasn't rip-stinkin' drunk.")

Making fun of politicians is a pastime practically as old as politics itself. Before the Greeks got around to inventing romantic comedy, they amused themselves by lampooning their leaders; in Aristophanes' "The Knights," for instance, the Athenian despot Cleon is replaced in office by a sausage seller. (Standard garb for actors in the days of "old comedy" was a padded suit and a large red leather phallus.) The Romans, too, loved a witty put-down, like this one, aimed at Caesar and reported by Dio Cassius: "If you behave well, you will be punished; if you behave badly, you will be king."

What sets contemporary political humor apart is its curious—one is tempted to say unprecedented—configuration. In the new comic order, the most devastating joke is circulated not by an irreverent observer or a sly opponent but by the target himself, who appears on national television solely in order to deliver it. There seem to be two ways to look at this trend: as a sign of how seriously we now take light entertainment or as an indication of how lightly we have come to regard politics. Either way, it's an unsettling development. Perhaps Triumph, the Insult Comic Dog, put it best when he was given a better time slot than Senator John Kerry, of Massachusetts, recently on the "Tonight Show."

"John Kerry, a war veteran, has to follow a freaking dog puppet!" he shrieked. "What's going on in America?"

• • •

Not long ago, I went to the Museum of Television and Radio, on West Fifty-second Street, to see episode No. 15 of "Rowan & Martin's Laugh-In." When the episode originally aired, on September 16, 1968, "Laugh-In" was just beginning its first full season—it had débuted eight months earlier, as a mid-season replacement—but was about to become the No. 1 show on television. The program begins with all the usual "Laugh-In" mayhem. "It must be 'Sock it to me' time," a youthful Goldie Hawn announces, before hitting herself over the head with a plastic mallet. The mayor of Burbank gets pelted with Ping-Pong balls; Joanne Worley is doused with water; Ruth Buzzi is crushed by a stage set; and Judy Carne is pelted, doused, crushed, and then sprayed by a skunk. Still wet, she answers a phone, and on the other end (ostensibly) is Governor Nelson Rockefeller. "Oh, no, I don't think we could get Mr. Nixon to stand still for a 'Sock it to me,' " she chirps, at which point the show cuts away to Richard Nixon.

Nixon's appearance on "Laugh-In" lasts four seconds. At first, he is looking stage right; then he turns toward the camera. He widens his eyes in what seems to be an effort at feigned surprise but comes off looking more like mock dismay. "Sock it to me?" he asks, drawing out the "me?" in a way that suggests he has perhaps never heard the line before.

Episode No. 15 was broadcast at the height of Nixon's (ultimately successful) campaign against Vice-President Hubert Humphrey, and was an immediate sensation. George Schlatter, the creator of "Laugh-In," now runs a television production company in Los Angeles. He told me that Nixon had been extremely reluctant to be on the show; although the producers had repeatedly entreated him to appear, his campaign aides had even more insistently urged him not to. Eventually, the race brought Nixon out to Los Angeles. He gave a press conference, and Schlatter and one of "Laugh-In" 's writers, Paul Keyes, who happened to be a close friend of the former Vice-President's, went over to watch it, bringing a TV camera with them.

"While his advisers were telling him not to do it, Paul was telling him how much it would mean to his career," Schlatter recalled. "And we went in, and he said, 'Sock it to me.' It took about six takes, because it sounded angry: 'Sock-it-to-me!' After that, we grabbed the tape and escaped before his advisers got to him.

"Then, realizing what we had done—because he did come out looking like a nice guy—we pursued Humphrey all over the country, trying to get him to say, 'I'll sock it to you, Dick!' " Schlatter went on. "And Humphrey later said that not doing it may have cost him the election. "We didn't realize how effective it was going to be. But there were other factors in the election, too—I can't take all the blame."

Nixon on "Laugh-In" is often cited as a watershed moment in the history of television—the unthinking man's version of Nixon in China. What had once seemed antithetical—parody and power—had proved not to be. Was the joke on Nixon or on his hosts? Who could say? But, if the episode announced the new order, many people, including Nixon himself, seemed not to have noticed. As President, he never went near "Laugh-In," or anything like it. Indeed, according to Schlatter, he became critical of the show and eventually pressured NBC into muffling its politics.

"Laugh-In" 's godchild "Saturday Night Live" premièred in the fall of 1975. Its approach to political satire was less staccato and more sustained. Week after week, Chevy Chase portrayed Gerald Ford, a former college football star, as an irredeemable klutz. The following spring, Ford's press secretary, Ron Nessen, agreed to appear on "S.N.L." as a guest host. In one sketch, Nessen, playing himself, looked on indulgently as Chase, playing Ford, lurched around the set, stapling his ear and signing his hand instead of a piece of tax legislation. Nessen's participation in the show was widely criticized—reportedly by the head of NBC, among others— as demeaning to the Presidency, even though, in an early example of life imitating parody, Ford himself appeared in the same episode, on tape, to recite a variation of Chase's signature line: "I'm Gerald Ford and you're not." ("There's really nothing you can do in that situation," Ford said years later. "You can't stand up and say, 'I was the best athlete' and all that stuff.")

The next four years were a period of strict separation: Jimmy Carter avoided humor, at least of the purposeful variety, whenever possible. (Jerome Doolittle, a White House speechwriter who sometimes composed funny lines for Carter, likened his role to that of Franklin Roosevelt's tap-dance coach.) "Who do they think they elected?" Carter supposedly once asked a staff member who was urging him to be more lighthearted. "Fred Allen?"

• • •

A few days after watching Richard Nixon on "Laugh-In," I went down to Washington to meet Landon Parvin. Parvin, who is fifty-five, is a slight man with pale-blue eyes, prominent ears, and gray hair that sticks up from the top of his head, like Homer Price's. He has an earnest manner, which tends to surprise people who have first been introduced to him, as it were, through his work. Depending on how you look at things, Parvin is either the capital's funniest serious speechwriter or its most serious funny one. He is particularly in demand during what is referred to in Washington as the "silly season," when the nation's leaders gather at a series of dinners to listen to the powerful crack jokes. If the program consists of four speeches, it is not uncommon for Parvin to have written three of them, and it is not unheard of for him to have written all four. In January, for instance, for the annual dinner of the Alfalfa Club—an association of political and corporate bigwigs named for the plant whose roots, according to club lore, "will do anything for a drink"—Parvin wrote the speech delivered by President Bush, and the one delivered by Jack Valenti, the Alfalfa nominee for President of the United States, and also the one delivered by the outgoing club president, Vernon Jordan. "As I look around the room, I am reminded that it is a long way from the public-housing projects of Atlanta to the presidency of Alfalfa," Jordan said in his remarks, which, in keeping with capital tradition, were labelled "off the record," then extensively reported anyway. "I only wish my daddy—Strom Thurmond—could see me tonight!"

I had been urged to visit Parvin by people who remembered or, perhaps more accurately, remembered having heard about a groundbreaking bit he wrote back in 1982, when he was working as a speechwriter in the Reagan White House. That spring, Nancy Reagan had decided to sing a song at the Gridiron Club dinner, and it fell to Parvin to come up with the lyrics. The assignment was an unpromising one. The Gridiron Club, an association made up of assorted members of the Washington media élite, exists solely in order to spoof the even more powerful. Among the numerous public-relations debacles of Mrs. Reagan's first year had been a trip to England during which she was photographed wearing fifteen different outfits and the purchase, in the midst of a national recession, of a set of china valued at two hundred thousand dollars. The first lyrics that Parvin wrote, to the tune of "Second Hand Rose," Mrs. Reagan rejected as too easy on her, so in the next set he took aim directly at the First Lady's image problems. "Even though they tell me that I'm no longer queen/Did Ronnie have to buy me that new sewing machine?" she asked plaintively. Then she smashed a plate on the floor. The number—entitled "Second Hand Clothes"—was such a hit that Mrs. Reagan had to sing it twice; Parvin hadn't thought to write her an encore. When, in the months that followed, the First Lady began to receive better press coverage, the shift was attributed to her song-and-dance routine.

Mrs. Reagan's success makes sense only by the logic of self-parody, according to which, as in fairy tales, straw is gold. The First Lady didn't answer her critics' charges; she merely repeated them, in the process emptying them of one kind of significance and filling them with another. As Parvin put it to me, if a politician can make fun of his faults he is, in effect, saying, "I'm not really worried about it; you shouldn't be, either."

"What most people don't realize is there are two kinds of political humor," Parvin went on. "There is the kind satirists do.

Then, there's what I do. The easiest thing in the world, I learned in the White House, is to get a zinger on the evening news. The press will pick it up like that. But what I learned over the years is that that doesn't necessarily serve the politician's purpose, because what you want is for him to be better liked. Really, that is the purpose of political humor for a politician: to be better liked."

Parvin left the White House in 1984, and in the years since has written hundreds of speeches, for scores of politicians. He prefers straight speeches, like the inaugural address he composed last fall for Governor Arnold Schwarzenegger, of California, but he is constantly getting calls from people who want him to repeat the trick he performed for Mrs. Reagan.

"A politician will be in some trouble and he'll say, 'Will you do me some lines on it?,' because he's heard that humor can get him out of trouble," Parvin told me. Sometimes he can help, and sometimes the trouble—misuse of public funds, for example—is intractable. "I tell them, depending on the situation, 'No, this is trouble. You should not make fun of this.' "

• • •

On March 1, 2000, shortly before the New York Presidential primary, George Bush, then the governor of Texas, made the first of his election-year appearances on the "Late Show with David Letterman." It was an educational experience for him. Bush seems to have only half understood why he was there, and so he came prepared with several jokes about Letterman, who had recently undergone heart bypass surgery. "It's about time you had the heart to invite me," Bush said early in the show, prompting a round of boos. Later, Letterman asked what he meant by his slogan "I'm a uniter, not a divider." Bush replied, "It means when it comes time to sew up your chest cavity, we use stitches," a line that elicited more boos from the audience. At one point, when the conversation grew particularly testy, Letterman said to Bush: "Let me remind you of one thing, Governor: the road to Washington runs through me." Bush at least knew enough not to argue with this. At the end of the interview, he held up a "Dweebs for Bush" T-shirt that he had had specially made for the occasion.

Bush did not make the same mistake again. Later in the campaign, appearing as himself to introduce a special election edition of "Saturday Night Live," he announced, "When they asked me to help introduce tonight's special, I felt fairly ambilavent. Although I'm a big fan, I've seen things on the show I thought were, in a word, offensive." He also gamely went on the "Tonight Show" to misspeak, pronouncing the word "flammable," for instance, "flammam-ababable." And when he went back on "Letterman" he vowed that, if elected, he would "make sure the White House library has lots of books with big print and pictures." Meanwhile, Vice-President Al Gore was similarly making the late-night-comedy rounds, poking fun at his woodenness, his pedantry, and his tendency to exaggerate his own achievements. "Remember, America: I gave you the Internet, and I can take it away," he said on "Letterman." On the election edition of "S.N.L.," which aired just two days before voters went to the polls, he declared, "I was one of the very first to be offended by material on 'Saturday Night Live.' " Even after losing, Gore continued to make the comedic rounds, appearing, for example, on "S.N.L." again, in December, 2002, to sit, half naked, in a hot tub.

One frequently offered explanation for what happened between Nixon's going on "Laugh-In" and Bush's and Gore's going on everything is the shift in American viewing habits. In 1968, thirty-five million Americans tuned in every night to the network news, out of a total TV-owning audience of fifty-six million households. Although by 1992, when Bill Clinton went on "The Arsenio Hall Show" to play "Heartbreak Hotel" on his sax, network-news viewership had increased slightly to thirty-nine million, the total TV audience had nearly doubled, to 92.1 million. By 2000, network-news viewership had dropped to twenty-nine million, while the total audience continued to increase, to a hundred and one million households.

A few months ago, the Pew Research Center for the People and the Press set out to quantify how Americans were getting information about the current Presidential campaign. In a randomized survey, fifteen hundred adults were presented with a list of possible sources and asked which ones they were "regularly learning" something from. Among all age groups, the network news shows were cited by thirty-five per cent and daily newspapers by thirty-one per cent. Among respondents under the age of thirty, those figures both drop to twenty-three per cent. Comedy shows, meanwhile, were cited by twenty-one per cent of young people as a source that they regularly "learned" something from. And these numbers, disconcerting as they may be, only begin to tell the story.

Owing to the way that elections operate, the most sought-after voters also tend to be the most indifferent ones—those who, deep into a campaign, still don't have a clear impression of the candidates in contention. "My guess is that ninety-five per cent of the people watching 'Meet the Press' already have decided whom they're going to vote for," Jon Macks, a former political consultant who now writes for Jay Leno, told me. "Nothing is going to make them change their mind. But there's a lot of people that watch the 'Tonight Show,' or any of the shows like it, who are going to see someone and they are going to connect."

Looked at in these terms, an exercise like delivering the Top Ten list comes to seem just another way of reaching a critical demographic, like touring a senior citizens' center or learning Spanish. The indignity of it is simply the price the candidate pays to achieve his purpose, which is always to "connect." What this account misses, however, is the extent to which indignity *is* the purpose.

Consider, for example, President Bush's recent jokes about the U.S.'s failure to find weapons of mass destruction in Iraq. At the annual Radio and Television Correspondents' dinner last month, the President presented a slide show in which he appeared as a hapless dupe, rummaging under the furniture in the Oval Office, as if for a set of lost keys. "Those weapons of mass destruction have got to be somewhere," he said brightly. The sketch, which Landon Parvin helped write, made no sense as an appeal to the youth vote—it was presented to an audience of reporters. But it was entirely consistent with the notion of preëmptive self-mockery. (When the slide show provoked outrage, a White House spokeswoman declared that the President was just "poking fun at himself," as if no further defense were needed.)

As I spoke to people who write political comedy, I kept hearing versions of Parvin's theory. Mark Katz, who recently published a memoir about his experiences writing jokes for the Clinton White House, told me, "Humor is all about acquiring political capital through likability." Al Franken, who has written for, among others, Gore and Hillary Clinton, put it this way: "Americans don't want their President or their senators to be the funniest person in the world. They just want to see that their senator or their President has a sense of humor and is a human being."

As has often been observed, one of the ways in which television has changed politics is by collapsing distinctions—enlarging the trivial and trivializing the large. In this context—the context of no context—any claim to significance is fated to descend into parody. While aspiring to be likable, or just a human being, seems a modest goal for the leader of the free world, it may, at this point, be the best that can be hoped for. When Humphrey declined to say, "I'll sock it to you, Dick!," a reluctance to compromise one's dignity could still be claimed as a political virtue. Now it can be seen for what it is: a liability that needs to be corrected by appearing, say, after a dog puppet.

Discussion Questions

1. How does politicians' participation in popular culture (e.g., appearing on entertainment programs) affect the way we think about and respond to political issues?
2. What are your dominant mental pictures of contemporary politicians? Do many of the images that come to mind originate in popular culture, or do they come from more traditional political contexts (e.g., debates, speeches, congressional hearings)? How do these images differ from those you have of politicians from previous eras?
3. Given the interpenetration of politics and entertainment Kolbert describes, how do you now understand politics? For you, what issues shouldn't be treated as fuel for satire?

Writing Activities

1. Imagine you're an advisor to a current or past politician who is concerned about public perceptions. Write a memo to this political figure with advice on how to use humor to anticipate and defuse criticism and shape public opinion of the politician's character.
2. Write a sketch featuring a prospective voter watching a politician's appearance on a comedy show (e.g., *The Daily Show* or *Saturday Night Live*). Your scene should include both what the viewer sees and how the viewer reacts to the politician's performance.

Ridicule: An Instrument in the War on Terrorism

Public Diplomacy White Paper No. 7

J. MICHAEL WALLER

Headnotes/Things to Look For

J. Michael Waller is secretary of the Institute of World Politics, directing the Institute's graduate programs in public diplomacy and political warfare. His work has appeared in journals and newspapers, including Insight, *the* Washington Times, *and the* Wall Street Journal, *and his books include* Dismantling Tyranny: Transitioning

Beyond Totalitarian Regimes. *His blog,* Fourth World War, *focuses on issues related to the war on terrorism.*

Note how Waller draws from a wide range of historical and contemporary examples to make a case for ridicule as a potentially valuable weapon against terrorism.

✦

INTRODUCTION

Demonization of the enemy is the general default position of American message-making against international threats. The history of warfare shows, however, that while demonization can build and maintain alliances and coalitions, and is important to maintain national unity in a protracted conflict, it can inadvertently aid the enemy's own war aims.

Incessant, morbid portrayals of an individual, movement, or nation as a mortal enemy might rally support for the American side, but they have a shelf-life that gets tired over time. Constant specters of unrelenting dangers risk sowing defeatism and chipping away at our own morale. Abroad they risk making the U.S. look like a bully in some places and surrender the propaganda advantage to the other side. The questions at this stage of the war are:

- Do we inadvertently aid our enemies and potential enemies by taking them too seriously?
- Does our relentless portrayal of individuals, ideologies, movements and philosophies as mortal dangers to America enhance the enemies' status and prestige?
- Is it an unsound political strategy to hype the image and power of the enemy and the few leaders who personify it?
- Is there something else the United States and its allies should be doing in their attempts to discredit, undermine and defeat the enemy?

This paper argues in the affirmative. It suggests that U.S. strategy includes undermining the political and psychological strengths of adversaries and enemies by employing ridicule as a standard operating tool of national strategy. Ridicule is an underappreciated weapon not only against terrorists, but against weapons proliferators, despots, and international undesirables in general. Ridicule serves several purposes:

- Ridicule raises morale at home.
- Ridicule strips the enemy/adversary of his mystique and prestige.
- Ridicule erodes the enemy's claim to justice.
- Ridicule eliminates the enemy's image of invincibility.
- Directed properly at an enemy, ridicule can be a fate worse than death.

THE POWER OF RIDICULE

Used as a means of positive persuasion, humor can be an important public diplomacy tool. "If I can get you to laugh with me," said comedian John Cleese, "you like me better, which makes you more open to my ideas. And if I can persuade you to laugh at the particular point I make, by laughing at it you acknowledge the truth."[1]

Humor is an excellent means of making policy points and building constructive relations abroad. Everybody wins. Laughing *at* someone—ridicule—is another matter. It is the use of humor at someone else's expense. It is a zero-sum game destructive to one of the parties involved. Like a gun, it is a dangerous weapon. Even in trained hands, it can misfire. Used carelessly or indiscriminately, ridicule can create enemies were there were none, and deepen hostilities among the very peoples whom the user seeks to win over.

In nearly every aspect of society and across cultures and time, ridicule works. Ridicule leverages the emotions and simplifies the complicated and takes on the powerful, in politics, business, law, entertainment, literature, culture, sports and romance. Ridicule can tear down faster than the other side can rebuild. One might counter an argument, an image, or even a kinetic force, but one can marshal few defenses against the well-aimed barbs that bleed humiliation and drip contempt. Politicians fear ridicule. Some take ridicule well and emerge stronger for it; others never recover from it. The perpetual circle of democracy absorbs and even breeds ridicule against individuals and ideas, while the system itself remains intact. While ridicule can be a healthy part of democracy, it can weaken the tyrant.

THE ANCIENTS AND RIDICULE

We get the word "satire" from the ancient Greek *satyr*, the mythical drunk, hedonistic or otherwise naughty man-goat. Satyrs performed the fourth and final part of a tetralogy drama, usually in a burlesque performance that poked fun at the preceding serious or tragic trilogy. The audience would leave the performance satisfied and upbeat.

Prominent Classical literary figures used satire and ridicule against war. Poet-playwright Aristophanes, for example, in 425 B.C., satirized Athenian policy of the Peloponnesian War in *The Acharnians,* and mocked government, society and war in subsequent plays; he filled his plays with invective and *ad hominem* attacks as well as sexual humor. Greek society, irrespective of the type of government, placed boundaries on the types and intensity of ridicule, as did other ancients.

While permitted under certain circumstances, ridicule was seen as such a devastatingly powerful weapon that the ancients proscribed its use except in extreme situations. Roman Emperor Augustus Caesar banned jokes about the emperor.

In Christianity, ridicule of another person is considered uncharitable and can even be sinful, except, one reasons, in time of war when violence and killing can be morally permissible. In the Talmud, the basis of Jewish law, the ancient Hebrews proclaimed, "All mockery (*leitzanut*) is prohibited except for mockery of idol worship (*avoday zarah*)," as mockery is so destructive it can be used only against evil.[2]

Muhammad, the founder of Islam, personally used ridicule as a weapon of war early after he announced his prophethood.[3] Islamic poets were not mere literary artists; they were often warriors who wrote satire and ridicule of the enemy as an important weapon of offensive warfare. Muhammad banned the faithful from drawing human images, including his own, in large part to stamp out idolatry. Violent Muslim overreactions in early 2006 to some European cartoons depicting Muhammad appear to be less manifestations of offended sensitivities than of vulnerability to the power of ridicule.[4]

TYRANTS, TERRORISTS AND RIDICULE

Dictators, tyrants, and those who aspire to seize and keep power by intimidation and force can tolerate no public ridicule. They generally harbor grandiose self-images with little bearing on how people really think of them. They require a controlled political environment, reinforced by sycophants and toadies, to preserve an impenetrable image. Some are more tolerant of reasoned or principled opposition but few of satire or ridicule. The size of their egos may be seen as inversely proportional to the thickness of their skin. However, few are true madmen; most are rational and serious.[5]

Saddam Hussein had a strong sense of humor, and is known to have told mildly self-deprecating stories about himself in public.[6] That is not to say he accepted others' stories; Saddam's storytelling was under his own control. Hence the vulnerability: Control is the essence of an authoritarian movement or dictatorship.

Jokes and contempt know no philosophy and a good laugh, even of the gallows humor variety, spreads virally, almost impossible to control. Russian émigré comedian Yakov Smirnov often referred to the Soviet government's "Department of Jokes" that censored all spoken and written humor. While we have found no evidence of a Soviet unit with that specific name, we do know that the Communist Party Central Committee's Propaganda Department and the KGB Fifth Chief Directorate respectively set and enforced ideological discipline in which a "Department of Jokes" or its equivalent would reside. "No great movement designed to change the world can bear to be laughed at or belittled."

Czechoslovakian novelist Milan Kundera wrote in *The Joke*, "because laughter is the rust that corrodes every thing."[7]

Fidel Castro understood the principle when, six months after seizing power in 1959, he had signs placed in all official buildings that read, "Counter-revolutionary jokes forbidden here." One of the first Cuban publications that Castro shut down was *Zig Zag*, a magazine of humor.[8]

While the Russians ultimately did away with a department of jokes, their president, Boris Yeltsin, could laugh at his political opponents' innovative, irreverent and wildly popular political satire TV puppet show, *Kukly*. But the sense of humor of his tough-minded successor, former KGB Lt. Col. Vladimir Putin, has no such ability. Putin shut down *Kukly* and the NTV television channel that produced it. In Putin's Russia, mocking or insulting the president is a crime punishable by imprisonment.

Venezuelan strongman Hugo Chavez pushed through a similar law to protect him from open ridicule. In the 1980s, the Islamic Republic of Iran went so far as to assassinate jokesters abroad, even in western Europe, where the regime murdered an exiled humorist in Germany and a London merchant who sold CD recordings that mocked the mullahs.

Humor survives repression; in the words of Professor Luis Aguilar of Georgetown University, repression "only drives it underground. For repressed people, it is a subtle form of rebellion; a collective means to pay back the oppressor; the last resort; the last laugh."[9]

EMPOWERING THE POWERLESS

That collective payback, that last laugh, can empower the powerless. It need not be expressed outwardly, where doing so could mean punishment or even death. In Iran, friends take taxi rides just to share jokes away from informers in their schools and places of work. Even quiet or inward expression remains alive, ready to flame with the first breath of oxygen. Jokes are a release of the fearful, a rewarding act of defiance, a rhetorical rock hurled at the oppressor.

The best ones spread because they speak the truth, and the truth leads to freedom. The joke is quietly shared and spread; the people know that they are not alone. "Every joke is a tiny revolution," said George Orwell. "Whatever destroys dignity, and brings down the mighty from their seats, preferably with a bump, is funny."[10]

RIDICULE AS AN OFFENSIVE WEAPON

Like rifles and satellites, submarines and propaganda, ridicule is a neutral piece of technology. It can soften up entrenched and hardened targets, especially when those targets have alienated large parts of the population, or even small but loud elements in society.

French revolutionaries preceded their overthrow and murder of the king and his family through relentless campaigns of ridicule in the politically rather open society of late 18th century Paris. Constant, vicious, often crude parody and mockery of the king as an individual and the monarchy as a system, the aristocracy, and the Church, arguably motivated and radicalized the public more than the high-minded philosophies of the revolutionaries. Combined with positive philosophical, reasoned and inspiring campaigns of *Liberté, Egalité, Fraternité*, the abuse stripped away the moral legitimacy the monarchy had from the outwardly respectful French subjects, and made the king the butt of constant sexual and scatological humor that, along with the excesses of the time, reduced the monarchy in many French eyes to a contemptible canker that required and deserved destruction. Popular history falsely remembers the pious Marie Antoinette as her French executioners caricatured her. Mass murderers can still have a good laugh, but usually at others' expense. Adolf Hitler's sense of humor knew no self-deprecation; his was what the Germans call *schadenfreude*, a word that has no English equivalent but can be understood as taking malicious pleasure at others' misfortune. Hitler loved cruel jokes on his own ministers, especially on Foreign Minister Ribbentrop,[11] but always away from public view. He could never laugh at himself. His propagandists in 1933 tried to appeal to the satirical German public by issuing a compendium of tame political cartoons, but the effort went nowhere.

The Nazis and fascists required either adulation or fear; their leaders and their causes were vulnerable to well-aimed ridicule. Hitler with his Charlie Chaplin–style toothbrush mustache (a former aide later said it made him look like he had a cold), his uniform-loving Hermann Goering, and his club-footed propaganda chief Joseph Goebbels made great caricatures of their own, as did the flamboyant Benito Mussolini, who rehearsed his oratorical gesticulations—which could be impressive in person or on film, but made to look silly in still frames—before a mirror. German jokes about the Nazis quickly went underground, but resurfaced when the people saw the regime near collapse toward the end of the war.

DEFENSIVE WEAPON

Little if any American World War ll–era ridicule had much effect on continental Europe, but it was still vital to the war effort. Ridicule can be a defensive weapon if it helps calm the fears of the public at home and gives hope that they can indeed defeat the enemy. British and American boys sang anti-Hitler songs, mostly mocking the fuehrer's private parts, as one might expect from adolescents, but laughing at the enemy during wartime helps one become less fearful and more optimistic of victory.

Popular culture also mocked the Axis powers—not after a decent interval following a given incident or atrocity, but from the start. The Three Stooges, one of the most popular comic groups in cinema at the time, performed the first parodies of the enemy in 1940, with slapstick episodes of Moe making ridiculous impressions of Hitler; Larry heiling as propaganda minister, and Curly dressed as Goering with his belly and buttocks festooned with medals. Moe also impersonated a laughable Tojo. One episode poked fun at Stalin, who was allied with Hitler when the film was made.

Others in Hollywood also helped the war effort through humor and ridicule. Charlie Chaplin's famous full-length movie, *The Great Dictator*, though developed years before, followed the first Stooges episode in 1940. Chaplin—complaining that Hitler had stolen his trademark mustache—starred as fuehrer lookalike Adenoid Hynkel, accompanied by his sidekick Benzoni Napolini, dictator of Bacteria.

Like many in Hollywood did at the time, the cartoon studios put their talent at the disposal of the war effort. Disney's Donald Duck, in the 1942 short "Donald Duck In Nutziland" (retitled "Der Fuehrer's Face"), won an Academy Award after the unhappy duck dreamed he was stuck in Nazi Germany. Disney produced dozens of anti-Axis cartoons, as did Warner Bros. starring Bugs Bunny and Daffy Duck. Both studios have released some of the cartoon shorts on video but limited the rebroadcast and banned the re-release of some on what critics call political correctness grounds.[12]

Current anti-terrorist ridicule that worries little of political correctness is *Team America: World Police,* a clever animated marionette show about a covert counterterrorism force that patriotically if clumsily fights Islamist terrorists and North Korean dictator Kim Jong-il.[13] *Team America* is a brilliant work that plays on the obvious faults of an insecure and lonely Kim, the absurdity of United Nations diplomacy in the person of weapons inspector Hans Blix, and on popular stereotypes about Islamist terrorists and Hollywood anti-war personalities. Developed by the creators of the South Park cartoon, *Team America* limits its effectiveness, as well as the size of its audience, with extremely crude adolescent (some might call it "adult") humor.[14] Nevertheless, it is a masterpiece of over-the-top ridicule that could be to the current young generation what the irreverent *Monty Python and the Holy Grail* was to young people thirty years ago. *Team America* puts the bad guys in their place and shows that, as clumsy and arrogant as Americans might be to many people, they are still the good guys.

The United States occasionally used ridicule and satire in film to influence elections abroad. Large-scale American intervention in Italy's 1948 election, in which the Communist Party was believed able to win a parliamentary plurality, saved the day for the Christian Democrats. Among the many instruments the

U.S. used to convince Italians to vote against the Communist Popular Front was the romantic comedy *Ninotchka,* a parody of life in the Soviet Union starring Greta Garbo and Melvyn Douglas. "This film, which hilariously satirized life in Russia, tended to leave an audience with a feeling that if this is Russia please deliver us from such a society," one observer reported. "Distributors provided double the usual number of copies of the film, and special arrangements were made so that the film would be shown immediately among the low-income-level population." The film was so effective that the Italian Communists tried to prevent it from being shown; after the Italians voted against the Communists, one party worker complained, "What licked us was *Ninotchka.*"[15]

RIDICULE AND US STRATEGY

Americans have used ridicule as a potent weapon to cut its enemies down to size since the Revolutionary War. Ridicule served two wartime purposes: to raise the people's morale by helping them to laugh at their enemies, and to dent the morale of enemy forces.

Despite their far superior training, discipline, skill and firepower, the British were unprepared for irregular combat with the colonists. The Americans were guerrilla fighters who had the bad form not to stand in formation on a battlefield and to shoot at enemy officers.

The British handily won the first engagement, the Battle of Lexington in April, 1775, but suffered heavy losses during their march from Concord back to Boston with Americans shooting at them from behind trees and rocks. Bostonians jeered. Among the many poems and ditties circulating around Boston after the opening shots of the war at Lexington and Concord was this one:

How brave you went out with muskets all bright,
And thought to befrighten the folks with the sight;
But when you got there how they powder'd your pums,
And all the way home how they pepper'd your bums,
And is it not, honies, a comical farce,
To be proud in the face, and be shot in the arse.[16]

Such mockery stung: the British army at the time was the finest, most experienced and most formidable in the world, its officers and men proud of their history, in their view, of gentlemanly warfighting. The practically un-trained, mostly un-uniformed, often un-disciplined, frequently uncouth, and generally low-class American riffraff, in British eyes, were no worthy adversary at all. With fife and drum as important means of battlefield coordination and communication, British troops ridiculed the Americans with songs like "Yankee Doodle," whose mocking lyrics the colonists changed and embraced as their own anthem. That counter-ridicule operation unsettled the Redcoats. One British soldier recorded, "After our rapid successes, we held the Yankees in great contempt, but it was not a little mortifying to hear them play this tune."[17]

Local patriots heaped abuse on British civilian and military officials. They directed a poem at General William Howe, whom George III had named royal military governor of Massachusetts in the winter of 1775 and took Mrs. Joshua Loring as his mistress:

> Sir William, he, snug as a flea,
> Lay all this time a-snoring
> Nor dreamed of harm, as he lay warm
> In bed with Mrs. ____.[18]

Benjamin Franklin was famous in the colonies and Europe as a colorful humorist as well as inventor and scientist. As a colonial agent in London, he used humor to win sympathy for the colonies' grievances, and tried persuasion through gentle satire, such as his 1773 essay on "Rules by Which a Great Empire May Be Reduced to a Small One," a blueprint that showed how, through poor treatment of its colonies, the British government was destroying its imperium.

Franklin at the time viewed himself as an Englishman from Pennsylvania, and did not support the idea of American independence. He also used ridicule as a weapon at home as a printer, writer and patriot, and later in France as a diplomat, propagandist and intelligence officer.[19]

RIDICULE IN 21st CENTURY CONFLICT

With the proliferation of communications technology, ridicule is a cheap and easy way to wage conflicts short of war, or to undermine an enemy in time of war. Thin-skinned dictators include Castro of Cuba, Kim Jong-il of North Korea, Alexander Lukashenko of Belarus, Hugo Chavez of Venezuela, and the regimes of China, Vietnam, and many predominantly Muslim countries.

The more extreme the leader, the more vulnerable he tends to be to ridicule. Being a declared adversary—even enemy—of the United States is a status symbol among the world's terrorists, dictators, and political extremists. By taking that enemy too seriously, by hyping it up as a threat, the United States is unintentionally credentializing a heretofore insignificant individual or group, and giving it the stature it needs to rise above its own society, establish itself, attract recruits, and gain influence.

Ridicule can cut the enemy down to size. Arab, Persian and other predominantly Islamic cultures have long traditions of using ridicule for political and military purposes, presenting the U.S. with ample opportunities. The practice of militaristic ridicule dates from the third to fifth years of Muhammad's annunciation as prophet, when he employed ridicule aggressively against enemies, ahead of his invading forces. Poets wrote not so much for entertainment or storytelling as for psychological purposes to help achieve military ends. The popularity of some medieval Arab poets has been undergoing a revival since the 1980s, where the most extreme have provided intellectual and ideological foundations for Wahhabi/Salafi brands of militant Islamism and their terrorist manifestations.

Muslims around the world have ridiculed Islamist extremists and their terroristic interpretations of the Koran as few American writers, comedians and broadcasters would ever dare. Pakistani TV has run shows mocking the extremists. Political satire in literature, music and movies are some of the biggest sellers in the Arabic-speaking markets. Arab, Iranian and Indonesian stand-up comics already perform stinging political satire but few are well-known and even fewer have outlets, though if they were "discovered" their listenership could be in the hundreds of millions.

The previous Iranian government tolerated some forms of political satire, but Iran's top political impersonator Ali Dean, who did hilarious impressions of various mullahs, was forced to an American exile. Private Farsi-language TV stations in North America lampoon Iranian leaders. The most influential station, NITV, is owned by an exiled Iranian rock star, with Dean as its top humorist, broadcasting into Iran.[20]

U.S. policymakers must incorporate ridicule into their strategic thinking. Ridicule is a tool that they can use without trying to control. It exists naturally in its native environments in ways beneficial to the interests of the nation and cause of freedom. Its practitioners are natural allies, even if we do not always appreciate what they say or how they say it.

The United States need do little more than give them publicity and play on its official and semi-official global radio, TV and Internet media, and help them become "discovered." And it should be relentless about it. In his California exile from Iran, Ali Dean studies the mullahs' sermons and speeches for his material. "They hate me because they don't like nobody impersonate them," he says. "To them, they are untouchable. To me, there is no untouchable."[21]

CONCLUSION

Ridicule is a powerful weapon of warfare. It can be a strategic weapon. The United States must take advantage of it against terrorists, proliferators, and other threats. Ridicule is vital because:

- It sticks.
- The target can't refute it.
- It is almost impossible to repress, even if driven underground.
- It spreads on its own and multiplies naturally.
- It gets better with each re-telling.
- It boosts morale at home.
- Our enemy shows far greater intolerance to ridicule than we.
- Ridicule divides the enemy, damages its morale, and makes it less attractive to supporters and prospective recruits.
- The ridicule-armed warrior need not fix a physical sight on the target. Ridicule will find its own way to the targeted individual. To the enemy, being ridiculed means losing respect. It means losing influence. It means losing followers and repelling potential new backers.
- To the enemy, ridicule can be worse than death. At least many enemies find death to be a supernatural martyrdom. Ridicule is much worse: destruction without martyrdom: A fate worse than death. And they have to live with it.

Notes

1. Harry Mills, *Artful Persuasion* (American Management Association, 2000), p. 131.
2. Rabbi Uri Cohen, "Balak—God's Laughter: Making Fun of Balaam," *Nishmat*, Jerusalem Center for Advanced Study of Jewish Women, accessed January 18, 2006 at http://www.nishmat.net/article.

php?id=155&heading=0. Rabbi Cohen, a professor at Princeton University, is also a stand-up comedian.

3. Chronology of Islam, Canadian Society of Muslims (Toronto) http://muslim-canada.org/chronol.htm

4. Were one to use cartoons against Islamist extremists, one would seek to marginalize the extremists from their support base and from the rest of Islam. The cartoonist would make the extremists' own appearance and behavior the object of ridicule, and never the Islamic religion or its founder themselves. In addition to betraying the principles of freedom of religion and respect for other religions, making fun of another's religion is counterproductive to the war effort. For more on this, see White Paper No. 6 in this series, "Splitting the Opposition."

5. See Jerrold M. Post, *Leaders and their Followers in a Dangerous World: The Psychology of Political Behavior* (Cornell University Press, 2004).

6. Mark Bowden, "Tales of the Tyrant," *The Atlantic*, May 2002, pp. 36–37.

7. Milan Kundera, *The Joke*, trans. Henry Heim (Harper & Row, 1984). The author acknowledges writer Ben MacIntyre for locating the Kundera reference and others in his column, "Saddam Has Only Got One Ball," *The Times*, 26 August 2005, p. 24.

8. Luis E. Aguilar, *"Chistes"—Political Humor in Cuba* (Cuban-American National Foundation, 1989), p. i.

9. Ibid.

10. George Orwell, "Funny, but Not Vulgar," *Leader*, 28 July 1945, in Sonia Orwell and Ian Angus, eds., *Orwell: As I Please, 1943–1945, The Collected Essays, Journals and Letters* (Nonpareil, 2000), pp. 283–288.

11. Albert Speer, *Inside the Third Reich* (Simon & Schuster, 1970).

12. *Bugs & Daffy Wartime Cartoons* (Warner Bros., 1942–45; released on VHS video, 1998); *Walt Disney Treasures—On the Front Lines* (Disney DVD, 2004).

13. *Team America: World Police* (Paramount DVD, 2005).

14. One must not discount the value of adolescent humor in winning the war of ideas. While many find it patently offensive, it can appeal to adolescent boys and young men unlike any other form of propaganda, and by its nature is self-replicating. In the global war of ideas, the young male demographic is one of the most important yet, to date, impenetrable markets for counterterrorism strategists.

15. *Ninotchka* (MGM, 1939; Warner Home Video DVD, 2005).

16. Philip M. Taylor, *Munitions of the Mind* (Manchester University Press, 2003), p. 135.

17. Ibid., p. 135.
18. A. J. Langguth, *Patriots: The Men Who Started the American Revolution* (Simon & Schuster, 1988), p. 313.
19. J. Michael Waller, "The American way of propaganda: Lessons from the founding fathers," Public Diplomacy White Paper No. 1, Institute of World Politics, November 2005/January 2006.
20. Author's interview with Zia Atabay, President, NITV.
21. Bob Simon, "Lights, Camera, Revolution," CBS News, 18 June 2003. Accessed at: http://www.cbsnews.com/stories/2002/10/22/60ll/main526501.shtml.

Discussion Questions

1. The key term in this white paper is "ridicule" rather than comedy, as Waller describes a corollary to the self-mocking strategy of politicians Kolbert describes. How effective is ridicule as a strategy in the war on terror?
2. Waller begins by warning that demonization of the enemy can backfire, even aiding the target. What is the danger of portraying an enemy as a powerful threat?
3. Describe the point about laughter and argument that the quotation from British comic John Cleese makes.
4. What benefit does Waller suggest in using Muslim comics as part of this campaign of ridicule?

Writing Activity

1. Choose an enemy to ridicule. This enemy can be personal, social, political, or cultural. Use ridicule to show the target as vulnerable and unworthy of respect and fear.

Light-Bulb Jokes: Charting an Era
Daniel Harris

Headnotes/Things to Look For

This article appeared in The New York Times Magazine *in 1997. Daniel Harris has published articles in many magazines, including the* Nation *and the* Baffler. *He serves as a contributing editor for* Harper's Magazine, *specializing in topics related to popular culture. His books include* The Rise and Fall of Gay Culture *and* Cute, Quaint, Hungry, and Romantic: The Aesthetics of Consumerism.

Harris assesses how light-bulb jokes reveal a range of social tensions in relation to technology, race, and class. Note how Harris builds his case for how light-bulb jokes function after providing a slew of examples labeled by year. Consider how he carefully analyzes every component of the basic formula.

———————————— ✦ ————————————

CIRCA 1950
How many Polacks does it take to screw in a light bulb?
Five—one to stand on a table and hold the bulb in the socket and four to rotate the table.

1960s
How many psychiatrists does it take to screw in a light bulb?
Only one, but the light bulb has to really *want* to change.

CIRCA 1970
How many feminists does it take to screw in a light bulb?
One, and that's *not funny!*

1980s
How many Reagan aides does it take to screw in a light bulb?
None—they like to keep him in the dark.

1980s
How many Holocaust revisionists does it take to screw in a light bulb?
None—they just deny that the bulb ever went out in the first place.

1980s
How many Communists does it take to screw in a light bulb?
One, but it takes him about 30 years to realize that the old one has burned out.

1986
How many Ukrainians does it take to screw in a light bulb?
They don't need light bulbs—they glow in the dark.

DATE UNKNOWN
How many Surrealists does it take to screw in a light bulb?
A fish.

EARLY 1990s
How many baby boomers does it take to screw in a light bulb?
Ten—six to talk about how great it is that they've all come together to do this, one to screw it in, one to film it for the news, one to plan a marketing strategy based on it and one to reminisce about mass naked bulb-screwing in the 60s.

How many Gen X'ers does it take to screw in a light bulb?
Two—one to shoplift the bulb so the boomers have something to screw in and the other to screw it in for minimum wage.

1990s
How many Microsoft executives does it take to screw in a light bulb?
None—Bill Gates will just redefine Darkness™ as the industry standard.

CIRCA 1991
How many L.A. cops does it take to screw in a light bulb?
Six—one to do it and five to smash the old bulb to splinters.

1995
How many O.J. jurors does it take to screw in a light bulb?
None of them believe it is broken.

1997
How many Dolly clones does it take to screw in a light bulb?
As many as you'd like. As many as you'd like.

Unlike knock-knock jokes, dead-baby jokes, dumb-blonde jokes and why-did-the-chicken-cross-the-road jokes, the light-bulb joke is uniquely political. Not only does it make references to current events (how many Canadian separatists, how many Branch Davidians), it also summarizes, in epigrammatic form, the history of the second half of the 20th century, excoriating in virtually the same breath the illegal immigrant and the gainfully employed bureaucrat, big government and big business, homosexuals and homophobes, shrinks and paranoids. And because the light-bulb joke involves a piece of electrical equipment, it mirrors our ambivalent attitudes toward technology, which, ever since Thomas Edison invented the incandescent bulb in 1879, has become so complex that we can no longer install and repair our appliances without enlisting the services of price-gouging experts. In the light-bulb joke, the ancient literary genre of the riddle demonstrates its versatility and wickedly dissects the problems of the machine age.

The crux of the joke's humor lies in the words "how many," since in most instances changing a light bulb requires only one person—not the teeming hordes of support technicians and service providers who crowd around the ladder protesting unsafe working conditions and developing special bulb-insertion software. The light-bulb joke is, in spirit, both anticorporate and anti-Federal, providing a perfect vehicle for satirizing byzantine bureaucracies. It is the ideal joke of an era of upsizing, in which both large corporations and government agencies have bloated staffs that will allow the bulb to be changed only after the completion of environmental impact statements, ergonomic reports and Civil Service examinations conducted for the Light Bulb Administrator position. It is a deeply American joke, full of the rage of the Republican rebel who despises the social welfare state and advocates instead a pioneering philosophy of self-rule. At the risk of overstatement, you might suggest that the historical roots of the joke's libertarian agenda lie in the colonists' rejection of royalist tyranny and the 19th-century frontiersmen's love of personal initiative.

The light-bulb joke is also well suited to an age of consumer-protection campaigns and media exposés of the potentially life-threatening dangers of defective products, from exploding gas tanks to leaking silicone breast implants. It resonates with our suspicion of the rapaciousness of specialists eager to make a quick buck at the expense of both our pocketbooks and our physical safety, like the six garage mechanics, five of whom hold the ladder while the other gives the estimate at the end of the month. Within the context of its virtually infinite permutations, the joke transforms the light bulb into a kind of symbolic Every Commodity, whose purchase and installation is complicated by malfunctioning components and hidden costs. (How many I.B.M. PC owners? Only one, but the purchase of the light-bulb adapter card is extra.)

The joke is peculiarly modern because it makes sense only in an era in which the middle-class homeowner maintains his own property and is unable to afford the servants who, in a long-lost age of cheap immigrant labor, would have changed his bulbs for him. It is at once the epitaph for an obsolete class of household slaves and the patriotic battle hymn of the bedraggled housewife and the diligent handyman who cut their own lawns and unclog their own sinks. In the late 20th century, we are all bulb changers, participants in a pedestrian task that unites the rich with the poor.

The light bulb is a highly charged ideological object in our aging democracy—an emblem of normality, of a society that stigmatizes its exceptional citizens, reviling their lack of conformity and mechanical ineptitude as unpardonable evidence of their elitism. The ability to perform this simple household chore becomes a test of one's humanity, and those outcasts who fail are immediately interned in the menagerie of buffoons that the light-bulb joke so mercilessly pillories.

The joke singles out two contrasting groups in its role as an equal-opportunity leveler. On the one hand, it ridicules bungling minorities whose spatulate fingers are ill equipped to handle this fragile glass object, smashing the bulb with a hammer, cutting it in two with a chain saw or getting drunk until the room spins. On the other hand, it is increasingly used to satirize overeducated scientists who intellectualize a task that involves a mere twist of the wrist, compiling libraries of software documentation or defining Darkness™ as a new industry standard. Simultaneously snobbish and anti-elitist, the joke reflects an identity crisis occurring among angry white males. Hemmed in from below by destitute ethnic groups and from above by incomprehensible aristocracies of white-collar intellectuals, the average citizen holds himself up as the exemplar of common sense, which inevitably prevails over those who refuse to turn the bulb without first completing the software upgrade and drawing up forbiddingly complex contracts governing brownouts or pratfalls.

The fact that a single joke is used to belittle the supposed deficiencies of minorities and the esoteric skills of the intelligentsia suggests that, in some sense, we equate the tensions caused by ethnic conflicts with the tensions caused by the new hierarchies of knowledge. Both ethnic diversity and profound inequalities of information and know-how are contributing to social unrest, to the demoralizing feelings of inadequacy and competitiveness that are tearing apart a nation already fractured by intolerance. It is not an accident that the same joke is used to ridicule the homeboy and the software designer; both are viewed with distrust as members of subversive minorities.

One of the most surprising features of the light-bulb joke is how the lowly bulb has been used to make fun of the exalted computer, spawning scores of light-bulb jokes about Silicon Valley. (How many hardware engineers? Thirty—but of course just five years ago all it took was a couple of kids in a garage in Palo Alto.) Far from streamlining the modern environment, mechanization has made our lives more complex and has needlessly confused straightforward tasks like setting the clocks on our VCRs, paralyzing us with the cerebral intricacies of a chore it has turned into an indecipherable electronic puzzle. The joke catches the machine age in the nostalgic act of clarifying its original purpose—that of making things simpler, faster, easier to use.

The light-bulb joke reflects another form of social unrest. In the not too distant past, it was an uncensored forum for socially acceptable expressions of racism, homophobia, anti-Semitism and misogyny. (How many feminists? Two—one to declare that the bulb has violated the socket and one to secretly wish that *she* were the socket.) In the 1990s, however, the joke is being turned against its traditional tellers by a gang of comic vigilantes bent on evening the score. It is a joke in turmoil, the battleground of a small civil war in which minorities, who for decades remained in tight-lipped silence as loud-mouthed Archie Bunkers taunted them in public, are now talking back, lambasting such groups as homophobes, who change the bulb with sterile rubber gloves because it is possible that a gay person with AIDS just touched it. The scapegoats have been elevated from the butt of the joke to the joke tellers, a promotion that mirrors their increasing integration into society. While very little has been done from 1879 to the age of the politically incorrect to improve Edison's invention, the light-bulb joke has been constantly reinvented.

Discussion Questions

1. What kinds of jokes are you familiar with that serve any of the political and cultural purposes Harris describes for light-bulb jokes?

2. Specifically, Harris connects light-bulb jokes to "ambivalent attitudes toward technology" as well to current events and cultural changes. What purpose does joking about these changes serve?

3. What do you think of Harris's claim that the light-bulb joke is "a joke in turmoil"? What does he mean by this?

4. What comment about academic analysis of jokes is Harris making by stretching his analysis of light-bulb jokes to such extremes?

Writing Activities

1. Look at a newspaper or online news source (e.g., Google News). Drawing from the headlines, write some light-bulb jokes illuminating current social concerns or anxieties.

2. Brainstorm a new genre of jokes that could serve purposes similar to those Harris ascribes to light-bulb jokes. Here's a possible form: How many _____s does it take to _____?

The Joke

J. DAVID STEVENS

Headnotes/Things to Look For

J. David Stevens teaches at the University of Richmond. Recent work has appeared in Harper's Magazine, The North American Review, The Iowa Review, The Paris Review, Mid-American Review, *and* Notre Dame Review. *He has published a collection of stories,* Mexico is Missing, *and a book of literary criticism,* The Word Rides Again: Rereading the Frontier in American Fiction.

Note how Stevens takes off from a standard joke premise to explore some darker and more complicated dimensions of how jokes function both internally and in the wider culture in which it seeks laughs.

—————————— ✦ ——————————

A priest, a housewife, a chicken, and a bag of chocolate bars are on the bank of a river. They are not sure how they got there but know, collectively, that they are there for the purpose of the joke yet to be told. Uncomfortable as a unit, they take up different positions on the riverbank, waiting for the joke to commence. The sun shines brightly, but a breeze off the river cools the skin. There is a boat nearby: a rowboat, red with white and yellow splashes of paint. The trees on the river's far side bear fruit, though from a distance no one can tell what kind of fruit it is.

Meanwhile the joker is not telling his joke. He sees the characters in his head: an oversexed priest, a voluptuous housewife, a chicken with a Napoleon complex, some chocolate. But he cannot figure out where to go with them. He's had a rough day at work. He's knocked back a few gin-and-tonics already—less tonic, more gin. He promises himself to try again tomorrow.

Things grow restless on the riverbank. The priest has missed afternoon confession, and the housewife—whose name is Lila—worries that she forgot to turn off the oven. The chicken, who has been watching the Asian markets and contemplating a major purchase in Chinese poultry feed, curses the malevolent spirit that caused him to leave the coop without his cell phone. Only the bag of candy seems calm. A few feet from the rest of the group, it discovers its own sentience and repeatedly counts the number of chocolate bars it contains. It wonders if the others recognize its new level of consciousness. It resolves to learn how to speak. Days pass. The chicken would give his tail feathers for a single glimpse at the S&P Index. Lila has unbuttoned much of her shirt and tied the bottom in a knot. She describes the riverbank as an adventure that she often longs for but never undertakes. Her husband is a corporate lawyer with a Jaguar and a seven handicap who gets free T-shirts and gym bags from the tobacco companies he defends. Lila worries about her two sons—fears they will smoke, then hang out with leather-clad women, get tattooed, drop out of school, buy an RV. Her breasts heave slightly. The priest, whose name is Father Ron, watches the heaving breasts. The bag of candy composes, in a difficult Italian meter, an ode in which the river serves as a metaphor for their situation: both movement and stasis. It longs to recite its ode to the others. It pities Lila, and it pities Father Ron, who is now thinking about leather-clad women and an RV known to its neighbors as *Lovin' On Wheels*.

The joker cannot get the characters out of his head. At work, he sits in front of a computer screen all day, entering tiny numbers into tiny charts that he has been told are instrumental to corporate success. Sometimes he receives messages from friends, usually of the hey-how-you-doing-isn't-life-boring-as-hell ilk, but sometimes jokes. Funny jokes. Complex jokes. Joke lists. Listservs. He is on many lists. He cannot laugh out loud because his boss's secretary might hear him. She knows numbers are not funny. She does not like him because he is somewhat fat, and deep down they both know that fat men are supposed to be funny. In a man, fat without funny is just . . . well, fat. Or Winston Churchill. Or Alfred Hitchcock. He thinks that maybe there is humor in such a realization. His boss's secretary looks up from her *Southern Living*, testing the air. He reverts to numbers. Thinks chicken, candy, housewife, priest.

The chicken decides that the joke is a hell of his own making. Hubris compels him to believe that, if he can resolve the joke from the inside, he might break out of it. He tries the conventional approach. Why did the chicken cross the road? But here there are no roads, only a river. Somewhere from his youth he remembers a riddle about a farmer with a fox, a goose, and a bag of grain that must all ford a stream in a particular order to prevent any from eating the other. His mind works out variations. In the rowboat he paddles priest, housewife, and candy across in different permutations—making sure never to leave priest alone with housewife, housewife alone with chocolate. The task is daunting. The oars are insecure. The chicken's muscles ache, and his red comb becomes redder beneath the midsummer sun. The fruit trees on the opposite shore turn out to be lemon trees, ripe with yellow fire. The silence of the lemons makes the chicken uneasy. He thinks of recipes in which he might use their gutted pulp. Lemonade. Lemon Chess Pie. Lemon drops. Lemon . . . *chicken.* When nothing has changed by dusk, the chicken piles everyone back into the rowboat and returns them to the original shore. He learns to sleep with one eye open, trained on the lemon branches whose shadows reach like dark arms across the water's surface.

The mind is stuck on itself, he decides. It thinks that the world cannot function without it. If a housewife falls in a river but there is no one to hear her scream, no priest to pull her out . . . well, the mind sees the world merely as an extension of such musing. It says, hypothetically, that a chicken walks into a bar. But if a chicken *actually* walked into a bar and made a ranting beeline for the back table where the mind was talking up a couple of Rutgers coeds, it's unlikely that the mind could continue to see the universe as a place of its own invention. In fact, it's likely that the mind would do a screaming tarantella atop the back table until the bartender shooed the chicken out with a broom. This assumes, of course, that the chicken is not a bar regular, and that one of the coeds is not his steady girl, Henrietta, and that most of the bar's patrons do not want to buy him a Sam Adams because he is a well-known power broker around town. The mind would have trouble wrapping around such a chicken, but it would be one hell of a joke.

Meanwhile, Father Ron observes the supple curves of Lila's body. They have now been stranded together for weeks, but she has shown no interest in him. Or, more precisely, she has shown interest in him only as a spiritual confidant—someone with whom she can share all of the problems of her marriage, including her unrequited sexual needs. Father Ron thinks of Job. He wonders if the joke is a test of his spiritual resolve. Thinking along these lines, he notices the chicken, the supple curves of the chicken's body. He tells himself that he is not thinking in a serious way, but in a trapped-on-a-riverbank-with-only-these-questions-to-keep-me-sane way. This is philosophy. He begins to understand why women are called "chicks"—breasts, thighs, white meat, dark. He starts to dream about chicken. He wonders how egregious some sins might seem before God. The chicken, sensing something amiss, gives up on sleep altogether.

There is only frustration. Frustration and desire, the joker tells himself, which are really the same thing in the end. He watches the popular men at the bar whose jokes rise above the smoke and waft into the corner where he sits alone with his domestic beer. How do they begin? Two sisters in Montana must buy a bull for their ranch. An old Jew and a Chinese man are sitting on a park bench. Three hobos eat corn on a train. A doctor's office. A farmer's daughter. A moose. These are items ripe with humor, but when he envisions his joke, he can manage only slight changes: a duck, a rabbi, a librarian, a cherry pie. In the end the joke is futilely the same. Returning from the restroom, he steals a dart from the dart board and scratches his name into the oak table—then adds some eyes, a nose, and a mouth that resemble a once-famous cartoon cat. His mother always liked his drawings. She hung a few around the house and called him her *artiste*. She said that they would take a trip to France one day, though the closest they ever got was flipping through some travel brochures on Quebec at a rest stop near his cousin's place in Syracuse. At home, after last call at the bar, he will leave two Hungry Man dinners to thaw on the counter of his un-air-conditioned kitchen, then eat them both for breakfast the following morning without cooking them. Later he'll have a bagel at the office, extra cream cheese.

Egocentrism gets them only so far. At last they decide that the joke is not designed to punish any of them individually. It is merely a random confluence of cosmic forces, the teapot tempest in which they are tossed. They assume that they will be freed eventually, but, in the name of order and civilization, agree to establish rules by which their small society might run. After several halting drafts, they create a constitutional theocracy with the chicken as president, Father Ron as chancellor, and Lila as minister of culture and good taste. The bag of chocolate bars, because someone must, becomes the democratic masses. It redoubles its efforts at speech and thinks of the best way for a bag of candy to communicate with the outer world. It could pop its cellophane on a rock and attract throngs of approbative ants. It could melt into symbols on the sand. The First National Assembly is scheduled for a year hence: Father Ron will lead the country in prayer, followed by the chicken's address on the health-care system, then Lila's unveiling of the new army uniforms made of couch grass and lemon rind. The candy plans a Homeric hymn to commemorate the founding of the state. If it has time, it will fashion some scenery for its performance—perhaps a frieze of the chicken and

Father Ron commuting their household gods across the river and onto the riverbank promised in the mystical covenants of their forebears.

Of course, a joke should be easier to tell. He finally decides that the problem is his mother. When he was a child, she trained him to laugh at misfortune—every accident met with a smile. In this way he learned that pain was comedy. Pratfalls. Pies to the face. A well-placed boot in the groin. He imagines the chicken writhing on the sand, wings to his crotch, moaning, "Oh, my nuggets," and he cannot help smiling. His apartment is dark except for the late-night TV. His undershirt rides up his belly where he sticks his hand beneath the elastic of his shorts and cradles his testicles, an unconscious gesture. He sucks an ice cube from his whiskey glass and spits it out the open window, wondering if it might kill a man twelve stories down. Gravity is hilarious, he decides, hefting his paunch with a forearm. The TV audience roars at the host's one-liners. He resolves to get a bigger chin.

But nothing can help at this point. Long before the National Assembly, friction arises when Father Ron abolishes the institution of marriage and criticizes the chicken's population control plan. They both fear Lila, who has taken to wearing the new army uniform, stockpiling stones, and telling stories of how the Amazons each burned off one breast so as not to impede their bowstrings. An uneasy truce is called. They doff their official vestments, sacrifice the candy bars to a recipe that Lila dubs Couch Grass S'mores, then part ways. As the chicken slips downriver in the rowboat, he dreams of the new society that he will form out of the misfits he finds along his way—characters from bad jokes or other jokes never to be told: one-legged midgets, gay hairdressers, most of Poland. From here on in, until his death, he will strive to view himself as a fowl in charge of his own destiny. But even years later, in his tent beneath the mountains—the sultana's warm body reposed beside him, the drifting incense, and the sound of their many camels spitting in the distance—he will wake with the irrational fear that he is still part of the joke, that he is still working toward some inevitable punch line. There is a spirit at the door of the tent, waiting to sweep in. The chicken stares through the darkness. He sees only the image of his youngest daughter—a red-haired, smoke-eyed beauty who maligns him when she is angry. *Silly bird*, she chastises. *Silly, silly bird.*

Fat man in a little car. Fat man bowling. Fat man in bikini briefs. Fat man doing the cha-cha. Cellulite, he concludes, is the sole of wit. In all honesty, he can do no more with these characters.

He detests the chicken and Father Ron. He desires the chocolate bars and Lila. He has grown too close to his material. He's trying too hard. Humor, he knows from somewhere, cannot be forced but must spring from the mind like snakebite. *It will come,* he assures himself. He just has to wait for it. And when his mind does manage to coil like a rattler, the world will finally see him for the hero that he is. The men will buy him drinks; the women will come home with him, and they will titter in the lavishness of their un-air-conditioned sweat. There will be no calories that laughter cannot melt away. They will love him high and low, the Bobos in their Versace drinking Sea Breezes by the Sound, the Guidos in their leather pants drinking forties down the shore. The elevator door opens onto his boss's secretary who greets him with a sneer. But he exalts in the stale office air, anticipating the day when he is boss and can send her back out because she has not brought a pickle with his egg salad. She, above all, will be forced to acknowledge her treachery, the wanton ignorance of her kind. When the new *him* arrives at the office one day—the joke, the wit, the mind itself—then she will know how wrong she has been. She will see him in the glory of a new light and swear that everywhere she goes they want to be like him: the Bobos, the Guidos, the bosses, the masses. He is his own religion and not the antimiracle she sees now. Fat man in a cubicle. Fat man at a desk. Fat man who sweats too much. Fat man in off-the-rack pants.

Discussion Questions

1. Stevens gives us the elements of the joke—the characters and the setting—but then stops the forward progress toward the punchline. What's the effect of making the priest, housewife, chicken, and bag of candy self-aware?

2. How does Stevens introduce the joker who is unable to bring the joke to fruition? What kinds of pressure does the joker face, and what does he project as the rewards of telling the joke?

3. What does the bag of candy do with its newfound self-awareness? How does the bag of candy differ from the other characters in its preoccupations?

4. The joker tells himself at one point that frustration and desire "are really the same thing in the end." At another point the joker muses on how he learned as a child that "pain was comedy." What elements of comedy's cultural role is Stevens exploring through the joker's thoughts?

5. The joker imagines ultimate triumph if he can only get the joke told—does comedy have the kind of cultural power the joker ascribes to it?

Writing Activities

1. Set up your own premise for a joke involving multiple characters and a setting, then follow Stevens's lead by giving the characters self-awareness.
   What kinds of things do your characters think about?
2. Cast yourself as a character in a stalled joke and try to think your way out of it.

Can an Ape Tell a Joke?
VICKI HEARNE

Headnotes/Things to Look For

*Animal trainer and writer Vicki Hearne (1946–2001) wrote books
including* Adam's Task: Calling Animals by Name, Animal
Happiness, *and* Bandit: Dossier of a Dangerous Dog.

*In this essay Hearne moves us beyond comedy that is strictly
human with her inquiry into whether orangutans can be considered
comics. Animal trainer Bobby Berosini insists that he collaborates
with the orangutans, and that their ideas for new jokes are sometimes better than his. Hearne puts a different spin on Bergson's
point regarding the mechanical encrusted on the human by challenging us to be worthy of engagement with the animals who share
the stage with Berosini.*

---◆---

W.H. Auden wrote that poetry survives in those places where
"executives would never want to tamper." Similarly, the
knowledge of animals survives in places where academics would
never want to tamper, even now that many of them have added
their voices to the babble that presently obscures the reality of
animals. It survives in the circus, eerily revealed by Mark Twain as
a place where truth is guarded by scams—by what most would
consider tawdry but which Huckleberry Finn embraced as
"gaudy." It lives in the shabbier parts of public parks where dog
obedience classes are conducted. And it lives at the racetrack,
where the beauty of the horses, glowing as though each were the
darling of the infinite god of detail, stands in sharp contrast to the
gray faces of the gamblers.

But perhaps the least likely place one would expect to find
deep knowledge about animals is in a trained-orangutan act on a

Las Vegas stage—specifically, in the act performed for many years by Bobby Berosini and his five orangutans at the Stardust Hotel and Casino. I first saw Bobby Berosini's Vegas act three years ago, shortly after he received an unwelcome dose of national celebrity. Now that I've spent a week with him and his orangutans, and watched a dozen of his performances, I'm convinced that he deserves his celebrity, though not for the reasons he has come by it.

I would not ordinarily have ventured to Las Vegas to watch a trained-orangutan show, but Bobby Berosini, who immigrated to the United States from his native Czechoslovakia in 1964, is no ordinary animal trainer. I had heard he'd won numerous comedy awards for his act, and that he had probably done more with orangutans—famously difficult animals to train—than any trainer ever has. But this was not the reason for his sudden notoriety. He had been accused in 1989 of abusing his orangutans by, among others, People for the Ethical Treatment of Animals. This in itself was not unusual: these days animal trainers are regularly attacked by animal-rights activists. What was unusual in this case was that the trainer had fought back, suing PETA for defamation and invasion of privacy. And, most unusual of all, he had won his case: after a five-week trial in which Berosini brought his orangutans into court, a jury found PETA, along with several individual activists, guilty of "reckless disregard of the truth" and awarded Berosini $3.1 million in damages. (The judgment is currently on appeal.)

Berosini did not sue for harassment, but while I was in Las Vegas his Australian-born wife, Joan, described to me the harrowing experience of receiving repeated death threats against themselves and their animals in the middle of the night; of spending six months living with armed security guards twenty-four hours a day; and of being forced to shop at a different supermarket each day, since some of the threats had detailed plans to poison the orangs' food. (Many animal-rights activists believe that wild animals are better off dead than confined in any way by humans.) Even today, the harassment continues: when Berosini recently moved his act to the Five Star Theatre in Branson, Missouri, the PETA picketers followed.

Mad as some of these tactics were, the charges against Bobby Berosini were not ones that could be summarily dismissed. PETA had circulated a videotape, made surreptitiously backstage by a Stardust dancer, that purported to document the abuse. The tape, which was broadcast on *Entertainment Tonight*, is of extremely poor quality, but it appears to show Berosini and his assistants on about a half-dozen occasions preparing the animals to go onstage. In each instance one of the orangutans—it's hard to tell, but it looks like the same orang each time—seems to act up and is then threatened, shaken, or struck by Berosini with a wand or baton of some kind.

Jeanne Roush, then PETA's director of research and investigations, and one of the losing defendants, charged that the orangs were routinely beaten into submission right before going onstage. Berosini said that, on each of the occasions videotaped, he had had to correct the orangutan backstage because a dancer was making sounds of distressed animals to rile the orangutans. Before I got to Las Vegas, it was impossible to sort out who was telling the truth, so I decided not to pay too much attention to what was being said on either side.

What I would pay attention to, I decided, was what I saw myself—and what, as an animal trainer, I know about animals. I know, for example, that the "correction" of an animal in training is an intricate and poorly understood subject. Properly applied at the right moment, a correction will cause the animal to stop aggressive behavior and perform happily and well. But a correction that expresses the trainer's anger, impatience, or fear, or that is applied when the animal is honestly confused rather than disobedient, will leave the animal unable to perform. Since no one had said that the orangs muffed their performances after the corrections we see on the tape, I can only assume that Berosini was using good judgment.

I assume this also from the uncontested fact that the animals were performing live, twice a night, six nights a week, at liberty—that is, without any physical restraint on an unguarded stage. Roger Fouts, a primatologist who testified in another performing-ape case, has said that "you can get anyone to do anything if you beat them," but, in fact, this is not so. You can perhaps accomplish a fair amount by beating an animal or person who cannot escape (though you can't thereby engage the victim's higher faculties), but not if you beat an animal or person you then leave at liberty.

These thoughts occurred to me before I had had a chance to watch Berosini work, so I came to Las Vegas prepared to doubt PETA's charges. And after spending a week with Berosini, watching twelve performances and joining him backstage before several of them, I saw nothing to make me think he was a cruel or phony trainer—no thumps, no fists. (Could Berosini have acted differently while I was around? Possibly, but any trainer who behaves differently in public than in private will soon lose the respect of his animals.)

What I did see, there amid the Vegas glitz and against the ugly backdrop of this furious animal-rights battle, was mastery, and even a kind of miracle. Berosini and his orangs are, to be sure, masters of much that is gaudy—his act is a half hour of animal slapstick and off-color skits sandwiched between the usual Vegas dancing girls and boys; the orangs wear shorts and funny hats and make obscene gestures to the audience. But Bobby Berosini and his orangs are masters of something else as well—of the miracle that was unavailable to Job, who, as the voice in the whirlwind thunderously reminded him, could not engage the wild animals in any fruitful, cooperative enterprise. Bobby Berosini can.

• • •

As well as being a gifted trainer, Berosini is a gifted comedian, though by his reckoning he is not the only comedian on the Stardust stage. When I asked him, between shows in the Stardust's coffee shop, what motivates his orangs to work, he said to me, passionately, "*We* are comedians. *We* are comedians. Do you understand me?"

Comedians? Orangutans? This is not a reasonable remark, from the point of view of either popular or institutionally sanctioned knowledge about animals. If, as many human-rights activists and academics believe, animals are capable of feeling and suffering but not of elaborate intentions and creative thought, then Berosini's orangs *must* be beaten into submission, since food rewards would not be powerful enough to motivate their complex actions. Besides, animals could not possibly know the mood or muse of comedy. They lack the conceptual apparatus to handle the mischievous shifts in meaning required for jokes.

When Berosini told me that his orangutans are comedians, I nodded my head vigorously; the enchantment of the act had not worn off. But what does it mean to say of an animal that he or she is a comedian? This question leads back onstage, to the act itself, and to the sorts of questions Berosini and his orangs toss about, invert, capsize, and rescue, only to turn them on their head, time and time again.

The running theme of the act is "How I Train Them." Berosini keeps saying to the audience, "People ask me how I get them to do things," or "People ask me how I train them," and then he supplies different "answers." At one point the answer is, "You have to show them who is boss." He brings Rusty out to show him who is boss, and Rusty not only refuses to jump onto the stool provided for the purpose but tricks his trainer into doing so by pretending incomprehension until Berosini finally demonstrates, jumping onto the stool himself. Once Berosini has dutifully jumped, Rusty invites the audience to applaud.

Berosini goes on to mock much scientific and popular wisdom about operant conditioning—training that relies more on the carrot than on the stick—by demonstrating how he doesn't need to train the orangutans at all because "I have magic orang cookies." A fast and lively slapstick round results from his failed attempts to get Bo to eat a cookie; the cookie is juggled, spit into the audience, hidden, fed to Berosini, but never eaten by the orangutan.

Then there is yet another variation on the theme: "People ask me how I train them. The truth is, I do not have to train them, because I just mesmerize them." Bo is then asked to come forward and be a hypnotic subject. There is much crooning of "You are getting very, very sleepy." Bo drops her shoulders, stands more and more still, and—wonder of wonders—closes her eyes. Pleased with the trance, the "trainer" whispers, "Are you asleep?" All of a sudden Bo grins outrageously, nods her head vigorously, and then immediately droops back into her "mesmerized" posture. The joke, again, is on Berosini—or, rather, on the Berosini character, who, of course, stands for the audience and for our overblown ideas about our superior intelligence and ability to control the world.

• • •

As Berosini explains when he is offstage, the way he trains is not "traditional," in that he does not teach his animals "tricks" but rather teaches them through the flow of their intelligence interacting with his. He explains that whereas a suggestion for a move or gesture or gag often originates with him, it is just as likely to come from the orangutan; the trainer must be as adept at picking up cues from the animals as they are at picking up cues from him. And orangutans demand this kind of handling. "I do not train them to do what I know how to do," he told me, "because you just cannot do that. It doesn't work!" According to Berosini, orangutans are the hardest of all the apes to teach a trick to because they are so self-contained, so mentally poised. The same idea is expressed in scholarly literature on orangs with reference to their marked lack of social interaction in the wild. Unlike most other apes, they are not dependent on social support and approval, which vastly complicates the training relationship. An orangutan is irredeemably his or her own person—"the most poetic of the apes," as primate researcher Lyn Miles once told me. Miles had in mind the difference between orangutans and chimps. Chimps are much admired for their use of tools and their problem-solving relationship with things as they find them. A chimp looks inferential, ingenious, and ever so active while taking the various IQ tests that science presents him with—a hexagonal peg, say, and several holes of different shapes, only one of them hexagonal. Here, the chimp shows his tremendous initiative right away, holding the peg this way and that, trying out this, that, and the other hole; this, that, and the other angle. He *experiments*, he is filled with the inventor's work ethic; he tries, essays, tests, probes, he is full of the integrity of logic, or if not logic then at least something very American: he is so enterprising, so resourceful.

Give your orangutan the hexagonal peg and the several different holes, hide behind the two-way mirror, and watch how he engages the problem. And watch and watch and watch—because he will not engage the problem. He uses the peg to scratch his back, has a look-see at his right wrist, makes a halfhearted and soon abandoned attempt to use his fur for a macramé project, stares dreamily out the window if there is one and at nothing in particular if there is not, and the sun begins to set. (The sun will also set if you are observing a chimp, but the chimp is a lot busier, so you are less likely to mark the moment in your notes. An orangutan observer has plenty of time to be a student of the varieties of sunset.) You watch, and the orang dreams, and your notes perhaps consist of nothing more than memoranda on the behavior of the clock, when casually, and as if thinking of something else, the orangutan slips the hexagonal peg into the hexagonal hole. And continues staring off dreamily.

Professor Miles says that this sort of behavior contradicts the traditional finding that orangs are dumber than chimps. It is rather, she says, that chimps are problem-oriented whereas orangs are insight-oriented, the dreamers and visionaries of the world of the great apes. Which is all well and good, but how do you entertain five hundred people for half an hour twice a night, every night, six nights a week, for seven years, with animals whose forte is meditation, animals who do not do tricks? It's like trying to entertain a Las Vegas audience with five performing poets.

In the wild, too, orangs have not provided ethologists with the glamorous behaviors that, say, Jane Goodall's chimps have given her. I found no reports of orangs doing anything like the equivalent of fashioning special sticks to fish for termites, for instance. Orang observers instead report such exciting phenomena as the "fruit stare," which some people say is a function of the difficulty orangutans have foraging for food in the wild. Orangutans need to develop the fruit stare because trees can be coy about when, where, and how much they fruit, and the fruit is often hidden in the canopy of leaves. The fruit stare is an expression of reverie, but it is a reverie directed outward rather than inward—"like thinking with your eyes," naturalist Sy Montgomery has said. "That's why they are so spaced out."

But all this only explains why there are not many orangutan acts in the world and not how Bobby Berosini manages to put on an orangutan act night after night.

What Berosini says, again and again, is, "We are comedians. Do you understand me? Do you realize what I am telling you? We are comedians, my orangs and I." His voice is urgent now, but not frantic the way it is when PETA and the charges of abuse and the harassment are the topic. The act, he explains, is a collaboration: "Rusty will have an idea for a gag, and maybe I don't like his idea, but often I do, so I leave my gag aside and accept his idea, or maybe I sometimes insist that we still do it the other way. Or maybe Tiga insists that the old way was funnier, and then I have to laugh at myself and accept what she says. She has as many ideas as I do. She is an old campaigner, Tiga, she knows what she is doing."

I find the act screamingly funny, not only because the timing is so good but because the content is so intelligent, even if the orang humor can be a bit coarse. There are, for instance, the many sardonic jokes about "monkeys" and "monkey business." These are jokes about the audience, about humanity's ignorance about its fellow primates, because, of course, orangs are not monkeys—they are, along with chimps, gorillas, and humans, great apes. But this is the sort of detail people consistently get wrong. One witness in another performing-ape controversy told me a story about a zookeeper and an animal he referred to as "some sort of monkey." I pressed to discover what sort, and he said, "It doesn't matter. They're all monkeys, aren't they?"

Well, no, they are not, and it does matter, especially when you are claiming to speak with authority about the animals in question. I've listened to anthropologist Daniel Povinelli hold forth passionately about the importance of understanding the differences not only between monkeys and apes but also between different species of ape and different species of monkey. He says that there are pronounced morphological differences between monkeys and apes, and also pronounced psychological differences: "The apes are doing something different." For Povinelli, it is almost as radical a mistake to confuse monkeys with apes as it would be to confuse elephants with pigs or wolves with golden retrievers. "Evolution would be impossible without difference," Povinelli points out. "There can hardly be anything more fundamental than recognizing, studying, and appreciating the enormous differences, especially the psychological differences, among different animals."

Povinelli and Berosini are very different people, with very different relationships to animals, but they have in common a passionate belief that the details about an animal, whether psychological or morphological, are not merely pedantic decorations but should compel our respect. Berosini is a performer and Povinelli is a scientist, so they would probably disagree about what counts as a violation of this code, but they meet in insisting that there is such a code and that it matters. Indeed, when I told Povinelli that in his act Berosini calls his animals "monkeys" and makes no attempt to correct himself, he was somewhat shocked and not entirely reassured by my explanation of the dark comic irony of the usage.

Berosini, however, is nothing if not canny; it means something when he monkeys around. When Bo nods her head vigorously or applauds his "wit" when he makes a "monkey" joke, there is a sophisticated edge here, as if a physicist were joking around by blurring the difference between an atom and a molecule.

You have to know a great deal more than the bulk of the audience knows, or cares to know, about animals and the politics of animals in order to hear the sardonic implications in the reiteration of the "just monkeys" bit. These darker jibes ride on the back of traditional slapstick, but the jokes are, as perhaps true slapstick always is, constructed both from and about our intellectual ineptitude and hubris; every time one of the orangs makes a "monkey" out of Berosini, the joke is on us. Our brutishness and our intellectual incompetence are one.

But the act is comedy, true comedy, and not merely a collection of dark and sardonic jokes. The orangs and the audience and humanity itself, as represented by the character Berosini portrays, are redeemed in the end, in part by the sheer quicksilver beauty of the timing. When the audience laughs, at times with true joy, a joy free of malice, it is, after all, humanity that is being celebrated, since the ability to laugh without malice at one's own failings—and to see in those failings one's connection with everyone else in the room, a connection made through laughter—is no mean ethical feat.

If Berosini's act can be said to have one overriding theme, it is training—obedience—itself. "Obedience" comes from an old French word that means "to hear" or "to heed," "to pay attention to." The great trainers of every kind of animal, from parakeet to dog to elephant, have said for millennia that you cannot get an animal to heed you unless you heed the animal; obedience in this sense is a symmetrical relationship. In a given instance it may start with the human, who perhaps says to the dog, "Joe, sit!" Soon, however, the dog will take the command and turn it, use it to respond, to say something back. The dog might, for example, take to sitting in a sprightly fashion when one gets out a dumbbell, as if to say: "Yes, that's it, let's go!" It is at this moment that true training with any species, including humans, either begins or fails. If the human obeys, hears, heeds, responds to what the animal is now saying, then training begins. If the human "drops" the animal at this point, not realizing that the task has only begun, then the dog or orangutan will disobey.

Animals, like people, are motivated in many ways. Berosini's orangs are motivated offstage in the same way they appear to be motivated onstage: when they make a gesture, they get a response. Their trainer obeys them, unless they are committing mayhem. The intelligent responsiveness of animals is for us one of the most deeply attractive things about them, not only because we are a lonesome and threatened tribe but because intelligent responsiveness is a central, abiding good. The intelligent responsiveness of trainers, which some of them call respect, is what makes trainers attractive to animals, and may be the whole of the secret of "having a way with animals."

In the comic mismatch between the Berosini character's ideas about the orangs and the nature of the orangs themselves as they triumph continually over the would-be lordly "trainer," our fond hopes are mocked, but not cruelly. The world, which is to say the human project, is in trouble, but within the tiny world of Berosini's act a way is found, even if it is a stumbling, awkward way, to true responsiveness between ourselves and animals. Even the audience gets a response, as when Rusty invites us to applaud Berosini or when Tiga gives an audience member one of her "magic orang cookies," and does so gently, though without a hint of subservience.

Berosini also gets laughs by mocking the character of the orangs—Tiga's onstage character has a drinking problem and loose morals—but the "How I Train Them" series of gags is the most intellectually satisfying part of the act. Interestingly, Bo's simulation of the hypnotic trance is a play on the sort of spacy consciousness ethologists have observed in orangutans. There is the same dreaminess, the trance that frames the unpredictable moment of alert intelligence. Bo's eyes are closed, but otherwise she seems to be imitating the fruit stare in much the same way that a dressage horse—one so highly educated that we say he or she "dances"—imitates, with some variations, the postures and gestures of a horse in "nature."

The radical claim being made here is that the animals are "referring to," or at least imitating, these gestures deliberately, with some sense—if not precisely our sense—of the meaning of what they are doing. Berosini says that Bo is in on the joke, or at least on *some* joke, and that it is her interest and pleasure in such monkeying around that make it possible for him to work with her as he does. This is speculative, of course, but it could be argued that Berosini's is a more parsimonious explanation than an explanation based on conditioning would be. Indeed, it's questionable whether any model of conditioning, however elaborate, can explain behavior this complex, particularly since every performance the act changes, with both Berosini and the orangs offering improvisations. Talk of conditioned responses may be helpful in understanding part of a trained animal's development (or, for that matter, a dancer's or a poet's or an actor's or a philosopher's), but animal performance at this level makes more sense when viewed as rudimentary expressions of at least one primeval artistic impulse—the impulse to play with meaning.

Bo's trance-breaking grin is wonderfully timed, a case of high slapstick, if there can be such a thing; it is also, for me at least, an eerie instant of revelation in which I see something fairly exact in Berosini's claim that his orangs are comedians. But how might such an animal joke come about? Let's say that you are teaching the animal to be "mesmerized," and the animal spontaneously adds the mischievous nodding grin. This is a joke about who's in control, though not necessarily a joke about hypnosis. You accept the move and ask for it on purpose next time, and it becomes part of the routine. The animal offers it spontaneously at first, and then continues with it, perhaps for the same reason we repeat a phrase or a joke—because it felt so delicious the first time.

Berosini's act gives the orangs a point of view, one that I find credible as an animal point of view, and it gives their intelligence pride of place, as do other clever disobedience acts in the tradition— an ancient tradition going back to the Greeks, in which the *eiron,* or apparently lowly character, triumphs over the apparently noble character through wit, awareness, quickness of perception. (The word *eiron* gives us our word "irony.") In circus and movie tradition, the most familiar form of such comedy is the disobedient-dog act, in which the trainer character attempts to induce the dogs to display loyalty, nobility, and willing service; instead, they trip the trainer, disgrace the legacy of Rin Tin Tin by stealing a purse from an audience member, "bite" the trainer, and so on.

It is not Lassie and Rin Tin Tin themselves who are mocked by the disobedient-dog act but rather our own self-serving ideas of the selflessness of dogs, such as the pious notion that dogs "want to please" and work "for love of the handler." Berosini's orangs work with this sort of material wonderfully, displaying their intelligence against the backdrop of our ideas of their debasement.

If Berosini's comedy is somewhat dark and sharp-edged when you take a close look at it, that may be in part because of the tradition of comedy he inherits as a Czech, a tradition that has had to learn, over and over again, how to ensure the survival of intelligence in forms that escape the more violent scrutiny of various regimes. At any rate, the act I saw is one kind of shield for the mind, one kind of comic courage by means of which sanity survives amid social and political darkness.

One of Berosini's most famous monkey jokes occurred in court. During my stay in Las Vegas shortly after the 1990 trial, I heard it at least two dozen times. At one point during Berosini's testimony, PETA's lawyer asked him to tell the audience how he taught Bo to give the finger. He replied, "I'll give you a demonstration of how to give the finger if you want." This is just the way his orangs perform in his act, ragging him, continually foiling him with impudence, back talk, irreverence, impiety. And they give him the finger. In one way or another, most animals do give their trainers the finger—a great deal of animal humor is coarse, to put it mildly. I have long suspected that the real reason it was for so long heresy, an excommunicable offense, to say that animals have souls is that if you say they have souls, then their jokes and comments have meaning, and no bureaucratic or ecclesiastical or philanthropic dignity can survive animal vaudeville.

• • •

Joan Berosini told me that one juror, who asked to remain anonymous, said after the case was over, "It would be abuse to take the orangs away from Bobby." Is there anything to this, anything that can be understood without elevating Berosini to Patron Saint of Apes—a position that would destroy his comic art and that is, in any case, already held by Jane Goodall? Or, to turn the question around, what is the source of the improbable idea that the act's flow and liveliness and energy could possibly be achieved by beatings?

I do not think that the orangs mean their antics the way the audience interprets them. But I do think they mean *something* by them, and that they are motivated to stay onstage, rather than run loose in the audience, not by terror—which is a poor motivator—but by an interest in what they are doing.

So what *do* they mean, what are they doing? I am convinced that some animals—quite a few Airedales, for example, and also Border collies—are interested, and take pleasure, in something like the grammar of gesture itself, much as a dancer does. A bird dog in the field intends to retrieve the bird; the same dog cantering gaily after a dumbbell in an obedience ring "means" only that movement—not the retrieving of a bird, but the glorious gestures of retrieving. A Lippizaner means not to display himself before mares (which is what his movements would mean in "nature") but to call attention to the grandeur and intricacy of the display. These gestures are all metaphors, second inheritances of nature, in the same way poetry is a second inheritance of language. To call any of this—or poetry or dance, for that matter—"play," as some are wont to do, misses the point; it is work that is as serious as play, to borrow a phrase from the poet John Hollander. Such work is the highest use and pleasure of the mind, and orangutans plainly do have minds. The mind may remain satisfied in the wild, where the primitive problems of survival overwhelm other impulses, but if the other great apes are as close to us psychologically as some people claim and have minds, then it is good for those minds to develop.

And yet training in and of itself, apart from questions of abuse, makes people uneasy. In medieval times ecclesiasts believed that trained animals had devils in them—that dancing dogs were dancing satanically. In our time the idea of the "unnatural" has replaced the idea of the demonic, and for some it does not matter whether or not animals are abused, since keeping and training them is itself "unnatural" or "ethologically inappropriate," as though it were unnatural to develop the mind. These days the contemporary horror of the "unnatural" infects visions of life with domestic animals as well, but the possibility of the hearth—by which I mean a place where the human and animal may sit side by side—is much more likely to be denied when wild animals are in question.

Certainly you cannot have the same relationship with a wolf as with a dog, yet it does not follow from this that there can be *no* relationship. Today, at a time when the habitats of wild animals are rapidly disappearing, the terms of this relationship need to be reinvented, not abjured. We need to learn what we can from Berosini and other trainers—but particularly the wild-animal trainers—about how this might be done. A dog and her trainer, or a horse and his trainer, do not have to "meet each other halfway," because they already share the same social space. An orangutan and his trainer, however, must travel some conceptual distance to meet each other and work together. That this is possible, what it means that it is possible, what implications it has for the possibilities of mutual respect between wild animals and humans—this strikes me as a matter of urgent importance.

That is, I believe not only that the training of wild animals is acceptable but that the knowledge trainers have, which has been eschewed by science and philosophy and the church for millennia, may contain clues to imaginative and enlightened ways we might escape our age's violence and sentimentality toward the nonhuman world, and thereby genuinely take up the burden of our responsibility toward animals. In the Book of Job, the voice in the whirlwind points out that the wild goat and the unicorn and the ostrich and the warhorse are beyond Job. But the orangutan is not beyond Bobby Berosini, and it behooves us to understand why, to know that there is something to understand, and that the prurient contemplation of abuse, so popular in a self-servingly sentimental climate, will not open understanding here. Furthermore, the mongering of irresponsible images of abuse only obscures our views of the real cruelties that do exist.

James Thurber, who defended the intelligence of animals and animal wit as vigorously as anyone ever has, once wrote this about human wit: "The perfect tribute to perfection in comedy is not immediate laughter, but a curious and instantaneous tendency of the eyes to fill." This, I keep thinking, and not weepy displays of ignorant outrage and pity, is the tribute owed to Berosini's orangs. But be careful your vision does not mist too much. Bo and Rusty and Tiga and Niki and Benny are quite clear-eyed. Trainers speak often of how uncannily good animals are at "reading" people, and of training as a humbling activity. That's because when you train an animal you teach yourself and the animal a "language" by means of which the animal can tell you more than you may have wanted to know about what he or she sees in looking at you. If there is a moral to the act that the orangs are in on, it is this: be sure that when Tiga looks into your eyes she finds a clarity and amused intelligence fit to answer her own, lest she turn from you, leaving you in the foolish darkness yet again.

Discussion Questions

1. How does Hearne give value to what animals may know (about us, about themselves) through her account of Berosini's work with orangutans?
2. Why does Berosini claim that he works collaboratively with the orangutans? How would you describe the nature of their comic partnership?
3. How does Hearne build the case defending Berosini? How does she gradually expand her subject to incorporate a meditation on the relationship between people and animals?
4. Describe Hearne's persona in the essay. What kind of person does she seem to be? How does she establish her expert knowledge about animals and animal training?

Writing Activity

1. Write an essay expanding the boundary of what we consider to be comic, as Hearne does by agreeing with Berosini that the orangutans are comic performers. Bergson argued that comedy belongs only to the realm of the "strictly human." Where else might we find cause for laughter?

Chapter 2: Writing Prompts

Comic Arguments

1. Imagine you are a campaign manager or media consultant for a particular politician you're familiar with (this can be someone on the national scene or someone you've observed on the local or state level). Write a comic speech for this politician that aims to negate criticism by anticipating public criticisms or negative images.
2. Write a comic appreciation of a favorite performer (incorporating the comic strategies you are praising if you can). Think about how to blend close reading of the comic's work with contextual framing that shows the comic's personal and cultural importance.

Analysis

1. Write an analysis of a joke, a series of jokes, or a public event that deserves to be understood as comic. You can apply premises drawn from Bergson and Davis's work, and you can also draw from Harris for models.

2. Write an analysis of jokes you're familiar with from your youth, considering how they appealed to you then and how your understanding of them may have changed over time as you grew older.

3. Write an analysis of one or more of your favorite comic films or television shows, relating them to your understanding of the culture you live in.

4. Write an analysis of a comic performer, focusing on the attitudes the comic embodies and offers to the audience as a way of being in the world.

Research

1. Research the historical milestones in political humor Kolbert describes, beginning with Nixon's appearance on *Laugh-In*, then write an argument on the relationship of politics, popular culture, and comedy. You might choose instead to work backwards, researching the role of humor in politics prior to 1968, then writing an argument describing how politicians used humor before Nixon's appearance on a network comedy show.

2. Research a type of joke (e.g., knock-knock jokes, jokes about an ethnic group). Write an argument about the cultural role of such jokes.

3. Research the film comedies of a particular time period (e.g., the screwball comedies of the thirties, Bob Hope and Bing Crosby's Road pictures, Christopher Guest's mockumentaries) to develop an argument about their comic methods and cultural roles.

4. Research the career of a comic performer, making a case for the relationship of the comic's strategies and persona to their particular cultural context. You might choose a comic connected to the feminist movement, the civil rights movement, or any other movement for social change, focusing on the role of comedy in the movement and the cultural changes resulting from the movement.

CHAPTER 3

Modest and Immodest Proposals (deliberative rhetoric)

Introduction

Aristotle describes deliberative, or political, rhetoric as persuasion aimed at future action. This category thus includes policy proposals, campaign speeches, speeches delivered in governing bodies like Congress, and any calls for action in the public realm. As mentioned in the book's introduction, Aristotle further articulates that the major appeals in deliberative rhetoric generally involve invoking the expedient or the moral; that is, people can argue that something makes practical sense or that something is the right thing to do. These types of appeals often clash with each other, as can be seen in heated political debates about the torture of prisoners (recall the public discussion about the treatment of suspected terrorists held at Guantanamo Bay and the fictional situations portrayed in the Fox television show *24*), aid to victims of Hurricane Katrina, and the effect of tax cuts on federal programs that aid the poor.

Jonathan Swift's "A Modest Proposal" stands as perhaps the most famous example of political comic rhetoric, as Swift wields deadpan irony voiced through a carefully crafted persona to offer a calmly delivered but morally reprehensible proposal for political action; Swift's speaker uses a detached, logical tone to highlight the rationality of his plan. Jane Austen offers us another kind of proposal in her novel *Pride and Prejudice*, showing how a character can horribly misjudge the appeals that will persuade the object of his affection to agree to share her life with him. Joseph Addison addresses the sticky issue of giving advice at all, noting that human beings, especially those holding powerful positions, by nature don't like being put into the subordinate position of needing guidance. Oscar Wilde sidesteps this problem, not by following Addison's suggestion of weaving advice into stories, but rather by encapsulating his views into pithy phrases intended to guide the young. Also using comic strategies to make advice easier to accept, Scott Adams of *Dilbert* fame demonstrates how to behave at meetings. Finally, Molly Ivins issues a feisty call for appreciation of the many contributions of smokers to society.

A Modest Proposal for Preventing the Children of Poor People in Ireland, from Being a Burden on Their Parents or Country, and for Making Them Beneficial to the Publick

JONATHAN SWIFT

Headnotes/Things to Look For

Jonathan Swift (1667–1745) was born in Ireland. After graduating from Trinity College, he spent time in England before returning to Ireland to make his name as a writer of satire, notably Gulliver's Travels. *"A Modest Proposal," written in 1729, is perhaps his best-known piece.*

Note the rational tone of the gentleman who calmly delivers this proposal. While he emphasizes the practicality of the plan, he is also careful to point out that he has everyone's best interests at heart.

✦

It is a melancholy object to those, who walk through this great town, or travel in the country, when they see the streets, the roads and cabbin-doors crowded with beggars of the female sex, followed by three, four, or six children, all in rags, and importuning every passenger for an alms. These mothers instead of being able to work for their honest livelihood, are forced to employ all their time in stroling to beg sustenance for their helpless infants who, as they grow up, either turn thieves for want of work, or leave their dear native country, to fight for the Pretender in Spain, or sell themselves to the Barbadoes.

I think it is agreed by all parties, that this prodigious number of children in the arms, or on the backs, or at the heels of their mothers, and frequently of their fathers, is in the present deplorable state of the kingdom, a very great additional grievance; and therefore whoever could find out a fair, cheap and easy method of making these children sound and useful members of the common-wealth, would deserve so well of the publick, as to have his statue set up for a preserver of the nation.

But my intention is very far from being confined to provide only for the children of professed beggars: it is of a much greater extent, and shall take in the whole number of infants at a certain age, who are born of parents in effect as little able to support them, as those who demand our charity in the streets.

As to my own part, having turned my thoughts for many years, upon this important subject, and maturely weighed the several schemes of our projectors, I have always found them grossly mistaken in their computation. It is true, a child just dropt from its dam, may be supported by her milk, for a solar year, with little other nourishment: at most not above the value of two shillings, which the mother may certainly get, or the value in scraps, by her lawful occupation of begging; and it is exactly at one year old that I propose to provide for them in such a manner, as, instead of being a charge upon their parents, or the parish, or wanting food and raiment for the rest of their lives, they shall, on the contrary, contribute to the feeding, and partly to the cloathing of many thousands.

There is likewise another great advantage in my scheme, that it will prevent those voluntary abortions, and that horrid practice of women murdering their bastard children, alas! too frequent among us, sacrificing the poor innocent babes, I doubt, more to avoid the expence than the shame, which would move tears and pity in the most savage and inhuman breast.

The number of souls in this kingdom being usually reckoned one million and a half, of these I calculate there may be about two hundred thousand couple whose wives are breeders; from which number I subtract thirty thousand couple, who are able to maintain their own children, (although I apprehend there cannot be so many, under the present distresses of the kingdom) but this being granted, there will remain an hundred and seventy thousand breeders. I again subtract fifty thousand, for those women who miscarry, or whose children die by accident or disease within the year. There only remain an hundred and twenty thousand children of poor parents annually born. The question therefore is, How this number shall be reared, and provided for? which, as I have already said, under the present situation of affairs, is utterly impossible by all the methods hitherto proposed. For we can neither employ them in handicraft or agriculture; we neither build houses, (I mean in the country) nor cultivate land: they can very seldom pick up a livelihood by stealing till they arrive at six years old; except where they are of towardly parts, although I confess they learn the rudiments much earlier; during which time they can however be properly looked upon only as probationers: As I have been informed by a principal gentleman in the county of Cavan, who protested to me, that he never knew above one or two instances under the age of six, even in a part of the kingdom so renowned for the quickest proficiency in that art.

I am assured by our merchants, that a boy or a girl before twelve years old, is no saleable commodity, and even when they come to this age, they will not yield above three pounds, or three pounds and half a crown at most, on the exchange; which cannot turn to account either to the parents or kingdom, the charge of nutriments and rags having been at least four times that value.

I shall now therefore humbly propose my own thoughts, which I hope will not be liable to the least objection.

I have been assured by a very knowing American of my acquaintance in London, that a young healthy child well nursed, is, at a year old, a most delicious nourishing and wholesome food, whether stewed, roasted, baked, or boiled; and I make no doubt that it will equally serve in a fricasie, or a ragoust.

I do therefore humbly offer it to publick consideration, that of the hundred and twenty thousand children, already computed, twenty thousand may be reserved for breed, whereof only one fourth part to be males; which is more than we allow to sheep, black cattle, or swine, and my reason is, that these children are seldom the fruits of marriage, a circumstance not much regarded by our savages, therefore, one male will be sufficient to serve four females. That the remaining hundred thousand may, at a year old, be offered in sale to the persons of quality and fortune, through the kingdom, always advising the mother to let them suck plentifully in the last month, so as to render them plump, and fat for a good table. A child will make two dishes at an entertainment for friends, and when the family dines alone, the fore or hind quarter will make a reasonable dish, and seasoned with a little pepper or salt, will be very good boiled on the fourth day, especially in winter.

I have reckoned upon a medium, that a child just born will weigh 12 pounds, and in a solar year, if tolerably nursed, encreaseth to 28 pounds.

I grant this food will be somewhat dear, and therefore very proper for landlords, who, as they have already devoured most of the parents, seem to have the best title to the children.

Infant's flesh will be in season throughout the year, but more plentiful in March, and a little before and after; for we are told by a grave author, an eminent French physician, that fish being a prolifick dyet, there are more children born in Roman Catholick countries about nine months after Lent, the markets will be more glutted than usual, because the number of Popish infants, is at least three to one in this kingdom, and therefore it will have one other collateral advantage, by lessening the number of Papists among us.

I have already computed the charge of nursing a beggar's child (in which list I reckon all cottagers, labourers, and four-fifths of the farmers) to be about two shillings per annum, rags included; and I believe no gentleman would repine to give ten shillings for the carcass of a good fat child, which, as I have said, will make four dishes of excellent nutritive meat, when he hath only some particular friend, or his own family to dine with him. Thus the squire will learn to be a good landlord, and grow popular among his tenants, the mother will have eight shillings neat profit, and be fit for work till she produces another child.

Those who are more thrifty (as I must confess the times require) may flea the carcass; the skin of which, artificially dressed, will make admirable gloves for ladies, and summer boots for fine gentlemen.

As to our City of Dublin, shambles may be appointed for this purpose, in the most convenient parts of it, and butchers we may be assured will not be wanting; although I rather recommend buying the children alive, and dressing them hot from the knife, as we do roasting pigs.

A very worthy person, a true lover of his country, and whose virtues I highly esteem, was lately pleased, in discoursing on this matter, to offer a refinement upon my scheme. He said, that many gentlemen of this kingdom, having of late destroyed their deer, he conceived that the want of venison might be well supply'd by the bodies of young lads and maidens, not exceeding fourteen years of age, nor under twelve; so great a number of both sexes in every country being now ready to starve for want of work and service: And these to be disposed of by their parents if alive, or otherwise by their nearest relations. But with due deference to so excellent a friend, and so deserving a patriot, I cannot be altogether in his sentiments; for as to the males, my American acquaintance assured me from frequent experience, that their flesh was generally tough and lean, like that of our school-boys, by continual exercise, and their taste disagreeable, and to fatten them would not answer the charge. Then as to the females, it would, I think, with humble submission, be a loss to the publick, because they soon would become breeders themselves: And besides, it is not improbable that some scrupulous people might be apt to censure such a practice, (although indeed very unjustly) as a little bordering upon cruelty, which, I confess, hath always been with me the strongest objection against any project, how well soever intended.

But in order to justify my friend, he confessed, that this expedient was put into his head by the famous Salmanaazor, a native of the island Formosa, who came from thence to London, above twenty years ago, and in conversation told my friend, that in his country, when any young person happened to be put to death, the executioner sold the carcass to persons of quality, as a prime dainty; and that, in his time, the body of a plump girl of fifteen, who was crucified for an attempt to poison the Emperor, was sold to his imperial majesty's prime minister of state, and other great mandarins of the court in joints from the gibbet, at four hundred crowns. Neither indeed can I deny, that if the same use were made of several plump young girls in this town, who without one single groat to their fortunes, cannot stir abroad without a chair, and appear at a play-house and assemblies in foreign fineries which they never will pay for; the kingdom would not be the worse.

Some persons of a desponding spirit are in great concern about that vast number of poor people, who are aged, diseased, or maimed; and I have been desired to employ my thoughts what course may be taken, to ease the nation of so grievous an incumbrance. But I am not in the least pain upon that matter, because it is very well known, that they are every day dying, and rotting, by cold and famine, and filth, and vermin, as fast as can be reasonably expected. And as to the young labourers, they are now in almost as hopeful a condition. They cannot get work, and consequently pine away from want of nourishment, to a degree, that if at any time they are accidentally hired to common labour, they have not strength to perform it, and thus the country and themselves are happily delivered from the evils to come.

I have too long digressed, and therefore shall return to my subject. I think the advantages by the proposal which I have made are obvious and many, as well as of the highest importance. For first, as I have already observed, it would greatly lessen the number of Papists, with whom we are yearly over-run, being the principal breeders of the nation, as well as our most dangerous enemies, and who stay at home on purpose with a design to deliver the kingdom to the Pretender, hoping to take their advantage by the absence of so many good Protestants, who have chosen rather to leave their country, than stay at home and pay tithes against their conscience to an episcopal curate.

Secondly, The poorer tenants will have something valuable of their own, which by law may be made liable to a distress, and help to pay their landlord's rent, their corn and cattle being already seized, and money a thing unknown.

Thirdly, Whereas the maintainance of an hundred thousand children, from two years old, and upwards, cannot be computed at less than ten shillings a piece per annum, the nation's stock will be thereby encreased fifty thousand pounds per annum, besides the profit of a new dish, introduced to the tables of all gentlemen of fortune in the kingdom, who have any refinement in taste. And the money will circulate among our selves, the goods being entirely of our own growth and manufacture.

Fourthly, The constant breeders, besides the gain of eight shillings sterling per annum by the sale of their children, will be rid of the charge of maintaining them after the first year.

Fifthly, This food would likewise bring great custom to taverns, where the vintners will certainly be so prudent as to procure the best receipts for dressing it to perfection; and consequently have their houses frequented by all the fine gentlemen, who justly value themselves upon their knowledge in good eating; and a skilful cook, who understands how to oblige his guests, will contrive to make it as expensive as they please.

Sixthly, This would be a great inducement to marriage, which all wise nations have either encouraged by rewards, or enforced by laws and penalties. It would encrease the care and tenderness of mothers towards their children, when they were sure of a settlement for life to the poor babes, provided in some sort by the publick, to their annual profit instead of expence. We should soon see an honest emulation among the married women, which of them could bring the fattest child to the market. Men would become as fond of their wives, during the time of their pregnancy, as they are now of their mares in foal, their cows in calf, or sow when they are ready to farrow; nor offer to beat or kick them (as is too frequent a practice) for fear of a miscarriage. Many other advantages might be enumerated. For instance, the addition of some thousand carcasses in our exportation of barrel'd beef: the propagation of swine's flesh, and improvement in the art of making good bacon, so much wanted among us by the great destruction of pigs, too frequent at our tables; which are no way comparable in taste or magnificence to a well grown, fat yearly child, which roasted whole will make a considerable figure at a Lord Mayor's feast, or any other publick entertainment. But this, and many others, I omit, being studious of brevity.

Supposing that one thousand families in this city, would be constant customers for infants flesh, besides others who might have it at merry meetings, particularly at weddings and christenings, I compute that Dublin would take off annually about twenty thousand carcasses; and the rest of the kingdom (where probably they will be sold somewhat cheaper) the remaining eighty thousand.

I can think of no one objection, that will possibly be raised against this proposal, unless it should be urged, that the number of people will be thereby much lessened in the kingdom. This I freely own, and 'twas indeed one principal design in offering it to the world. I desire the reader will observe, that I calculate my remedy for this one individual Kingdom of Ireland, and for no other that ever was, is, or, I think, ever can be upon Earth. Therefore let no man talk to me of other expedients: Of taxing our absentees at five shillings a pound: Of using neither cloaths, nor houshold furniture, except what is of our own growth and manufacture: Of utterly rejecting the materials and instruments that promote foreign luxury: Of curing the expensiveness of pride, vanity, idleness, and gaming in our women: Of introducing a vein of parsimony, prudence and temperance: Of learning to love our country, wherein we differ even from Laplanders, and the inhabitants of Topinamboo: Of quitting our animosities and factions, nor acting any longer like the Jews, who were murdering one another at the very moment their city was taken: Of being a little cautious not to sell our country and consciences for nothing: Of teaching landlords to have at least one degree of mercy towards their tenants. Lastly, of putting a spirit of honesty, industry, and skill into our shop-keepers, who, if a resolution could now be taken to buy only our native goods, would immediately unite to cheat and exact upon us in the price, the measure, and the goodness, nor could ever yet be brought to make one fair proposal of just dealing, though often and earnestly invited to it.

Therefore I repeat, let no man talk to me of these and the like expedients, 'till he hath at least some glympse of hope, that there will ever be some hearty and sincere attempt to put them into practice.

But, as to my self, having been wearied out for many years with offering vain, idle, visionary thoughts, and at length utterly despairing of success, I fortunately fell upon this proposal, which, as it is wholly new, so it hath something solid and real, of no expence and little trouble, full in our own power, and whereby we can incur no danger in disobliging England. For this kind of commodity will not bear exportation, and flesh being of too tender a consistence, to admit a long continuance in salt, although perhaps I could name a country, which would be glad to eat up our whole nation without it.

After all, I am not so violently bent upon my own opinion, as to reject any offer, proposed by wise men, which shall be found equally innocent, cheap, easy, and effectual. But before something of that kind shall be advanced in contradiction to my scheme, and offering a better, I desire the author or authors will be pleased maturely to consider two points. First, As things now stand, how they will be able to find food and raiment for a hundred thousand useless mouths and backs. And secondly, There being a round million of creatures in humane figure throughout this kingdom, whose whole subsistence put into a common stock, would leave them in debt two million of pounds sterling, adding those who are beggars by profession, to the bulk of farmers, cottagers and labourers, with their wives and children, who are beggars in effect; I desire those politicians who dislike my overture, and may perhaps be so bold to attempt an answer, that they will first ask the parents of these mortals, whether they would not at this day think it a great happiness to have been sold for food at a year old, in the manner I prescribe, and thereby have avoided such a perpetual scene of misfortunes, as they have since gone through, by the oppression of landlords, the impossibility of paying rent without money or trade, the want of common sustenance, with neither house nor cloaths to cover them from the inclemencies of the weather, and the most inevitable prospect of intailing the like, or greater miseries, upon their breed for ever.

I profess, in the sincerity of my heart, that I have not the least personal interest in endeavouring to promote this necessary work, having no other motive than the publick good of my country, by advancing our trade, providing for infants, relieving the poor, and giving some pleasure to the rich. I have no children, by which

I can propose to get a single penny; the youngest being nine years old, and my wife past child-bearing.

Discussion Questions

1. What clues does Swift give about the character, or ethos, of the speaker before the proposal is made explicit?
2. How do the expedient and the moral relate to each other in the proposal? How does the proposer aim to satisfy the demands of both kinds of appeals in this kind of argument?
3. How does Swift weave in his actual proposal to address poverty in Ireland toward the end of the piece without abandoning the persona he has so carefully built from the start? Where else do you think the counterproposal could be placed?

Writing Activity

1. Write a proposal in which a reasonable-sounding proposer suggests an outrageous or morally reprehensible solution to a problem, striving to maintain a calm and rational tone.

Mr. Collins' Proposal from *Pride and Prejudice*

JANE AUSTEN

Headnotes/Things to Look For

Jane Austen (1775–1817) spent her whole life with her family in Hampshire, England, closely observing the society around her and ultimately putting her clear-eyed view into a series of novels, including Sense and Sensibility, Pride and Prejudice, Mansfield Park, Emma, Northanger Abbey, *and* Persuasion. *The durability of her gentle but telling critique of social and romantic customs can be seen in the regular release of film versions of her books.*

Note the interplay and opposition of logical and emotional appeals in the debate engaged in by Mr. Collins and Elizabeth Bennet, and how their arguments illustrate their dramatically different views of what marriage should be.

--- ✦ ---

The next day opened a new scene at Longbourn. Mr. Collins made his declaration in form. Having resolved to do it without loss of time, as his leave of absence extended only to the following Saturday, and having no feelings of diffidence to make it distressing to himself even at the moment, he set about it in a very orderly manner, with all the observances which he supposed a regular part of the business. On finding Mrs. Bennet, Elizabeth, and one of the younger girls together, soon after breakfast, he addressed the mother in these words: "May I hope, madam, for your interest with your fair daughter Elizabeth, when I solicit for the honour of a private audience with her in the course of this morning?"

Before Elizabeth had time for anything but a blush of surprise, Mrs. Bennet answered instantly, "Oh dear!—yes—certainly. I am sure Lizzy will be very happy—I am sure she can have no objection. Come, Kitty, I want you upstairs." And, gathering her work together, she was hastening away, when Elizabeth called out:

"Dear madam, do not go. I beg you will not go. Mr. Collins must excuse me. He can have nothing to say to me that anybody need not hear. I am going away myself."

"No, no, nonsense, Lizzy. I desire you to stay where you are." And upon Elizabeth's seeming really, with vexed and embarrassed looks, about to escape, she added: "Lizzy, I INSIST upon your staying and hearing Mr. Collins."

Elizabeth would not oppose such an injunction—and a moment's consideration making her also sensible that it would be wisest to get it over as soon and as quietly as possible, she sat down again and tried to conceal, by incessant employment, the feelings which were divided between distress and diversion. Mrs. Bennet and Kitty walked off, and as soon as they were gone, Mr. Collins began.

"Believe me, my dear Miss Elizabeth, that your modesty, so far from doing you any disservice, rather adds to your other perfections. You would have been less amiable in my eyes had there NOT been this little unwillingness; but allow me to assure you, that I have your respected mother's permission for this address. You can hardly doubt the purport of my discourse, however your natural delicacy may lead you to dissemble; my attentions have been too marked to be mistaken. Almost as soon as I entered the house, I singled you out as the companion of my future life. But before I am run away with by my feelings on this subject, perhaps it would be advisable for me to state my reasons for marrying—and, moreover, for coming into Hertfordshire with the design of selecting a wife, as I certainly did."

The idea of Mr. Collins, with all his solemn composure, being run away with by his feelings, made Elizabeth so near laughing, that she could not use the short pause he allowed in any attempt to stop him further, and he continued:

"My reasons for marrying are, first, that I think it a right thing for every clergyman in easy circumstances (like myself) to set the example of matrimony in his parish; secondly, that I am convinced that it will add very greatly to my happiness; and thirdly—which perhaps I ought to have mentioned earlier, that it is the particular advice and recommendation of the very noble lady whom I have the honour of calling patroness. Twice has she condescended to give me her opinion (unasked too!) on this subject; and it was but the very Saturday night before I left Hunsford—between our pools at quadrille, while Mrs. Jenkins was arranging Miss de Bourgh's footstool, that she said, 'Mr. Collins, you must marry. A clergyman like you must marry. Choose properly, choose a gentlewoman for MY sake; and for your OWN, let her be an active, useful sort of person, not brought up high, but able to make a small income go a good way. This is my advice. Find such a woman as soon as you can, bring her to Hunsford, and I will visit her.' Allow me, by the way, to observe, my fair cousin, that I do not reckon the notice and kindness of Lady Catherine de Bourgh as among the least of the advantages in my power to offer. You will find her manners beyond anything I can describe; and your wit and vivacity, I think, must be acceptable to her, especially when tempered with the silence and respect which her rank will inevitably excite. Thus much for my general intention in favour of matrimony; it remains to be told why my views were directed towards Longbourn instead of my own neighbourhood, where I can assure you there are many amiable young women. But the fact is, that being, as I am, to inherit this estate after the death of your honoured father (who, however, may live many years longer), I could not satisfy myself without resolving to choose a wife from among his daughters, that the loss to them might be as little as possible, when the melancholy event takes place—which, however, as I have already said, may not be for several years. This has been my motive, my fair cousin, and I flatter myself it will not sink me in your esteem. And now nothing remains but for me but to assure you in the most animated language of the violence of my affection. To fortune I am perfectly indifferent, and shall make no demand of that nature on your father, since I am well aware that it could not be complied with; and that one thousand pounds in the four per cents, which will not be yours till after your mother's decease, is all that you may ever be entitled to. On that head, therefore, I shall be uniformly silent; and you may assure yourself that no ungenerous reproach shall ever pass my lips when we are married."

It was absolutely necessary to interrupt him now.

"You are too hasty, sir," she cried. "You forget that I have made no answer. Let me do it without further loss of time. Accept my thanks for the compliment you are paying me. I am very sensible of the honour of your proposals, but it is impossible for me to do otherwise than to decline them."

"I am not now to learn," replied Mr. Collins, with a formal wave of the hand, "that it is usual with young ladies to reject the addresses of the man whom they secretly mean to accept, when he first applies for their favour; and that sometimes the refusal is repeated a second, or even a third time. I am therefore by no means discouraged by what you have just said, and shall hope to lead you to the altar ere long."

"Upon my word, sir," cried Elizabeth, "your hope is a rather extraordinary one after my declaration. I do assure you that I am not one of those young ladies (if such young ladies there are) who are so daring as to risk their happiness on the chance of being asked a second time. I am perfectly serious in my refusal. You could not make ME happy, and I am convinced that I am the last woman in the world who could make you so. Nay, were your friend Lady Catherine to know me, I am persuaded she would find me in every respect ill qualified for the situation."

"Were it certain that Lady Catherine would think so," said Mr. Collins very gravely—"but I cannot imagine that her ladyship would at all disapprove of you. And you may be certain when I have the honour of seeing her again, I shall speak in the very highest terms of your modesty, economy, and other amiable qualification."

"Indeed, Mr. Collins, all praise of me will be unnecessary. You must give me leave to judge for myself, and pay me the compliment of believing what I say. I wish you very happy and very rich, and by refusing your hand, do all in my power to prevent your being otherwise. In making me the offer, you must have satisfied the delicacy of your feelings with regard to my family, and may take possession of Longbourn estate whenever it falls, without any self-reproach. This matter may be considered, therefore, as finally settled." And rising as she thus spoke, she would have quitted the room, had Mr. Collins not thus addressed her:

"When I do myself the honour of speaking to you next on the subject, I shall hope to receive a more favourable answer than you have now given me; though I am far from accusing you of cruelty at present, because I know it to be the established custom of your sex to reject a man on the first application, and perhaps you have even now said as much to encourage my suit as would be consistent with the true delicacy of the female character."

"Really, Mr. Collins," cried Elizabeth with some warmth, "you puzzle me exceedingly. If what I have hitherto said can appear to you in the form of encouragement, I know not how to express my refusal in such a way as to convince you of its being one."

"You must give me leave to flatter myself, my dear cousin, that your refusal of my addresses is merely words of course. My reasons for believing it are briefly these: It does not appear to me that my hand is unworthy of your acceptance, or that the establishment I can offer would be any other than highly desirable. My situation in life, my connections with the family of de Bourgh, and my relationship to your own, are circumstances highly in my favour; and you should take it into further consideration, that in spite of your manifold attractions, it is by no means certain that another offer of marriage may ever be made you. Your portion is unhappily so small that it will in all likelihood undo the effects of your loveliness and amiable qualifications. As I must therefore conclude that you are not serious in your rejection of me, I shall choose to attribute it to your wish of increasing my love by suspense, according to the usual practice of elegant females."

"I do assure you, sir, that I have no pretensions whatever to that kind of elegance which consists in tormenting a respectable man. I would rather be paid the compliment of being believed sincere. I thank you again and again for the honour you have done me in your proposals, but to accept them is absolutely impossible. My feelings in every respect forbid it. Can I speak plainer? Do not consider me now as an elegant female, intending to plague you, but as a rational creature, speaking the truth from her heart."

"You are uniformly charming!" cried he, with an air of awkward gallantry; "and I am persuaded that when sanctioned by the express authority of both your excellent parents, my proposals will not fail of being acceptable."

To such perseverance in wilful self-deception Elizabeth would make no reply, and immediately and in silence withdrew, determined, that if he persisted in considering her repeated refusals as flattering encouragement, to apply to her father, whose negative might be uttered in such a manner as to be decisive, and whose behavior at least could not be mistaken for the affectation and coquetry of an elegant female.

Discussion Questions

1. Mr. Collins relies heavily on the social forms he believes should guide his actions. How do these conventions of behavior and speech shape his view of the world and his place in it?
2. What reasons does Mr. Collins offer for his proposal to Elizabeth? How do these reasons help Elizabeth (and us) form our sense of his ethos, or character?
3. How does Elizabeth's reply differ in emphasis from Mr. Collins' proposal? What concerns does she place first in contrast to him?
4. Both Mr. Collins and Elizabeth make claims to being rational people. Ultimately, which character seems more "rational" to you? Why?

Writing Activity

1. Write a contemporary proposal scene in which the characters have radically different views of the world, appropriate behavior, and each other. Through their words and actions, illuminate their understanding of social conventions and relationships.

On Giving Advice
The Spectator, No. 512

JOSEPH ADDISON

Headnotes/Things to Look For

Joseph Addison (1672–1719) was a poet and essayist, perhaps best known for his contributions to the Tatler *and his role in developing* The Spectator *magazine, in partnership with his friend Richard Steele. Addison stands as an important figure in the development of the essay, cultivating a clear, direct style which provides a window on the workings of a lively mind.*

Note how quickly Addison moves into his topic, leading with the blunt assertion that people don't like to receive advice. The form he's working in, that of the occasional essay, doesn't allow for leisurely introductions. You can see this same strategy in much of the writing that appears on op-ed pages and in weekly magazines to this day.

———————— ✦ ————————

Friday, October 17, 1712

Lectorem delectando pariterque monendo. *

HORACE

There is nothing which we receive with so much Reluctance as Advice. We look upon the Man who gives it us as offering an Affront to our Understanding, and treating us like Children or Idiots. We consider the Instruction as an implicit Censure, and the Zeal which any one shews for our Good on such an Occasion as a Piece of Presumption or Impertinence. The Truth of it is, the Person who pretends to advise, does, in that Particular, exercise a Superiority over us, and can have no other Reason for it, but that, in comparing us with himself, he thinks us defective either in our Conduct or our Understanding. For these Reasons, there is nothing so difficult as the Art of making Advice agreeable; and indeed all the Writers, both Ancient and Modern, have distinguished themselves among one another, according to the Perfection at which they have arrived in this Art. How many Devices have been made use of, to render this bitter Potion palatable? Some convey their Instructions to us in the best chosen Words, others in the most harmonious Numbers, some in Points of Wit, and others in short Proverbs.

But among all the different Ways of giving Counsel, I think the finest, and that which pleases the most universally, is Fable, in whatsoever Shape it appears. If we consider this way of instructing or giving Advice, it excells all others, because it is the least shocking, and the least subject to those Exceptions which I have before mentioned.

This will appear to us, if we reflect, in the first place, that upon the reading of a Fable we are made to believe we advise our selves. We peruse the Author for the sake of the Story, and consider the Precepts rather as our own Conclusions, than his Instructions. The Moral insinuates it self imperceptibly, we are taught by Surprise, and become wiser and better unawares. In

———————

*To equally entertain and instruct the reader.

short, by this Method a Man is so far over-reached as to think he is directing himself, whilst he is following the Dictates of another, and consequently is not sensible of that which is the most unpleasing Circumstance in Advice. In the next Place, if we look into Human Nature, we shall find that the Mind is never so much pleased, as when she exerts her self in any Action that gives her an Idea of her own Perfections and Abilities. This natural Pride and Ambition of the Soul is very much gratified in the reading of a Fable; for in Writings of this Kind, the Reader comes in for half of the Performance; Every thing appears to him like a Discovery of his own; he is busied all the while in applying Characters and Circumstances, and is in this respect both a Reader and a Composer. It is no wonder therefore that on such Occasions, when the Mind is thus pleased with it self, and amused with its own Discoveries, that it is highly delighted with the Writing which is the Occasion of it. For this Reason the Absalon and Achitophel was one of the most popular Poems that ever appeared in English. The Poetry is indeed very fine, but had it been much finer it would not have so much pleased, without a Plan which gave the Reader an Opportunity of exerting his own Talents.

This oblique manner of giving Advice is so inoffensive, that if we look into ancient Histories, we find the Wise Men of old very often chose to give Counsel to their Kings in Fables. To omit many which will occur to every ones Memory, there is a pretty Instance of this Nature in a Turkish Tale, which I do not like the worse for that little Oriental Extravagance which is mixed with it.

We are told that the Sultan Mahmoud, by his perpetual Wars abroad, and his Tyranny at home had filled his Dominions with Ruin and Desolation and half-unpeopled the Persian Empire. The Visier to this great Sultan, (whether an Humourist or an Enthusiast we are not informed) pretended to have learned of a certain Dervise to understand the Language of Birds, so that there was not a Bird that could open his Mouth but the Visier knew what it was he said. As he was one Evening with the Emperor, in their Return from hunting, they saw a couple of Owls upon a Tree that grew near an old Wall out of an heap of Rubbish. I would fain know, says the Sultan, what those two Owls are saying to one another; listen to their Discourse, and give me an account of it. The Visier approached the Tree, pretending to be very attentive to the two Owls. Upon his Return to the Sultan, Sir, says he, I have heard part of their Conversation, but dare not tell you what it is. The Sultan would not be satisfied with such an Answer, but forced him to repeat Word for Word every thing the Owls had said. You must know then, said the Visier, that one of these Owls has a Son, and the other a Daughter, between whom they are now upon a Treaty of Marriage. The Father of the Son said to the Father of the Daughter, in my hearing, "Brother, I consent to this Marriage, provided you will settle upon your Daughter fifty ruined Villages for her Portion." To which the Father of the Daughter replied, "Instead of fifty I will give her five hundred, if you please. God grant a long life to Sultan Mahmoud! whilst he reigns over us we shall never want ruined Villages."

The Story says, the Sultan was so touched with the Fable, that he rebuilt the Towns and Villages which had been destroyed, and from that time forward consulted the Good of his People.

To fill up my Paper, I shall add a most ridiculous Piece of natural Magick, which was taught by no less a Philosopher than Democritus, namely, that if the Blood of certain Birds, which he mentioned, were mixed together, it would produce a Serpent of such a wonderful Virtue that whoever did eat it should be skill'd in the Language of Birds, and understand every thing they said to one another. Whether the Dervise above-mentioned might not have eaten such a Serpent, I shall leave to the Determinations of the Learned.

Discussion Questions

1. Do you agree with Addison's core premise regarding people's attitudes towards advice? Does the person giving advice automatically assume a position of superiority, or do certain situations change this dynamic?

2. Consider the several ways to give advice that Addison lists at the end of the first paragraph. What examples can you give from contemporary culture that connect to or build on the forms Addison offers? Have the forms of advice changed substantially since Addison's time?

3. Addison puts forward the fable as the best method of giving advice because it allows the audience to maintain self-esteem. Why is this so? What beliefs about one's self does the figuring out of a fable's meaning reinforce?

4. Addison includes an epigraph from the Roman writer Horace exhorting writers to entertain and instruct readers. To what degree does Addison succeed in doing this?

Writing Activity

1. Write a fable advising a political leader to change a policy.

Phrases and Philosophies for the Use of the Young

OSCAR WILDE

Headnotes/Things to Look For

Oscar Wilde (1854–1900), of Irish birth like Swift, was a star student at both Trinity College in Dublin and Magdalen College at Oxford. He later wrote poems, plays, novels, and stories, achieving great success as a playwright while cultivating his own celebrity. He was affiliated with both the aesthetic and decadent movements, and was convicted of "gross indecency" in connection with his homosexuality, spending time in jail.

Note how Wilde contradicts or stands on its head much of the standard advice the young are used to hearing from their elders. Consider whether this reversing of conventional wisdom leads to greater understanding of how to act (beyond the pleasure of thumbing one's nose at authority figures).

✦

The first duty in life is to be as artificial as possible. What the second duty is no one has as yet discovered.

Wickedness is a myth invented by good people to account for the curious attractiveness of others.

If the poor only had profiles there would be no difficulty in solving the problem of poverty.

Those who see any difference between soul and body have neither.

A really well-made buttonhole is the only link between Art and Nature.

Religions die when they are proved to be true. Science is the record of dead religions.

The well-bred contradict other people. The wise contradict themselves.

Nothing that actually occurs is of the smallest importance.

Dullness is the coming of age of seriousness.

In all unimportant matters, style, not sincerity, is the essential. In all important matters, style, not sincerity, is the essential.

If one tells the truth one is sure, sooner or later, to be found out.

Pleasure is the only thing one should live for. Nothing ages like happiness.

It is only by not paying one's bills that one can hope to live in the memory of the commercial classes.

No crime is vulgar, but all vulgarity is crime. Vulgarity is the conduct of others.

Only the shallow know themselves.

Time is waste of money.

One should always be a little improbable.

There is a fatality about all good resolutions. They are invariably made too soon.

The only way to atone for being occasionally a little overdressed is by being always absolutely overeducated.

To be premature is to be perfect.

Any preoccupation with ideas of what is right or wrong in conduct shows an arrested intellectual development.

Ambition is the last refuge of the failure.

A truth ceases to be true when more than one person believes in it.

In examinations the foolish ask questions that the wise cannot answer.

Greek dress was in its essence inartistic. Nothing should reveal the body but the body.

One should either be a work of art, or wear a work of art.

It is only the superficial qualities that last. Man's deeper nature is soon found out.

Industry is the root of all ugliness.

The ages live in history through their anachronisms.

It is only the gods who taste of death. Apollo has passed away, but Hyacinth, whom men say he slew, lives on. Nero and Narcissus are always with us.

The old believe everything: the middle-aged suspect everything; the young know everything.

The condition of perfection is idleness: the aim of perfection is youth.

Only the great masters of style ever succeeded in being obscure.

There is something tragic about the enormous number of young men there are in England at the present moment who start life with perfect profiles, and end by adopting some useful profession.

To love oneself is the beginning of a life-long romance.

Discussion Questions

1. Wilde praises the artificial and the superficial over what we're used to considering as more important and valuable aspects of life. Why does he value these things? Why does he put forward style as more important than sincerity?

2. Wilde insists on the value of the individual over the mass, connecting group behavior to vulgarity and asserting that truth disappears when believed by more than one person. Why does Wilde distrust beliefs held in common by society?

3. Wilde associates industry or purposeful action with ugliness and idleness with perfection. What are the dangers of working hard to achieve something, in Wilde's view? What kind of life is Wilde recommending for the young?

Writing Activity

1. Write some phrases or proverbs of your own, refuting the advice you've been given that you find less than helpful.

Surviving Meetings
Scott Adams

Headnotes/Things to Look For

Scott Adams is perhaps best-known as the creator of the Dilbert *comic strip. Before embarking on his career as a satirist skewering the ways of business, Adams earned his MBA from the Haas School of Business at UC-Berkeley. He is the author of* The Dilbert Principle, Dogbert's Top Secret Management Handbook, *and* The Dilbert Future, *among other books. The selection below is taken from* The Joy of Work.

Note how Adams's criticism seems to be aimed at the corporate culture that makes meetings mandatory rather than at any particular villain. In cases like these, who is responsible for the suffering, and who must change?

━━━━━━━━━━ ✦ ━━━━━━━━━━

Unless you work alone, one of the biggest assaults on your happiness is something called a meeting. A meeting is essentially a group of people staring at visual aids until the electrochemical activity in their brains ceases, at which point decisions are made. It's like being in suspended animation, except that people in suspended animation aren't in severe physical discomfort and praying for death.

If you attend many meetings, your life will disappear faster than a bag of cash falling off the back of an armored car in front of a homeless shelter for Olympic sprinters. But not everyone feels bored at meetings. The exception to this rule is the people who have such bad personal lives that they use meetings as a substitute for actual social interactions. Avoid these people if you can:

If you absolutely can't avoid meetings, learn how to enjoy them. Your body might have to sit motionless for hours, but you can train your brain to disengage and enjoy itself.

PERSONAL DIGITAL ASSISTANTS

If your co-workers are bringing PalmPilots and other personal digital assistants (PDAs) to meetings, get a Nintendo Gameboy and try to blend in with the crowd. You might want to paint your Gameboy dark gray and file off the logo. Interrupt the meeting to ask people their phone numbers and addresses. Press buttons randomly on your Gameboy to simulate data entry. If someone offers to transfer his business-card information via infrared signal to your PDA, play along. Point your Gameboy in the appropriate direction, then say, "Got it." When the other person complains that he did not receive your information, recommend that he get his PDA repaired. Once your credibility has been established, through the process of being an unscrupulous weasel, you can merrily play with your Gameboy throughout the meeting.

ROBOT VISUALIZATION

My favorite technique for keeping my brain from burrowing out of my head during meetings is what I call the robot visualization. The way this works is that you imagine your body is a gigantic robot and you are a tiny captain inside it, in the control room. Imagine the control room being like the bridge of the Starship Enterprise. The forward screens are the view out of your eyes. Every movement of your huge robotic body becomes fun that way. You hear your little captain issue the command, "Turn neck thirty degrees starboard." When your neck actually turns, it's very cool. You're the captain of this excellent robot. It's just you in the control room, alone with the attractive and ambitious Ensign Raquel. (Adjust the gender to suit your preferences.) There's no end to the robotic possibilities once the two of you start getting frisky and end up on the weapons control panel.

EMBARRASSING THE PRESENTER

If one of your co-workers is making a presentation, amuse yourself by asking questions that are impossible to answer. Don't limit yourself to questions that make any sense or have any relevance. The objective of this game is to make your co-worker get that "please shoot me" expression in front of a roomful of people. For example, if he is doing a presentation on the budget, ask this sort of question:

"Correct me if I'm wrong, but isn't the depreciation rate a good indication of the declining EVA projection from the perspective of a long-term strategy, vis-à-vis the budget gap?"

When your co-worker's eyes start to look like two pie plates with an olive in the middle of each one, make a dissatisfied face and say, "That's okay. I'll ask someone knowledgeable."

It's also fun to raise issues that will create extra work for the presenter. Compete with the other people at your table to see who can make the presenter work the hardest after the meeting. The key is to look earnest and concerned, so your issue seems impossible to ignore. Here are some good issues that fit almost any situation. Any one of these would require more work than could ever be justified, yet they sound almost important.

ANNOYING ISSUES

"What's the impact on all the other departments in our company? Have you checked with them?"

"How would the numbers look if you did 5 percent less of whatever it is that you were talking about? Could you run those numbers for next week?"

"Maybe you should produce a skit to describe your plan and distribute the videotape throughout the company."

The following story is allegedly true, but sounds more like an urban legend. Either way, it suggests a fun joke to pull on a vendor if you can get your co-workers to collude.

From: [name withheld]
To: scottadams@aol.com

This happened at the headquarters of a large mid-Atlantic bank. A vendor came in to talk about some new software. He set up an overhead projector to use with his computer and asked someone to shut off the lights in the conference room. Everyone just sat there. So he looked around for the light switch but couldn't find it.

Finally someone explained that the company replaced the
light switches with motion sensors because people were
always leaving the conference-room lights on.

When he asked the employees what they did when they
had presentations, they replied that they just "sat real still"
until the lights went out.

Discussion Questions

1. Definition is a standard rhetorical strategy used to set up the terms of an
   argument. How does Adams use definition to announce both his topic and
   his comic intention early in the essay?
2. How do the various survival strategies Adams offer extend his critique of the
   office culture that dominates many corporate settings?
3. Adams takes a risk in the essay in terms of the persona he projects. How
   would you describe the character of this persona? Why does Adams believe
   that his satirical target warrants this kind of tone and behavior in response?

Writing Activity

1. Choose an activity that many people must participate in regularly (e.g.,
   attending classes, eating meals with family) and write a survival manual.

The Lung-Impaired Liberation Movement
MOLLY IVINS

Headnotes/Things to Look For

*Molly Ivins (1944–2007) was raised in Texas before earning degrees
at Smith College and Columbia. She served as editor and writer for
many newspapers and magazines, notably* The Texas Observer *and
the* New York Times, *and her essays appeared in* Esquire, The
Atlantic, The Nation, *and* Harper's. *Her books of political commentary include* Molly Ivins Can't Say That, Can She?, Nothin' But
Good Times Ahead, You Got to Dance with Them What Brung

You: Politics in the Clinton Years, *and* Shrub: The Short But Happy Political Life of George W. Bush.

Note how Ivins creates a movement for a group that on first glance doesn't quite fit the profile of a persecuted community, immediately adapting the language of political activism to advance her cause.

——————— ✦ ———————

We in the Smoking Community (we prefer to be known as "tobacco co-dependents" or "the lung-impaired" rather than by the tobacconist tag "nicotine addicts") are having terrible self-esteem problems these days. I'm sure all you health fascists are happy to hear this, but I'm warning you right now, our concerns had damn well better be your concerns because we're paying for health-care reform. And don't you forget it. We want respect. We demand gratitude. And we'd also like to have a few planes we could smoke in again.

Our growing list of non-negotiable demands now includes the manufacture and prominent television advertising of a toothpaste that will yellow your teeth. All this white-teeth propaganda you see all over the networks is a threat to our self-esteem. We want affirmative action in the hiring of television characters who will popularize the attractive hacking morning cough.

We want a Smokers' History Week. We demand that school-children be taught the stories of our community's heroes—Bogey and Bette and Duke and FDR. We want schoolchildren (who are currently the victims of so much anti-smoking propaganda that even little ones of 5 or 7 believe they're entitled to tell grown-ups, "Ooo, yuck, that stinks.") taught that politics in this country have gone to hell since the smoke-filled room was declared illegal.

We want it noted that we in the smoking community now spend more time outdoors than the most dedicated environmentalists. We care. We field-strip our butts when in the wilderness and later deposit them in appropriate containers.

The great sociologist of smoking, Susan Sharlot, has long since irrefutably (more or less) proved our positive impact on society. We smokers are an intense breed: We work hard, we pay incredible sums in taxes, and we die young. We are a net savings to society, particularly in Social Security and Medicaid costs. Kiss our butts.

Of course, we have our extremist fringe: I, myself, oppose the public smoking of bad cigars. But a good cigar, ah, a great cigar is one of the things that makes life worth living—even if it does help life end a little early.

The chewing-tobacco aficionados are, I grant you, an unsightly lot. Nevertheless, the National Pastime would be dead without them and the no-caps-on-salaries provision, so the greater good calls for their continued freedom. Besides, the mouth-cancer specialists need patients.

It's my belief that you health fascists are going about this in entirely the wrong way. Of course, there are people with legitimate reasons to object to smoking. But if you add together all the asthmatics and smoke-allergy sufferers and even throw in people whose nearest and dearest have recently died of a horrible, lingering illness caused by smoking, they're still only a tiny fraction of the populace compared to the Smoking Community. Why not segregate them instead of segregating us? Why not have an asthmatics, allergies and small babies' section in the restaurant?

You may not have considered the fact that the national security is at stake here. I point out to you that Aldrich Ames, the CIA guy who sold out to the Soviets, reports that the reason he was able to pass such a variety of information along to the KGB, on topics far afield from the desk to which he was assigned, was because he picked up the info while standing outside CIA headquarters with other smoking CIA agents. Yes!

Consider as well the cordial exchange of opinion and information among smokers witnessed outside the recent Republican and Democratic state conventions. Democrats talking to Republicans! Liberals talking to Conservatives! Fundamentalists talking to Episcopalians! All of us bound together in the bonds of brotherhood and sisterhood by our mutual oppression as smokers. Standing there, puffing in the rain, our fellowship overcoming the boundaries of such ancient and trifling differences as labor and management, Longhorns and Aggies, bikers and Bach-lovers. (Lung cancer does not discriminate on grounds of race, creed, color or sex.)

We in the Smoking Community, bound together by increasingly cruel forms of segregation, discrimination and tobacconism, are subject to undue stress and alarm. No wonder we need to smoke. I, myself, have been driven to seek medical counsel twice in recent years because of Smokers' Fear; in the first instance, it proved to be a case of pimples on my throat and, in the second, calluses on my vocal cords. (Shows you what a hard worker I am—calluses on my vocal cords.)

I write this to warn y'all of the increasing unrest in the Smoking Community. If you're going to saddle us with the cost of national health insurance, we, by God, want respect and gratitude. That, or we form the Smokers' Liberation Movement.

Discussion Questions

1. What specific language from political movements does Ivins appropriate in building her case for smokers' rights?
2. How does Ivins concede in her argument that not all tobacco-related products or users are worth defending? How does this strategy make her seem more reasonable?
3. How do Ivins's repeated mentions of lung cancer and premature death function in her call to action?

Writing Activity

1. Write a manifesto or founding document for a group of defamed citizens, defending their behavior and making a case for how they contribute to society in unappreciated ways.

Making the Case
with Comedy
(forensic rhetoric)

Introduction

Forensic, or judicial, rhetoric, according to Aristotle, determines the facts about what happened in the past along with the rightness or wrongness of past behavior. As countless courtroom dramas attest, this form of rhetoric remains compelling; we seem to crave the revelation not only of who committed the crime but also the pronouncement of judgment that metes out the appropriate punishment. As Bergson points out, however, the ceremonial always carries with it a latent comic element waiting for the comic to expose it. Courtrooms and judicial proceedings in general cast people in set roles (judge, prosecutor, defense attorney, bailiff, witness), giving them rote language to use and established actions to perform ("all rise," for instance, or swearing to tell the truth). We have learned from Bergson that humans acting according to a script, no matter how good their reasons, can become the targets of laughter.

In the classic slapstick comedy *Duck Soup*, the Marx Brothers explode the solemnity of the courtroom (as well as a lot of other things, including several countries in the final scenes). Groucho begins the scene presiding over the court, but soon jumps over the bench to interrogate Chico, on trial for espionage; together they delight in the anarchy they bring to the rule-bound setting. We see similar outbursts in the more recent movies *Liar, Liar,* in which attorney Jim Carrey disrupts the court by having to tell the truth and nothing but the truth, and *My Cousin Vinny,* in which Joe Pesci brings a big-city attitude to a polite southern court to defend his young cousin against false charges. The essays in this chapter have fun not only with the formulas of courtroom proceedings but also other elements of the legal world.

Benjamin Franklin takes on the persona of Polly Baker to teach the court a lesson about the limits of the law. Anton Chekhov shows a less happy outcome for a defendant, showing that the legal system often ignores the compelling motivations of people's actions. Ian Frazier brings together the conventions of legal documents with manic cartoon characters familiar to generations of TV-watching children. Jim Stallard offers us images of Supreme Court justices, among the most rule-bound legal figures in the culture, contending with each other on the basketball court to reach their decisions. Finally, Frazier, Madeleine Begun Kane, and Chris Harris address the legal aspects of relationships between parents and children, proving perhaps that the wheels of justice turn everywhere, even in domestic settings.

'What Are the Poor Young Women to Do?' The Speech of Polly Baker

BENJAMIN FRANKLIN

Headnotes/Things to Look For

Benjamin Franklin (1706–1790), along with being recognized as one of the Founding Fathers of the United States, distinguished himself in many other areas as well; he was a writer and publisher, a practicing politician who theorized about politics, a scientist and inventor who did groundbreaking work with electricity, and a diplomat who helped make the American Revolution possible through his cultivation of French support.

Like Swift in "A Modest Proposal," Franklin takes on a persona, in this case that of a woman brought before the court to answer for her "immoral" behavior after delivering five babies without benefit of marriage. Note how Franklin's strategy relies on a different kind of irony than Swift's, as Polly Baker plainly states the discrepancy between what the law demands of her and of men.

◆

1747

The speech of Miss Polly Baker before a Court of Judicature, at Connecticut near Boston in New England; where she was prosecuted the fifth time for having a bastard child: Which influenced the court to dispense with her punishment, and which induced one of her judges to marry her the next day—by whom she had fifteen children.

"May it please the honorable bench to indulge me in a few words: I am a poor, unhappy woman, who have no money to fee lawyers to plead for me, being hard put to it to get a living. I shall not trouble your honors with long speeches; for I have not the presumption to expect that you may, by any means, be prevailed on to deviate in your sentence from the law, in my favor. All I humbly hope is that your honors would charitably move the governor's goodness on my behalf, that my fine may be remitted. This is the fifth time, gentlemen, that I have been dragged before your court on the same account; twice I have paid heavy fines, and twice have been brought to public punishment, for want of money to pay those fines. This may have been agreeable to the laws, and I don't dispute it; but since laws are sometimes unreasonable in themselves, and therefore repealed; and others bear too hard on the subject in particular circumstances, and therefore there is left a power somewhere to dispense with the execution of them; I take the liberty to say that I think this law, by which I am punished, both unreasonable in itself, and particularly severe with regard to me, who have always lived an inoffensive life in the neighborhood where I was born, and defy my enemies (if I have any) to say I ever wronged any man, woman, or child. Abstracted from the law, I cannot conceive (may it please your honors) what the nature of my offense is. I have brought five fine children into the world, at the risk of my life; I have maintained them well by my own industry, without burdening the township, and would have done it better if it had not been for the heavy charges and fines I have paid. Can it be a crime (in the nature of things, I mean) to add to the king's subjects, in a new country, that really wants people? I own it, I should think it rather a praiseworthy than a punishable action. I have debauched no other woman's husband, nor enticed any other youth; these things I never was charged with; nor has anyone the least cause of complaint against me, unless, perhaps, the ministers of justice, because I have had children without being married, by which they have missed a wedding fee. But can this be a fault of mine? I appeal to your honors. You are pleased to allow I don't want sense; but I must be stupefied to the last degree, not to prefer the honorable state of wedlock to the condition I have lived in. I always was, and still am, willing to enter into it; and doubt not my behaving well in it, having all the industry, frugality, fertility, and skill in economy appertaining to a good wife's character. I defy anyone to say I ever refused an offer of the sort: on the contrary, I readily consented to the only proposal of marriage that ever was made me, which was when I was a virgin, but too easily confiding in the person's sincerity that made it, I unhappily lost my honor by trusting to his; for he got me with child, and then forsook me.

"That very person, you all know, he is now become a magistrate of this country; and I had hopes he would have appeared this day on the bench, and have endeavored to moderate the court in my favor; then I should have scorned to have mentioned it; but I must now complain of it, as unjust and unequal, that my betrayer and undoer, the first cause of all my faults and miscarriages (if they must be deemed such), should be advanced to honor and power in this government that punishes my misfortunes with stripes and infamy. I should be told, 'tis like, that were there no act of assembly in the case, the precepts of religion are violated by my transgressions. If mine is a religious offense, leave it to religious punishments. You have already excluded me from the comforts of your church communion. Is not that sufficient? You believe I have offended heaven, and must suffer eternal fire: Will not that be sufficient? What need is there then of your additional fines and whipping? I own I do not think as you do, for, if I thought what you call a sin was really such, I could not presumptuously commit it. But, how can it be believed that heaven is angry at my having children, when to the little done by me toward it, God has been pleased to add his divine skill and admirable workmanship in the formation of their bodies, and crowned the whole by furnishing them with rational and immortal souls?

"Forgive me, gentlemen, if I talk a little extravagantly on these matters; I am no divine, but if you, gentlemen, must be making laws, do not turn natural and useful actions into crimes by your prohibitions. But take into your wise consideration the great and growing number of bachelors in the country, many of whom, from the mean fear of the expenses of a family, have never sincerely and honorably courted a woman in their lives; and by their manner of living leave unproduced (which is little better than murder) hundreds of their posterity to the thousandth generation. Is not this a greater offense against the public good than mine? Compel them, then, by law, either to marriage, or to pay double the fine of fornication every year. What must poor young women do, whom customs and nature forbid to solicit the men, and who cannot force themselves upon husbands, when the laws take no care to provide them any, and yet severely punish them if they do their duty without them; the duty of the first and great command of nature and nature's God, *increase and multiply*; a duty, from the steady performance of which nothing has been able to deter me, but for its sake I have hazarded the loss of the public esteem, and have frequently endured public disgrace and punishment; and therefore ought, in my humble opinion, instead of a whipping, to have a statue erected to my memory."

Discussion Questions

1. How does Franklin establish the character of Polly Baker in her opening remarks? In other words, how does she create a space in this setting for herself to speak to the presiding judges?
2. While presenting Polly Baker as a poor (and likely uneducated) woman, Franklin has her call the authority and wisdom of the law into question. How do Polly's arguments make a case for the law being unreasonable and unjust?
3. As noted earlier, Franklin employs a kind of irony in how Polly assesses the actions of men in her society (both of the man who betrayed her and of young men in general). What claims does she make regarding how men are allowed to behave and the double standard in play?
4. How does Franklin have Polly address the religious and moral issues, separating them from the legal issues of her case?

Writing Activity

1. Write a speech by the judge who is moved to marry Polly after hearing her address to the court, or, if you prefer, write a speech by a judge who is not persuaded by the speech.

A Malefactor

ANTON CHEKHOV

Headnotes/Things to Look For

Anton Chekhov (1860–1904) originally began writing short humorous stories to support his family. He also trained to be a doctor and practiced medicine throughout his life, though he made his living through his literary work. As he matured as an artist, Chekhov's fiction became more serious and layered in its portrayal of Russian society, and he wrote a series of plays that are performed to this day, including The Seagull, Uncle Vanya, Three Sisters, *and* The Cherry Orchard.

Note Chekhov's focus on two very different worlds coming into contact in this short story. Even at the end of the tale, the peasant Denis Grigoryev doesn't understand the legal imperatives that lead to his imprisonment.

———————— ✦ ————————

An exceedingly lean little peasant, in a striped hempen shirt and patched drawers, stands facing the investigating magistrate. His face overgrown with hair and pitted with smallpox, and his eyes scarcely visible under thick, overhanging eyebrows have an expression of sullen moroseness. On his head there is a perfect mop of tangled, unkempt hair, which gives him an even more spider-like air of moroseness. He is barefooted.

"Denis Grigoryev!" the magistrate begins. "Come nearer, and answer my questions. On the seventh of this July the railway watchman, Ivan Semyonovitch Akinfov, going along the line in the morning, found you at the hundred-and-forty-first mile engaged in unscrewing a nut by which the rails are made fast to the sleepers. Here it is, the nut! . . . With the aforesaid nut he detained you. Was that so?"

"Wha-at?"

"Was this all as Akinfov states?"

"To be sure, it was."

"Very good; well, what were you unscrewing the nut for?"

"Wha-at?"

"Drop that 'wha-at' and answer the question; what were you unscrewing the nut for?"

"If I hadn't wanted it I shouldn't have unscrewed it," croaks Denis, looking at the ceiling.

"What did you want that nut for?"

"The nut? We make weights out of those nuts for our lines."

"Who is 'we'?"

"We, people. . . . The Klimovo peasants, that is."

"Listen, my man; don't play the idiot to me, but speak sensibly. It's no use telling lies here about weights!"

"I've never been a liar from a child, and now I'm telling lies . . ." mutters Denis, blinking. "But can you do without a weight, your honour? If you put live bait or maggots on a hook, would it go to the bottom without a weight? . . . I am telling lies," grins Denis. . . . "What the devil is the use of the worm if it swims on the surface! The perch and the pike and the eel-pout always go to the bottom, and a bait on the surface is only taken by a shillisper, not very often then, and there are no shillispers in our river. . . . That fish likes plenty of room."

"Why are you telling me about shillispers?"

"Wha-at? Why, you asked me yourself! The gentry catch fish that way too in our parts. The silliest little boy would not try to catch a fish without a weight. Of course anyone who did not understand might go to fish without a weight. There is no rule for a fool."

"So you say you unscrewed this nut to make a weight for your fishing line out of it?"

"What else for? It wasn't to play knuckle-bones with!"

"But you might have taken lead, a bullet . . . a nail of some sort. . . ."

"You don't pick up lead in the road, you have to buy it, and a nail's no good. You can't find anything better than a nut. . . . It's heavy, and there's a hole in it."

"He keeps pretending to be a fool! as though he'd been born yesterday or dropped from heaven! Don't you understand, you blockhead, what unscrewing these nuts leads to? If the watchman had not noticed it the train might have run off the rails, people would have been killed—you would have killed people."

"God forbid, your honour! What should I kill them for? Are we heathens or wicked people? Thank God, good gentlemen, we have lived all our lives without ever dreaming of such a thing. . . . Save, and have mercy on us, Queen of Heaven! . . . What are you saying?"

"And what do you suppose railway accidents do come from? Unscrew two or three nuts and you have an accident."

Denis grins, and screws up his eye at the magistrate incredulously.

"Why! how many years have we all in the village been unscrewing nuts, and the Lord has been merciful; and you talk of accidents, killing people. If I had carried away a rail or put a log across the line, say, then maybe it might have upset the train, but . . . pouf! a nut!"

"But you must understand that the nut holds the rail fast to the sleepers!"

"We understand that . . . We don't unscrew them all . . . we leave some . . . We don't do it thoughtlessly . . . we understand. . . ."

Denis yawns and makes the sign of the cross over his mouth.

"Last year the train went off the rails here," says the magistrate. "Now I see why!"

"What do you say, your honour?"

"I am telling you that now I see why the train went off the rails last year. . . . I understand!"

"That's what you are educated people for, to understand, you kind gentlemen. The Lord knows to whom to give understanding. . . . Here you have reasoned how and what, but the watchman, a peasant like ourselves, with no understanding at all, catches one by the collar and hauls one along. . . . You should reason first and then haul me off. It's a saying that a peasant has a peasant's wit. . . . Write down, too, your honour, that he hit me twice—in the jaw and in the chest."

"When your hut was searched they found another nut. . . . At what spot did you unscrew that, and when?"

"You mean the nut which lay under the red box?"

"I don't know where it was lying, only it was found. When did you unscrew it?"

"I didn't unscrew it; Ignashka, the son of one-eyed Semyon, gave it me. I mean the one which was under the box, but the one which was in the sledge in the yard Mitrofan and I unscrewed together."

"What Mitrofan?"

"Mitrofan Petrov . . . Haven't you heard of him? He makes nets in our village and sells them to the gentry. He needs a lot of those nuts. Reckon a matter of ten for each net."

"Listen. Article 1081 of the Penal Code lays down that every wilful damage of the railway line committed when it can expose the traffic on that line to danger, and the guilty party knows that an accident must be caused by it . . . (Do you understand? Knows! And you could not help knowing what this unscrewing would lead to . . .) is liable to penal servitude."

"Of course, you know best. . . . We are ignorant people. . . . What do we understand?"

"You understand all about it! You are lying, shamming!"

"What should I lie for? Ask in the village if you don't believe me. Only a bleak is caught without a weight, and there is no fish worse than a gudgeon, yet even that won't bite without a weight."

"You'd better tell me about the shillisper next," said the magistrate, smiling.

"There are no shillispers in our parts. . . . We cast our line without a weight on the top of the water with a butterfly; a mullet may be caught that way, though that is not often."

"Come, hold your tongue."

A silence follows. Denis shifts from one foot to the other, looks at the table with the green cloth on it, and blinks his eyes violently as though what was before him was not the cloth but the sun. The magistrate writes rapidly.

"Can I go?" asks Denis after a long silence.

"No. I must take you under guard and send you to prison."

Denis leaves off blinking and, raising his thick eyebrows, looks inquiringly at the magistrate.

"How do you mean, to prison? Your honour! I have no time to spare, I must go to the fair; I must get three roubles from Yegor for some tallow! . . ."

"Hold your tongue; don't interrupt."

"To prison. . . . If there was something to go for, I'd go; but just to go for nothing! What for? I haven't stolen anything, I believe, and I've not been fighting. . . . If you are in doubt about the arrears, your honour, don't believe the elder. . . . You ask the agent . . . he's a regular heathen, the elder, you know."

"Hold your tongue."

"I am holding my tongue, as it is," mutters Denis, "but that the elder has lied over the account, I'll take my oath for it. . . . There are three of us brothers: Kuzma Grigoryev, then Yegor Grigoryev, and me, Denis Grigoryev."

"You are hindering me. . . . Hey, Semyon," cries the magistrate, "take him away!"

"There are three of us brothers," mutters Denis, as two stalwart soldiers take him and lead him out of the room. "A brother is not responsible for a brother. Kuzma does not pay, so you, Denis, must answer for it. . . . Judges indeed! Our master the general is dead—the Kingdom of Heaven be his—or he would have shown you judges. . . . You ought to judge sensibly, not at random. . . . Flog if you like, but flog someone who deserves it, flog with conscience."

Discussion Questions

1. How does the opening description of Denis Grigoryev set up the central conflict of the story? What elements show that he is out of place in this courtroom setting?

2. How does Chekhov use Denis Grigoryev's testimony to bring the world of the peasants into the courtroom? What are the rules, or laws, of this world?

3. What principles guide the magistrate? Does he have any sympathy at all for Denis Grigoryev, or is there no room in the legal world the magistrate represents for the peasant's experience?

Writing Activity

1. Write a story about two worlds coming into conversation in a courtroom, using the questioning of a witness to show the differences between the two worlds.

Coyote v. Acme

In the United States District Court, Southwestern District, Tempe, Arizona Case No. B19294, Judge Joan Kujava, Presiding

WILE E. COYOTE, Plaintiff
-V.-
ACME COMPANY, Defendant

IAN FRAZIER

Headnotes/Things to Look For

Ian Frazier was born in Cleveland, Ohio, in 1951. While attending Harvard, he wrote for the Harvard Lampoon, *the cradle of many noted American humorists. On the staff of* The New Yorker, *another breeding ground for comic writers, he wrote features for* "The Talk of the Town" *section. His books include* Dating Your Mom, On the Rez, Great Plains, *and* Family.

Note how Frazier brings together two very different worlds, the legal setting governed by contractual obligations and the cartoon realm of eternal pursuit and failure, in this exercise in legal rhetoric.

◆

Opening Statement of Mr. Harold Schoff, attorney for Mr. Coyote: My client, Mr. Wile E. Coyote, a resident of Arizona and contiguous states, does hereby bring suit for damages against the Acme Company, manufacturer and retail distributor of assorted merchandise, incorporated in Delaware and doing business in every state, district, and territory. Mr. Coyote seeks compensation for personal injuries, loss of business income, and mental suffering caused as a direct result of the actions and/or gross negligence of said company, under Title 15 of the United States Code, Chapter 47, section 2072, subsection (a), relating to product liability.

Mr. Coyote states that on eighty-five separate occasions he has purchased of the Acme Company (hereinafter, "Defendant"), through that company's mail-order department, certain products which did cause him bodily injury due to defects in manufacture or improper cautionary labelling. Sales slips made out to Mr. Coyote as proof of purchase are at present in the possession of the Court, marked Exhibit A. Such injuries sustained by Mr. Coyote have temporarily restricted his ability to make a living in his profession of predator. Mr. Coyote is self-employed and thus not eligible for Workmen's Compensation.

Mr. Coyote states that on December 13th he received of Defendant via parcel post one Acme Rocket Sled. The intention of Mr. Coyote was to use the Rocket Sled to aid him in pursuit of his prey. Upon receipt of the Rocket Sled Mr. Coyote removed it from its wooden shipping crate and, sighting his prey in the distance, activated the ignition. As Mr. Coyote gripped the handlebars, the Rocket Sled accelerated with such sudden and precipitate force as to stretch Mr. Coyote's forelimbs to a length of fifty feet. Subsequently, the rest of Mr. Coyote's body shot forward with a violent jolt, causing severe strain to his back and neck and placing him unexpectedly astride the Rocket Sled. Disappearing over the horizon at such speed as to leave a diminishing jet trail along its path, the Rocket Sled soon brought Mr. Coyote abreast of his prey. At that moment the animal he was pursuing veered sharply to the right. Mr. Coyote vigorously attempted to follow this maneuver but was unable to, due to poorly designed steering on the Rocket Sled and a faulty or nonexistent braking system. Shortly thereafter, the unchecked progress of the Rocket Sled brought it and Mr. Coyote into collision with the side of a mesa.

Paragraph One of the Report of Attending Physician (Exhibit B), prepared by Dr. Ernest Grosscup, M.D., D.O., details the multiple fractures, contusions, and tissue damage suffered by Mr. Coyote as a result of this collision. Repair of the injuries required a full bandage around the head (excluding the ears), a neck brace, and full or partial casts on all four legs.

Hampered by these injuries, Mr. Coyote was nevertheless obliged to support himself. With this in mind, he purchased of Defendant as an aid to mobility one pair of Acme Rocket Skates. When he attempted to use this product, however, he became involved in an accident remarkably similar to that which occurred with the Rocket Sled. Again, Defendant sold over the counter, without caveat, a product which attached powerful jet engines (in this case, two) to inadequate vehicles, with little or no provision for passenger safety. Encumbered by his heavy casts, Mr. Coyote lost control of the Rocket Skates soon after strapping them on, and collided with a roadside billboard so violently as to leave a hole in the shape of his full silhouette.

Mr. Coyote states that on occasions too numerous to list in this document he has suffered mishaps with explosives purchased of Defendant: the Acme "Little Giant" Firecracker, the Acme Self-Guided Aerial Bomb, etc. (For a full listing, see the Acme Mail Order Explosives Catalogue and attached deposition, entered in evidence as Exhibit C.) Indeed, it is safe to say that not once has an explosive purchased of Defendant by Mr. Coyote performed in an expected manner. To cite just one example: At the expense of much time and personal effort, Mr. Coyote constructed around the outer rim of a butte a wooden trough beginning at the top of the butte and spiralling downward around it to some few feet above a black X painted on the desert floor. The trough was designed in such a way that a spherical explosive of the type sold by Defendant would roll easily and swiftly down to the point of detonation indicated by the X. Mr. Coyote placed a generous pile of birdseed directly on the X, and then, carrying the spherical Acme Bomb (Catalogue # 78-832), climbed to the top of the butte. Mr. Coyote's prey, seeing the birdseed, approached, and Mr. Coyote proceeded to light the fuse. In an instant, the fuse burned down to the stem, causing the bomb to detonate.

In addition to reducing all Mr. Coyote's careful preparations to naught, the premature detonation of Defendant's product resulted in the following disfigurements to Mr. Coyote:

1. Severe singeing of the hair on the head, neck, and muzzle.
2. Sooty discoloration.
3. Fracture of the left ear at the stem, causing the ear to dangle in the aftershock with a creaking noise.

4. Full or partial combustion of whiskers, producing kinking, frazzling, and ashy disintegration.

5. Radical widening of the eyes, due to brow and lid charring.

We come now to the Acme Spring-Powered Shoes. The remains of a pair of these purchased by Mr. Coyote on June 23rd are Plaintiff's Exhibit D. Selected fragments have been shipped to the metallurgical laboratories of the University of California at Santa Barbara for analysis, but to date no explanation has been found for this product's sudden and extreme malfunction. As advertised by Defendant, this product is simplicity itself: two wood-and-metal sandals, each attached to milled-steel springs of high tensile strength and compressed in a tightly coiled position by a cocking device with a lanyard release. Mr. Coyote believed that this product would enable him to pounce upon his prey in the initial moments of the chase, when swift reflexes are at a premium.

To increase the shoes' thrusting power still further, Mr. Coyote affixed them by their bottoms to the side of a large boulder. Adjacent to the boulder was a path which Mr. Coyote's prey was known to frequent. Mr. Coyote put his hind feet in the wood-and-metal sandals and crouched in readiness, his right forepaw holding firmly to the lanyard release. Within a short time Mr. Coyote's prey did indeed appear on the path coming toward him. Unsuspecting, the prey stopped near Mr. Coyote, well within range of the springs at full extension. Mr. Coyote gauged the distance with care and proceeded to pull the lanyard release.

At this point, Defendant's product should have thrust Mr. Coyote forward and away from the boulder. Instead, for reasons yet unknown, the Acme Spring-Powered Shoes thrust the boulder away from Mr. Coyote. As the intended prey looked on unharmed, Mr. Coyote hung suspended in air. Then the twin springs recoiled, bringing Mr. Coyote to a violent feet-first collision with the boulder, the full weight of his head and forequarters falling upon his lower extremities.

The force of this impact then caused the springs to rebound, whereupon Mr. Coyote was thrust skyward. A second recoil and collision followed. The boulder, meanwhile, which was roughly ovoid in shape, had begun to bounce down a hillside, the coiling and recoiling of the springs adding to its velocity. At each bounce, Mr. Coyote came into contact with the boulder, or the boulder came into contact with Mr. Coyote, or both came into contact with the ground. As the grade was a long one, this process continued for some time.

The sequence of collisions resulted in systemic physical damage to Mr. Coyote, viz., flattening of the cranium, sideways displacement of the tongue, reduction of length of legs and upper body, and compression of vertebrae from base of tail to head. Repetition of blows along a vertical axis produced a series of regular horizontal folds in Mr. Coyote's body tissues—a rare and painful condition which caused Mr. Coyote to expand upward and contract downward alternately as he walked, and to emit an off-key, accordionlike wheezing with every step. The distracting and embarrassing nature of this symptom has been a major impediment to Mr. Coyote's pursuit of a normal social life.

As the Court is no doubt aware, Defendant has a virtual monopoly of manufacture and sale of goods required by Mr. Coyote's work. It is our contention that Defendant has used its market advantage to the detriment of the consumer of such specialized products as itching powder, giant kites, Burmese tiger traps, anvils, and two-hundred-foot-long rubber bands. Much as he has come to mistrust Defendant's products, Mr. Coyote has no other domestic source of supply to which to turn. One can only wonder what our trading partners in Western Europe and Japan would make of such a situation, where a giant company is allowed to victimize the consumer in the most reckless and wrongful manner over and over again.

Mr. Coyote respectfully requests that the Court regard these larger economic implications and assess punitive damages in the amount of seventeen million dollars. In addition, Mr. Coyote seeks actual damages (missed meals, medical expenses, days lost from professional occupation) of one million dollars; general damages (mental suffering, injury to reputation) of twenty million dollars; and attorney's fees of seven hundred and fifty thousand dollars. Total damages: thirty-eight million seven hundred and fifty thousand dollars. By awarding Mr. Coyote the full amount, this Court will censure Defendant, its directors, officers, shareholders, successors, and assigns, in the only language they understand, and reaffirm the right of the individual predator to equal protection under the law.

Discussion Questions

1. When do the two contexts Frazier is working with first generate comic effects?
2. To what degree does the pleasure the reader takes in Frazier's comic strategy depend on knowing both contexts well?

3. What particular conventions of legal language are most effective in this piece when brought into conversation with cartoon images from Saturday morning television?

Writing Activity

1. Think of another conflict from literature or popular culture that hasn't had its day in court and write an opening statement or transcript of a legal proceeding based on it.

No Justice, No Foul

JIM STALLARD

Headnotes/Things to Look For

Jim Stallard writes regularly for McSweeney's, *a journal founded by Dave Eggers and based in San Francisco. Stallard worked in the vicinity of the Supreme Court in the '80s, and he vouches for the existence of a basketball court in the building.*

This piece stands in the book as one of the most full-blown and complex examples of bringing two systems into conversation with each other for comic effect. Note how elaborately Stallard works out the premise of the justices deciding court cases on a literal basketball court.

◆

Whenever I hear some historian on PBS prattling about the Supreme Court, I have to step outside for air. I know it's a matter of seconds before the stock phrases—judicial review, legal precedent, activist court—will start rolling out, and I'll feel my blood coming to a boil as I hear the scamming of yet another generation.

Are you sitting down? Everything you were taught about the Supreme Court and its decisions is bunk. For most of the nineteenth century and all of the twentieth, our biggest, most far-reaching legal decisions have been decided not by careful examination of facts and reference to precedent but by contests of game and sport between the justices. The games varied through the years—cribbage, chess, horseshoes, darts—even a brief, disastrous flirtation with polo. (Now do you understand *Plessy v. Ferguson?*)

But ever since 1923, basketball has been the only game, and as the years rolled by and the decisions came down, the whole thing has settled nicely into place. Basketball has shaped the way our society is today, every contour, every legality, every way that one person relates to another in an official, sanctioned sense.

I know, I know—you're thinking I got this stuff from radio signals in my head. Actually, the reason I'm privy to this info is really quite mundane. My father was a Supreme Court maintenance worker from 1925 until he retired forty years later. He started sneaking me in to see games when I was eight. I saw my share (though none of the landmarks) and heard from many sources about countless others.

Oliver Wendell Holmes hit on the basketball idea after attending a collegiate game in New York during the Court's Christmas recess in 1922. He thought he had finally identified the type of contest that could involve all the justices, could be played indoors when the Court was in "session," and, most important of all, did not involve horses.

Holmes brought the idea back to Washington and pitched it to Chief Justice Taft. The corpulent chief had been lobbying for Greco-Roman wrestling, but he was starting to realize none of his colleagues would go for a sport in which they might be killed. (The Fatty Arbuckle incident was fresh on everyone's minds.) Taft finally agreed that basketball offered a superior form of jurisprudence.

After a little tinkering, the procedure came down to this: whenever the justices were evenly split over a judgment (four to four with one judge abstaining) and the deadlock persisted for more than a week, the issue would move to the hardwood. In general, the "teams" could be described as liberal vs. conservative, although as court watchers know, legal philosophies cannot be reduced to such simplistic terms. The justice voted most valuable player in the game was allowed the choice of writing the opinion or—in the case of a political hot potato—making someone else do it.

For the first twelve years, the justices scrapped in a dreary gymnasium tucked in the basement of the Capitol building. The floor was cement and the baskets were mounted flush on the walls so that every fast break or layup carried the threat of a concussion. (Owen Roberts became notorious for his short-term memory and was constantly being carried off the floor.)

When the new Court building went up across the street in 1935, the justices insisted that the fourth floor remain mostly vacant to house the real highest court in the land. Because of a mix-up in the architectural plans, the room had a ceiling that was far too low—a fact that made Chief Justice Charles Evans Hughes livid and which has left its imprint on American history: many landmark decisions might have gone differently if the room could have accommodated justices with a high arc on their shot—Stanley Reed, Robert Jackson, and, most tragically, Abe Fortas.

Mind you, everything leading up to the actual decision was, and is, legitimate. The Court still accepted petitions on merit, they still read the briefs, listened (or dozed) during oral argument and then went into conference prepared to vote one way or another. When the deadlock came, however, the bifocals came off and the hightops went on.

Let's look at some of the landmark games, with impressions gleaned from those lucky few who witnessed them:

NEAR V. MINNESOTA (1931)

A First Amendment ruling that came down in favor of a sleazy Minnesota newspaper being sued for libel after using ethnic slurs. Charles Evans Hughes (twenty-eight points, thirteen rebounds, seven steals) thought some of the newspaper's comments were pretty funny, so he set out to win the MVP and the opinion that followed. "He was good, and he loved to talk out there," said one observer. "I'm no choirboy, but some of the things he was saying had my face turning red. The ref finally gave him a technical to quiet him down." Hughes's mouth finally got him in trouble in the waning moments. After hitting nothing but net, he pointed at Justice Pierce Butler—a bookish sort who had been the subject of persistent rumors—waited a few beats . . . and then yelled "Swish!" The observer recalled, "It was the only time I've ever seen a referee give two technicals at once to the same guy: One, two, gone."

HIRABAYASHI V. UNITED STATES (1943)
(SEE FIG. 1)

The case involved the rights of a Japanese-American citizen as the wartime government was herding his kind around California, but it turned out to be about so much more. Harlan Stone lured Robert Jackson into committing three charging fouls and turned the game around with a steal, a blocked shot, and a wicked bounce pass to Felix Frankfurter that left Owen Roberts and Stanley Reed glued to the floor, their mouths agape. Stone is

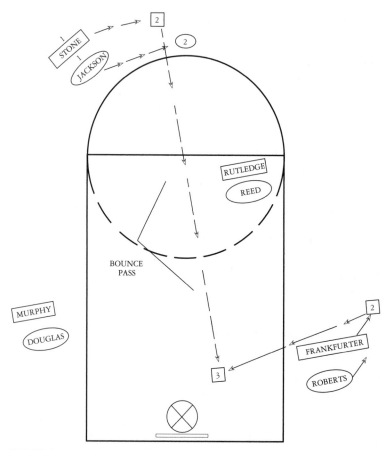

FIGURE 1 Pivotal play in *Hirabayashi v. United States* occurred with 1:23 left in the game, when Harlan Stone (1) dribbled to his left toward the top of the key (2) and then threw a behind-the-back bounce pass to Felix Frankfurter (3), who had faked outside and then cut back into the lane. Reed was busy trying to deny Rutledge the ball and so did not react in time to stop the pass.

credited by more than one as the person who remade the legal landscape in this century. "That was the start of a new kind of law," says one observer who was privy to the Court's biggest cases over decades. "No longer were people standing and taking two-handed set shots. No law is going to survive without being innovative and flexible."

BROWN V. BOARD OF EDUCATION (1954)

Those who watched remembered Earl Warren, "The Aircraft Carrier," posting up and calling for the ball four, five times in a row and kicking it back out until he saw a hairline crack in the defense or a teammate left completely undefended for a jump shot. "So agile for a big man," said one clerk. "They underestimated him at first, then they learned to play him tough. Not that it did them any good." (Interesting side note: Rumor has it that during oral arguments for the case, Warren was sizing up Thurgood Marshall, pleading for the appellants, and sent a page scurrying off to find out how tall he was.)

GRISWOLD V. CONNECTICUT (1964) (SEE FIG. 2)

The case that made contraception safe for America was a nail-biter. Thirty-three years later, a man who watched the game while clerking for Hugo Black was still bitter as he recalled the improbable thirty-foot shot William O. Douglas made at the buzzer: "Two defenders hanging all over him, absolutely no arc, and it goes in— I mean, he should have apologized to everyone. But instead of acknowledging he was lucky, he goes and writes that crap about the 'penumbra of privacy' to rub our noses in it. What a prick."

MIRANDA V. ARIZONA (1966)

The case leading to the requirement that criminal suspects be informed of their rights. Warren again (fourteen points, nine rebounds, twenty-one assists), making it seem like there were eight players on his team instead of four. He also blocked out Stewart and defended Byron White so effectively that White threw the ball at Warren's head and drew a costly technical. The Court's legal historian put it in perspective: "Some justices—I'm thinking of Oliver Wendell Holmes here—had really high point totals, but their teammates suffered because of it. Earl made everyone else play better, and three men playing great is better than one any day."

NEW YORK TIME`S V. UNITED STATES (1971)

The "Pentagon Papers" game, in which Hugo Black and William O. Douglas, teammates for once, shared MVP honors. More than one clerk said that Black clearly was the game's outstanding

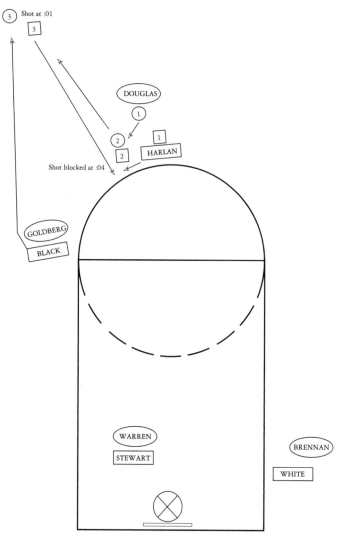

FIGURE 2 In the final frantic moments of *Griswold* v. *Connecticut*, with the game tied, William O. Douglas of the liberal bloc (ovals) had the ball at the top of the key being guarded by John Harlan of the conservative bloc (square).

1. 00:05 Seeing that teammates William Brennan, Earl Warren and Joseph Goldberg are all closely covered, Douglas begins a drive to his right, with Harlan sliding left.

2. 00:04 Douglas pulls up for a jumper only to have it blocked by Harlan, which sends the ball in the opposite direction. Douglas gives chase, with Harlan on his heels. Hugo Black leaves his man (Goldberg) in an attempt to trap Douglas, knowing there's time only for a desperation shot, not a pass.

3. 00:01 With Black and Harlan draped over him Douglas throws up a low trajectory shot that goes in.

player but that Douglas burned an indelible image into every brain with a monster dunk midway through the second half. "It got completely quiet for a few seconds, and then everyone—justices, clerks, refs—started to applaud. Then we had to wait another twenty minutes while they fixed the rim."

FURMAN V. GEORGIA (1972)

The death penalty game, when everything went to hell. Not only did several fistfights break out between sides, but justices were furious at their own teammates. After a while there was no passing; it got to be like a playground game where every person who grabbed a rebound turned and tried to take it himself to the other end. The result: a 16–16 final score, not even a pretense of choosing an MVP, and nine separate opinions. Bad law all around, which was overturned just a few years later. A disgusted clerk who witnessed the game summed it up: "I don't care how many lives are at stake—you don't play like a bunch of municipal court thugs. A lot of my idealism died that day."

ROE V. WADE (1973)

"I've never seen someone take control of a game the way [Harry] Blackmun did that day," said one of his clerks. "He was on a mission. You could tell he had stopped being intimidated and had come into his own. He ran up and down the court for forty minutes, and after the first fifteen the conservatives were just holding their sides and wheezing. Nobody there was thinking about abortion or right-to-privacy—it was just, 'Look at Harry go!' "

BAKKE V. CALIFORNIA (1978)

Bakke wasn't the only one standing up to be heard; this was Lewis Powell's coming-out party as a player. He surprised everyone with his finesse, so fluid and graceful—almost courtly, in his Southern way, the way he ran the floor, dishing assists, getting everyone their points. But every time the defense collapsed on him and dared him to hit from outside, he arced shots that would melt in your mouth. Marshall was baiting him the entire game—understandable when you consider that the case threatened affirmative action—but Powell wouldn't bite, even after being elbowed again and again. Nobody remembers him hitting the rim the entire game.

BOWERS V. HARDWICK (1986)

Was a Georgia law against sodomy in violation of the Constitution? Perhaps more to the point, why couldn't Byron "Whizzer" White realize he didn't have it anymore as an athlete? His teammates voted him MVP to keep him happy, even though he was cherry-picking the entire game. Brennan, whom White was supposed to be guarding, was scoring from all over, but all Whizzer cared about was his own total. His teammates were banking on his hints that he was about to retire and thought giving him the honor would speed him out the door. It still took seven long years.

• • •

As you can see, the games have their own rich history, sometimes even overlapping with the Official Truth that made it into textbooks. Oliver Wendell Holmes actually did make the notorious statement, "Three generations of imbeciles are enough," but he was not, as widely believed, referring to the state-sanctioned sterilization of a retarded woman. He directed it at a referee, the grandson of an official whose incorrect interpretation of the rule book gave Chief Justice Roger Taney an extra throw in the Dred Scott horseshoe match. (The ref was a bit touchy about the whole subject; nobody wants to hear that their granddad prolonged slavery, so Holmes got tossed.) And, yes, Potter Stewart did say "I know it when I see it," but he was not talking about pornography, he was arguing with a ref about what constitutes traveling. The official did not accept his definition and responded, "Why don't you try playing defense and see how you like it?"

But enough about justices running their mouths. Let's focus on overall athletic skills. Since this is the first written account to make it to the public, a lot of inside info on earlier justices has died with the men who knew it firsthand. But with most former clerks of the past few decades . . . still alive, it's possible to piece together fairly accurate descriptions of the recent ones. The consensus is that, as in the outside world, the modern players have it all over their counterparts from sixty years ago. It's a markedly different game. Dunks are so common now that no one bats an eye. It's also impossible to ignore the influence that steroids have had on the players. (Needless to say, Supreme Court justices do not submit to drug tests.) Strength and conditioning regimens allow the players to bring off athletic displays that were unimaginable in the thirties and forties.

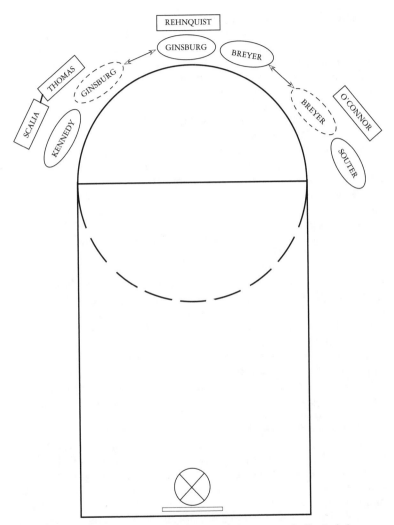

FIGURE 3 The "S-T Zone" (for "Scalia-Thomas") has been used effectively by moderates to force turnovers. With Scalia and Thomas inseparable, moderates can use one man (usually Kennedy) to defend them both, leaving an extra moderate player for double-teams. In this example, Rehnquist has the ball on top, guarded by Ginsburg and Breyer. When he passes to a fellow conservative, one of the two slides over to double-team the recipient, with the other defender staying put. Lately, Rehnquist and O'Connor have been able to negate the defensive scheme with back-door cuts. (Stevens: abstaining.)

Still, steroids and conditioning only get you so far. As any sports fan knows, a lot depends on how well you play as a team and what you're willing to give after tip-off. After years of what they considered judicial overstepping by the Warren Court, conservative justices had high hopes for Warren Burger's boys. But when the games were on the line, the conservatives in the Burger Court just didn't want it as much.

Of course, they weren't helped by the fact that Burger was the worst player of all time. He was as bad as Ben Cardozo, but Cardozo could at least make free throws. Once, after Burger missed his eighth consecutive shot from the line, White gave him a withering look and said, "Thank you, Nixon."

Blackmun, though he had flashes of brilliance, was too often timid. White, of course, was still a formidable athlete when Kennedy appointed him, but he had lost a lot by the 1970s, even if he refused to admit it. (Marshall and Brennan constantly bickered over who got to guard him.)

The liberal holdovers from the Warren Court liked to torment the more conservative newcomers just to show who was boss. One example stands out in particular: It was said that Marshall, cantankerous in his final years, enjoyed taunting Scalia by mocking his fondness for hypothetical questions during oral argument. During one-on-one games that they played strictly for pride, every possession became an opportunity for Marshall to humiliate him: "What if one justice were to back in slowly—like this, say—dribbling the ball methodically, while his fellow justice stood there powerless to stop him? And what if the first justice then dunked over him, like . . . this?"

As for scouting reports on the current nine:

Chief Justice William Rehnquist: Bad back, hates to reach low for balls. Tends to turn it over if you force him to go to his left. Still, no one is able to see the whole court better. Opponents often think he's not even paying attention, and suddenly he's stolen the ball from them.

David Souter: Finesse player; doesn't like to bang. Moves well without the ball; it's almost impossible to keep track of him. Drives defenders nuts and wears them out.

John Paul Stevens: Often wants to switch teams halfway through the game; it's hard to count on him in the late minutes.

Anthony Kennedy: Nondescript and workmanlike out there, but within the first week on the Court, he had memorized the dead spots on the floor and began forcing dribblers into them.

Sandra Day O'Connor: Got pushed around at first, but now uses her speed, and elbows. Runs the point well.

Antonin Scalia: Real trash talker. Constantly comparing himself to Warren, Black, and the other "maestros." Even the refs hate him.

Clarence Thomas: Was held in disdain by the other justices until his first game, when he let loose an eye-popping barrage of three-pointers. (The "Natural Law Fury from Above," as he called it.)

Ruth Bader Ginsburg: One of the best passers ever. Hooks up with Breyer in no-look alley-oops.

Stephen Breyer: Well-liked because he refuses to play dirty, even after taking cheap shots. Boxes out well.

• • •

Anyway, there you have the truth; it's up to you to handle it as best you can. And remember: I'll be judged by history. I don't know where the Court will go from here, now that the secret's out. Will they continue issuing opinions detailing how the votes broke down with faux precision? Will people be so outraged that political pressures will force—God forbid—an actual Supreme Court that tries to thrash out legal decisions based on logic?

The best we can hope is that everyone will submit to the higher power and let the shots fall where they may. Because at those critical moments when time stands still, as six of the justices clear out of the lane and one stands alone on top, dribbling the ball and eyeing the lone defender, this country reaches its full potential, a nation defined not by the past but by the moment. As the justice jukes and then brushes past his opponent and begins his rise to the goal, we all are lifted with him, knowing one thing at heart: If he can finish, so can we.

Discussion Questions

1. The legal system in the United States is known as an adversarial one, with advocates arguing for different positions in the hope of winning. What's incongruous, then, about the justices playing basketball to decide deadlocked cases?

2. How does Stallard build his comic appeals by integrating specific details drawn from history into this account of the court's operations?

3. How does Stallard blend the language of the Court with the language of the court?

4. The Court is generally considered a venue in which logic rules, with the justices representing the intellect unfettered by bias. How does the physical intrude on Stallard's rendering of the justices at play?

Writing Activity

1. Think of a well-respected institution and place its generally accepted way of conducting its business in a setting that makes us see it in a new light.

Laws Concerning Food and Drink; Household Principles; Lamentations of the Father

Ian Frazier

Headnotes/Things to Look For

Ian Frazier was born in Cleveland, Ohio, in 1951. While attending Harvard, he wrote for the Harvard Lampoon, *the cradle of many noted American humorists. On the staff of* The New Yorker, *another breeding ground for comic writers, he wrote features for "The Talk of the Town" section. His books include* Dating Your Mom, On the Rez, Great Plains, *and* Family.

Note how Frazier again brings together two dramatically different contexts, in this case the challenges of Yuppie parenthood and the magisterial cadences of biblical injunctions, another fine example of transposition as a comic strategy.

✦

SERMON ON THE TABLE

Of the beasts of the field, and of the fishes of the sea, and of all foods that are acceptable in my sight you may eat, but not in the living room. Of the hoofed animals, broiled or ground into burgers, you may eat, but not in the living room. Of the cloven-hoofed animal, plain or with cheese, you may eat, but not in the living room. Of the cereal, of the corn and of the wheat and of the oats, and of all the cereals that are of bright color and unknown provenance you may eat, but not in the living room. Of the quiescently frozen dessert and of all frozen after-meal treats you may eat, but absolutely not in the living room. Of the juices and other beverages, yes, even of those in sippy-cups, you may drink, but not in the living room, neither may you carry such therein. Indeed, when you reach the place where the living room carpet begins, of any food or beverage there you may not eat, neither may you drink. But if you are sick, and are lying down and watching something, then may you eat in the living room.

And if you are seated in your high chair, or in a chair such as a greater person might use, keep your legs and feet below you as they were. Neither raise up your knees, nor place your feet upon the table, for that is an abomination to me. Yes, even when you have an interesting bandage to show, your feet upon the table are an abomination, and worthy of rebuke. Drink your milk as it is given you, neither use on it any utensils, nor fork, nor knife, nor spoon, for that is not what they are for; if you will dip your blocks in the milk, and lick it off, you will be sent away. When you have drunk, let the empty cup then remain upon the table, and do not bite it upon its edge and by your teeth hold it to your face in order to make noises in it sounding like a duck; for you will be sent away. When you chew your food, keep your mouth closed until you have swallowed, and do not open it to show your brother or your sister what is within; I say to you, do not so, even if your brother or your sister has done the same to you. Eat your food only; do not eat that which is not food; neither seize the table between your jaws, nor use the raiment of the table to wipe your lips. I say again to you, do not touch it, but leave it as it is. And though your stick of carrot does indeed resemble a marker, draw not with it upon the table, even in pretend, for we do not do that, that is why. And though the pieces of broccoli are very like small trees, do not stand them upright to make a forest, because we do not do that, that is why. Sit just as I have told you, and do not lean to one side or the other, nor slide down until you are nearly slid away. Heed me; for if you sit like that, your hair will go into the syrup. And now behold, even as I have said, it has come to pass.

LAWS PERTAINING TO DESSERT

For we judge between the plate that is unclean and the plate that is clean, saying first, if the plate is clean, then you shall have dessert. But of the unclean plate, the laws are these: If you have eaten most of your meat, and two bites of your peas with each bite consisting of not less than three peas each, or in total six peas, eaten where I can see, and you have also eaten enough of your potatoes to fill two forks, both forkfuls eaten where I can see, then you shall have dessert. But if you eat a lesser number of peas, and yet you eat the potatoes, still you shall not have dessert; and if you eat the peas, yet leave the potatoes uneaten, you shall not have dessert, no, not even a small portion thereof. And if you try to deceive by moving the potatoes or peas around with a fork, that it may appear you have eaten what you have not, you will fall into iniquity. And I will know, and you shall have no dessert.

ON SCREAMING

Do not scream; for it is as if you scream all the time. If you are given a plate on which two foods you do not wish to touch each other are touching each other, your voice rises up even to the ceiling, while you point to the offense with the finger of your right hand; but I say to you, scream not, only remonstrate gently with the server, that the server may correct the fault. Likewise if you receive a portion of fish from which every piece of herbal seasoning has not been scraped off, and the herbal seasoning is loathsome to you, and steeped in vileness, again I say, refrain from screaming. Though the vileness overwhelm you, and cause you a faint unto death, make not that sound from within your throat, neither cover your face, nor press your fingers to your nose. For even now I have made the fish as it should be; behold, I eat of it myself, yet do not die.

CONCERNING FACE AND HANDS

Cast your countenance upward to the light, and lift your eyes to the hills, that I may more easily wash you off. For the stains are upon you; even to the very back of your head, there is rice thereon. And in the breast pocket of your garment, and upon the tie of your shoe, rice and other fragments are distributed in a manner wonderful to see. Only hold yourself still; hold still, I say. Give each finger in its turn for my examination thereof, and also each thumb. Lo, how iniquitous they appear. What I do is as it must be; and you shall not go hence until I have done.

VARIOUS OTHER LAWS, STATUTES, AND ORDINANCES

Bite not, lest you be cast into quiet time. Neither drink of your own bath water, nor of bath water of any kind; nor rub your feet on bread, even if it be in the package; nor rub yourself against cars, nor against any building; nor eat sand. Leave the cat alone, for what has the cat done, that you should so afflict it with tape? And hum not that humming in your nose as I read, nor stand between the light and the book. Indeed, you will drive me to madness. Nor forget what I said about the tape.

COMPLAINTS AND LAMENTATIONS

O my children, you are disobedient. For when I tell you what you must do, you argue and dispute hotly even to the littlest detail; and when I do not accede, you cry out, and hit and kick. Yes, and even sometimes do you spit, and shout "stupid-head" and other blasphemies, and hit and kick the wall and the molding thereof when you are sent to the corner. And though the law teaches that no one shall be sent to the corner for more minutes than he has years of age, yet I would leave you there all day, so mighty am I in anger. But upon being sent to the corner you ask straightaway, "Can I come out?" and I reply, "No, you may not come out." And again you ask, and again I give the same reply. But when you ask again a third time, then you may come out. Hear me, O my children, for the bills they kill me. I pay and pay again, even to the twelfth time in a year, and yet again they mount higher than before. For our health, that we may be covered, I give six hundred and twenty talents twelve times in a year; but even this covers not the fifteen hundred deductible for each member of the family within a calendar year. And yet for ordinary visits we still are not covered, nor for many medicines, nor for the teeth within our mouths. Guess not at what rage is in my mind, for surely you cannot know. For I will come to you at the first of the month and at the fifteenth of the month with the bills and a great whining and moan. And when the month of taxes comes, I will decry the wrong and unfairness of it, and mourn with wine and ashtrays, and rend my receipts. And you shall remember that I am that I am: before, after, and until you are twenty-one. Hear me then, and avoid me in my wrath, O children of me.

Discussion Questions

1. What biblical words, phrases, and stylistic features does Frazier use in this new gospel? What's the effect of blending the biblical diction and syntax with contemporary details of raising children?
2. The Old Testament deity is known for rages directed at recalcitrant people. How does Frazier mitigate the anger of the father in this essay? To what degree does he present a father who is to be obeyed out of fear of punishment? To what degree does he believe there's a chance that he will indeed be obeyed?
3. How would you describe life in the Frazier family, based on this essay?

Writing Activity

1. Using a biblical style, write a set of laws to guide a specific contemporary behavior you believe needs to be controlled.

A Pre-Musical Agreement
MADELEINE BEGUN KANE

Headnotes/Things to Look For

On her website MadKane (www.madkane.com), Madeleine Begun Kane describes herself as "a recovering lawyer." Her work has appeared in numerous anthologies of humor writing, including Life's a Stitch: The Best of Contemporary Women's Humor, Funny Times: The Best of the Best American Humor, *and* I Killed June Cleaver. *Her humor columns have been carried by the L.A. Times Syndicate and Knight-Ridder/Tribune.*

Note how Kane brings her legal training to bear on the domestic situation of a child wanting to take music lessons, providing another example of transposition in action.

---------- ✦ ----------

One afternoon your 10-year-old daughter comes home from school, enthused about learning to play an instrument. Your eyeballs start to throb. Your head begins to pulsate. You ask yourself whether tin ears are passed down from parents to their children. How do you resolve this dissonant dilemma?

Agreement entered into on the _____ day of _____, 20 _____, by noise-averse Parents and instrument wielding Child.

WHEREAS, Child has expressed an interest in studying the saxophone;

WHEREAS, Parents hate the sax and don't even consider it a real instrument;

WHEREAS, Child argues that playing the sax may lead to the presidency or at least to a shot on late-night TV;

WHEREAS, Parents concede the worthiness of such goals, but remind Child that after three years of piano lessons she didn't even master "Chopsticks" and, anyway, shouldn't Child play something feminine like the flute; and;

WHEREAS, Child's best friend's mother is letting her take up the sax, and if Parents let Child do this one little thing, she promises she will never again crush her cousin's accordion.

NOW, THEREFORE, Parents and Child agree to the following terms:

1. In lieu of studying the sax or the flute, Child shall play the clarinet, which is sort of like the sax but much less annoying. The parties further agree that if Child complies with this contract for a year, she may, if she deems it appropriate, switch to the sax. Parents feel safe in making this concession because Child has never complied with anything for longer than a nanosecond.

2. Parents shall pay all clarinet rental bills. Notwithstanding the foregoing, if Child doesn't practice at least one-half hour per day, the obligation to pay such bills shall revert to Child, who shall pay them out of her allowance, even if it takes the rest of her life. However, Child's duty to practice shall be void when her body temperature exceeds 101 degrees or when Parents are entertaining guests.

3. Practice sessions shall take place in Child's bedroom with the door rightly shut at all times. In the event a Parent is ill or had a bad day at the office, such session shall at Parent's option be canceled or be conducted in the basement tool closet. Child hereby waives any right she may have to claim that closet clarinet practice constitutes child abuse.

4. Phrases like "But I don't wanna practice" are hereby banned. Any utterance of same by Child shall increase her practice time, except in the event of a Parental headache.

5. Child shall not be required to regale relatives with clarinet renditions of "Do Re Mi," "Jingle Bells" or "Mary Had a

Little Lamb." Nor shall Child inflict same on guests without the mutual written agreement of all interested parties. If Child does in fact perform, phrases such as "she's such a cute little talent" shall be strictly prohibited, especially when accompanied by head-patting or cheek-pinching.

6. Child acknowledges that she will have to carry the clarinet to school twice a week for lessons and band practice. The weight of such instrument shall not entitle Child to a ride to or from school. Notwithstanding the foregoing, if Child carries more than four school books on any given day, she shall be given a lift by a Parent to be selected in rotation, provided that Child establishes, to said Parent's satisfaction, that Child used said books within fifteen hours of said ride. Parents concede that Child's arithmetic book is unusually heavy and that it should count as two books in making the aforesaid textbook calculation.

7. Child acknowledges that clarinet reeds are expensive and delicate and agrees to use them only for the purpose of emitting clarinet-type sounds. In return for Parents' agreement to supply her with reeds, Child agrees not to chew them, bend them or feed them to the dog.

8. Parents shall attend Child's band concerts and shall abstain from all embarrassing auditorium activity including but not limited to taking flash photos, jumping up and down in their seats and waving, or yelling, "That's my kid. Isn't she great?" Parents further agree to applaud with enthusiasm no matter how much their ears hurt.

9. Child promises that if she ever becomes a famous musician she will give Parents complete credit, especially when she accepts her first Grammy.

WHEREFORE, we affix our signatures.

_____

_____

Discussion Questions

1. How does Kane's use of the legal form of the prenuptial agreement shape our experience of this common parent–child situation?

2. How does Kane use the rhetorical trope of hyperbole (exaggeration) to convey the parents' exasperation with the child?

3. This legal agreement cuts both ways, putting restrictions on the parents as well as the child. What predictable behaviors of both parties need to be contained and controlled by the binding force of the document?

Writing Activity

1. Write a legal pre-_____ agreement to control a situation that requires such planning to make sure people behave well. This could be a family situation or a situation between friends or co-workers.

Why Are Kids So Dumb? A Defense
CHRIS HARRIS

Headnotes/Things to Look For

Chris Harris has been a writer for The Late Show with David Letterman, *and his comic essays have appeared in* The New Yorker, Spin Magazine, *and* McSweeney's, *among other publications.*

Note how Harris uses a particular brand of logic to argue that young people shouldn't be judged harshly by their elders. His logic may bear some resemblance to that described for us by Aristotle, but look for flaws in Harris's movement from premise to conclusion.

✦

Let us first extinguish any doubts: We're smarter than they are. Not only are we smarter now, but we were smarter as children too. Relative test scores? Don't bother; they can't even wear their baseball caps the right way. Teenagers have for years stood at the vanguard in the dumbing down of America, and this era's crop are no exception.

And now, yet another global survey has dumped our nation's progeny near the bottom of the educational trough. Children in countries we've never even heard of, like "Denmark" and "New Zealand," are beating us in geography. Undernourished waifs three countries from the nearest web connection are proving more adept in the sciences. And should any young Americans ever acquire the math skills needed to *understand* the global survey, they would find their math skills sorely lacking.

Why? Theories proliferate, including one that suggests those aforementioned caps squeeze their brains until they literally pop and slip right out of the bottoms of their baggy pants. But perhaps—have a seat, please—perhaps things aren't nearly as bad as they seem. And perhaps, lest things *become* as bad as they seem, we must consider some radical changes in educational theory. After an illuminating reevaluation of our children's skills, a series of remedial actions are herein proffered, upon which, if we are to check any trend toward density, we must act immediately.

HISTORY

The reason today's children know less history than previous generations is painfully evident: There's *more* of it. As one youth explained, "[older Americans] didn't have to learn about things like that World War and colonies and the Emaciation [sic] Procla-thing and all that because they *lived* through it" To keep the workload fair, a cut-off mark should be chosen—perhaps 1698—which moves with the current year and before which no history is taught. After all, history repeats itself anyway—there's no point in being redundant.

Those who argue that students in other countries have encountered no such difficulty are guilty of gross simplification. Certainly, Swedes know their nation's history better than our students know theirs, but what history does Sweden *have?* It gets cold; it gets less cold. It gets cold; it gets less cold. It gets cold again; you commit suicide. Of course they have a better grasp.

GEOGRAPHY

Balkans, Baltics, Baltimore—youth today hardly know the difference. But the map will be redrawn many times over—remember, even the continents shift—before they're in charge. One can argue that students' ignorance in this area is in fact *more* insightful than our own "knowledge" of arbitrary details like what country we live in, for it accurately reflects the uncertainty with which international borders are placed in these ever-changing times.

ENGLISH

The reputation of young people's vocabulary has been unfairly tarnished by an ageist, myopic definition of what constitutes *slang*. In years past, long, difficult words such as "extenuate" and "pugnacious" were the "hip lingo" of the times; these words now sound hopelessly dated, or "out." Today, really really short words (such as "cool" and "rad") are the speech pattern of choice. We can't reasonably expect them to use "lugubrious" or "obfuscate" any more than they do "groovy." The size of youth's vocabulary has also been criticized, proving that any statistic can fall victim to a negative spin. The plain fact is that kids today do not have a *smaller* vocabulary, they have a *more efficient* vocabulary. Over 240 words, for example, ranging from "stylish" to "titillating," can now be expressed with the omni-word "phat."

Besides, English and its grammatical components will be rendered obsolete by the year 2010 anyway, at which point all communication will have been distilled into chat room abbreviations. A typical conversation:

webdemon: hi

netfudge: wr ("wr" will stand for witty remark)

webdemon: LOL

netfudge: ? ("?" will stand for any question)

webdemon: xxx ("xxx" will stand for a series of sexual comments)

netfudge: bye

webdemon: bye

MATHEMATICS

The great irony of society is that the more and more powerful machines we create to do math for us, the more and more some people insist that math is essential for us to learn. Bull puckey! We have calculators, computers, ATMs, and CPAs: Math has never been *less* important to learn in the entire history of civilization. Kudos to the younger generation for recognizing this.

MOVING FORWARD

And yet, one is still left with the nagging feeling that today's youth are a bunch of meandering dullwits. Again, we must act immediately to confront the greater problems of our current educational system; at least three additional improvements warrant our prompt consideration:

To illustrate one flaw, let us employ a simple analogy. Think of teenagers as a diverse infestation of roaches in a home, and education a highly toxic poison. Our current high schools, then, are a scattering of storebought traps: Occasionally a roach wanders in and picks up some chemical toxins, but many do not eat enough, and some stay away entirely. Much more effective would be the hiring of an exterminator, who cleverly takes the *poison* to the *roaches*. It follows that we should not simply wait for students to accidentally stumble into schools, but instead douse them with education wherever they already are. In newly designed *mall schools*, for example, learning will be subversively incorporated into the everyday activities of "hanging out"—math at the cash registers, social studies in the food court, and foreign languages at Au Bon Pain.

Second, we must emphasize the positive, somehow take better advantage of the areas in which this generation excels, for it does excel at many things:

- Skateboard tricks
- Gunning down classmates
- Singing whiny pop songs

. . . Or, as an alternative, we can decide to *not* take advantage of these areas.

Third, and with only the slightest air of defeat, we must remember that youth have always been—well—kind of dumb. Romeo and Juliet thought that love was the greatest emotion. Ha! A young Michael Jackson sang that "people make the world go 'round." Ha! Ha! And in the sixties, students actually believed that life would be better without the massive economic might of the military-industrial machine. Ha ha! Ha! Time, we may note with relief, corrects this type of blatant naiveté on its own, crushing and conforming these puerile ideas of youth into our known and established—and *right*—societal standards.

With this in mind, then, perhaps our best course of action in addressing the stupidity of the young is *not* to act immediately at all, but instead to *lean back and do nothing*. Don't help them, don't encourage them, and please don't give them any hints. Eventually the real world—as it did with us—will force smartness upon our children, just in time for them to grab hold the reins of the world and kick us screaming off the carriage.

Fourth, and failing all else, we can always just turn off the television.

Discussion Questions

1. Harris offers a series of informal proofs in defense of youth. Try to set out his logical appeals in the form of what Aristotle calls an enthymeme, or informal logical proof. "If this premise is true, then this conclusion is true" is one way to think about the form of the enthymeme. What's wrong with Harris's arguments?

2. How does Harris let us know that he, as a representative of adults, is subject to the accusation of being dumb himself?

3. Harris includes a deliberative element in this essay, offering a proposal to solve the educational crisis facing the country. What are the merits of his solutions of mall schools and expansion of the curriculum to correspond with the interests of youth?

Writing Activity

1. Write a defense of a group needing a skilled rhetorician to speak out on their behalf, but be sure to show the rhetorical shortcomings of the advocate.

Comic Celebrations and Attacks (ceremonial rhetoric)

Introduction

Ceremonial, or epideictic, rhetoric allows us to praise and blame, to celebrate and censure. Aristotle focuses this form of discourse on the present—today, at this moment, this person or this action is worthy of praise, or not. Examples of ceremonial rhetoric include eulogies (note all the comic funerals portrayed in films and even in commercials, in which the expected praise suddenly turns to blame, or, in the case of the Chekhov story included in this chapter, the eulogy is about the wrong person), commencement addresses (note how often comics are asked to perk up these solemn occasions by standing the standard platitudes on their tasseled heads), and speeches given on public holidays such as Memorial or Veterans Day (in this chapter, Mark Twain finds himself responding to a toast at a military celebration).

Ceremonial rhetoric often tends to be less connected to specific settings than deliberative and forensic rhetoric. There is no legislative assembly, no courtroom, just the sprawling world in which we find much to like and dislike, and we're not shy about expressing these opinions. The second selection from Mark Twain is this kind of piece, in which he delivers his views on tobacco and those who claim to know what good tobacco is. Lewis Thomas finds much to praise and criticize in the way that writers use punctuation, while Laurie Anderson considers whether technology is worthy of celebration for its ubiquitous role in contemporary life. For the purposes of this chapter, I will also consider the memoir a form of ceremonial rhetoric: let's think of the past as a kind of eternal present we carry around with us, making judgments from moment to moment about what is to be praised and where we and others have failed and deserve blame. In this spirit, Anne Lamott assesses herself and the people she has encountered.

On Babies

At the Banquet, in Chicago, Given by the Army of the Tennessee to Their First Commander, General U.S. Grant, November, 1879

MARK TWAIN

Headnotes/Things to Look For

Mark Twain (1835–1910) was born Samuel Clemens in Missouri. Widely considered a major figure in the development of American literature, Twain began as a journalist before spreading out to nonfiction accounts of his travels and eventually novels, including The Adventures of Tom Sawyer *and* Adventures of Huckleberry Finn *(considered by many to be the great American novel). Later works include* A Connecticut Yankee in King Arthur's Court *and* The Mysterious Stranger.

Note that Twain is attending a banquet, a ceremonial event, and that he speaks in response to the fifteenth toast offered—to Babies. He takes some liberties with the form, sacrificing grand praise for plain talk about domestic life.

◆

The fifteenth regular toast was "The Babies—as they comfort us in our sorrows, let us not forget them in our festivities."

I like that. We have not all had the good fortune to be ladies. We have not all been generals, or poets, or statesmen; but when the toast works down to the babies, we stand on common ground. It is a shame that for a thousand years the world's banquets have utterly ignored the baby, as if he didn't amount to anything. If you will stop and think a minute—if you will go back fifty or one hundred years to your early married life and recontemplate your first baby—you will remember that he amounted to a great deal, and even something over. You soldiers all know that when the little fellow arrived at family headquarters you had to hand in your resignation. He took entire command. You became his lackey, his mere body servant, and you had to stand around, too. He was not a commander who made allowances for time, distance, weather, or anything else. You had to execute his order whether it was possible or not. And there was only one form of marching in his manual of tactics, and that was the double-quick. He treated you with every sort of insolence and disrespect, and the bravest of you didn't dare to say a word. You could face the death-storm at Donelson and Vicksburg, and give back blow for blow; but when he clawed your whiskers, and pulled your hair, and twisted your nose, you had to take it. When the thunders of war were sounding in your ears you set your faces toward the batteries, and advanced with steady tread; but when he turned on the terrors of his war-whoop you advanced in the other direction, and mighty glad of the chance, too. When he called for soothing-syrup, did you venture to throw out any side remarks about certain services being unbecoming an officer and a gentleman? No. You got and got it. When he ordered his pap-bottle and it was not warm, did you talk back? Not you. You went to work and warmed it. You even descended so far in your menial office as to take a suck at that warm, insipid stuff yourself, to see if it was right—three parts water to one of milk, a touch of sugar to modify the colic, and a drop of peppermint to kill those hiccoughs. I can taste that stuff yet. And how many things you learned as you went along! Sentimental young folks still take stock in that beautiful old saying that when the baby smiles in his sleep, it is because the angels are whispering to him. Very pretty, but too thin—simply wind on the stomach, my friends. If the baby proposed to take a walk at his usual hour, two o'clock in the morning, didn't you rise up promptly and remark, with a mental addition which would not improve a Sunday-school book much, that that was the very thing you were about to propose yourself? Oh! you were under good discipline, and as you went fluttering up and down the room in your undress uniform, you not only prattled undignified baby-talk, but even tuned up your martial voices and tried to sing!—"Rock-a-by baby in the treetop," for instance. What a spectacle for an Army of the Tennessee! And what an affliction for the neighbors, too; for it is not everybody within a mile around that likes military music at three in the morning. And when you had been keeping this sort of thing up two or three hours, and your little velvet-head intimated that nothing suited him like exercise and noise, what did you do? ["Go on!"] You simply went on until you dropped in the last ditch. The idea that a baby doesn't amount to anything! Why, one baby is just a house and a front yard full by itself. One baby can furnish more business than you and your whole Interior Department can attend to. He is enterprising, irrepressible, brimful of lawless activities. Do what you please, you can't make him stay on the reservation. Sufficient unto the day is one baby. As long as you are in your right mind don't you ever pray for twins. Twins amount to a permanent riot. And there ain't any real difference between triplets and an insurrection.

Yes, it was high time for a toast-master to recognize the importance of the babies. Think what is in store for the present crop! Fifty years from now we shall all be dead, I trust, and then this flag, if it still survive (and let us hope it may), will be floating over a Republic numbering 200,000,000 souls, according to the settled laws of our increase. Our present schooner of State will have grown into a political leviathan—a Great Eastern. The cradled babies of to-day will be on deck. Let them be well trained, for we are going to leave a big contract on their hands. Among the three or four million cradles now rocking in the land are some which this nation would preserve for ages as sacred things, if we could know which ones they are. In one of them cradles the unconscious Farragut of the future is at this moment teething—think of it!—and putting in a world of dead earnest, unarticulated, but perfectly justifiable profanity over it, too. In another the future renowned astronomer is blinking at the shining Milky Way with but a languid interest—poor little chap!—and wondering what has become of that other one they call the wet-nurse. In another the future great historian is lying—and doubtless will continue to lie until his earthly mission is ended. In another the future President is busying himself with no profounder problem of state than what the mischief has become of his hair so early; and in a mighty array of other cradles there are now some 60,000 future office-seekers, getting ready to furnish him occasion to grapple with that same old problem a second time. And in still one more cradle, somewhere under the flag, the future illustrious commander-in-chief of the American armies is so little burdened with his approaching grandeurs and responsibilities as to be giving his whole strategic mind at this moment to trying to find out some way to get his big toe into his mouth—an achievement which, meaning no disrespect, the illustrious guest of this evening turned his entire attention to some fifty-six years ago; and if the child is but a prophecy of the man, there are mighty few who will doubt that he succeeded.

Discussion Questions

1. As the banquet is given by and likely attended by military men, Twain offers a controlling metaphor to describe in grim detail how fathers must serve their babies. How well does this metaphor work, and why is it successful?
2. How does Twain play with the language of military life throughout the piece, bringing the military and the domestic into dialogue with each other? For instance, how are babies described as commanders, and fathers as lowly soldiers?
3. The second paragraph provides a meditation on the future. How does Twain use the elements and trappings of babyhood to give a fresh twist to this section?

Writing Activity

1. What other unacknowledged group deserves a toast in its honor? Imagine a ceremonial occasion featuring public proclamations, celebrating a segment of the population (e.g., teenagers, the elderly, people who exercise regularly).

Concerning Tobacco
MARK TWAIN

Headnotes/Things to Look For

Mark Twain (1835–1910) was born Samuel Clemens in Missouri. Widely considered a major figure in the development of American literature, Twain began as a journalist before spreading out to nonfiction accounts of his travels and eventually novels, including The Adventures of Tom Sawyer *and* Adventures of Huckleberry Finn *(considered by many to be the great American novel). Later works include* A Connecticut Yankee in King Arthur's Court *and* The Mysterious Stranger.

Twain was known for his iconoclastic wit, and he worked to cut through conventional pieties, even when they had to do with something incidental to the major issues of the day, as in this essay on tobacco. Note the immediate assertion of his thesis, which appears again at the conclusion, as a kind of bookend. In between the standard opening and closing, Twain uses a range of strategies.

——————————— ✦ ———————————

As concerns tobacco, there are many superstitions. And the chiefest is this—that there is a STANDARD governing the matter, whereas there is nothing of the kind. Each man's own preference is the only standard for him, the only one which he can accept, the only one which can command him. A congress of all the tobacco-lovers in the world could not elect a standard which would be binding upon you or me, or would even much influence us.

The next superstition is that a man has a standard of his own. He hasn't. He thinks he has, but he hasn't. He thinks he can tell what he regards as a good cigar from what he regards as a bad one—but he can't. He goes by the brand, yet imagines he goes by the flavor. One may palm off the worst counterfeit upon him; if it bears his brand he will smoke it contentedly and never suspect.

Children of twenty-five, who have seven years experience, try to tell me what is a good cigar and what isn't. Me, who never learned to smoke, but always smoked; me, who came into the world asking for a light.

No one can tell me what is a good cigar—for me. I am the only judge. People who claim to know say that I smoke the worst cigars in the world. They bring their own cigars when they come to my house. They betray an unmanly terror when I offer them a cigar; they tell lies and hurry away to meet engagements which they have not made when they are threatened with the hospitalities of my box. Now then, observe what superstition, assisted by a man's reputation, can do. I was to have twelve personal friends to supper one night. One of them was as notorious for costly and elegant cigars as I was for cheap and devilish ones. I called at his house and when no one was looking borrowed a double handful of his very choicest; cigars which cost him forty cents apiece and bore red-and-gold labels in sign of their nobility. I removed the labels and put the cigars into a box with my favorite brand on it—a brand which those people all knew, and which cowed them as men are cowed by an epidemic. They took these cigars when offered at the end of the supper, and lit them and sternly struggled with them—in dreary silence, for hilarity died when the fell brand came into view and started around—but their fortitude held for a short time only; then they made excuses and filed out, treading on one another's heels with indecent eagerness; and in the morning when I went out to observe results the cigars lay all between the front door and the gate. All except one—that one lay in the plate of the man from whom I had cabbaged the lot. One or two whiffs was all he could stand. He told me afterward that some day I would get shot for giving people that kind of cigars to smoke.

Am I certain of my own standard? Perfectly; yes, absolutely— unless somebody fools me by putting my brand on some other kind of cigar; for no doubt I am like the rest, and know my cigar by the brand instead of by the flavor. However, my standard is a pretty wide one and covers a good deal of territory. To me, almost any cigar is good that nobody else will smoke, and to me almost all cigars are bad that other people consider good. Nearly any cigar will do me, except a Havana. People think they hurt my feelings when they come to my house with their life preservers on— I mean, with their own cigars in their pockets. It is an error; I take care of myself in a similar way. When I go into danger—that is, into rich people's houses, where, in the nature of things, they will have high-tariff cigars, red-and-gilt girded and nested in a rosewood box along with a damp sponge, cigars which develop a dismal black ash and burn down the side and smell, and will grow hot to the fingers, and will go on growing hotter and hotter, and go on smelling more and more infamously and unendurably the deeper the fire tunnels down inside below the thimbleful of honest tobacco that is in the front end, the furnisher of it praising it all the time and telling you how much the deadly thing cost—yes, when I go into that sort of peril I carry my own defense along; I carry my own brand—twenty-seven cents a barrel—and I live to see my family again. I may seem to light his red-gartered cigar, but that is only for courtesy's sake; I smuggle it into my pocket for the poor, of whom I know many, and light one of my own; and while he praises it I join in, but when he says it cost forty-five cents I say nothing, for I know better.

However, to say true, my tastes are so catholic that I have never seen any cigars that I really could not smoke, except those that cost a dollar apiece. I have examined those and know that they are made of dog-hair, and not good dog-hair at that.

I have a thoroughly satisfactory time in Europe, for all over the Continent one finds cigars which not even the most hardened newsboys in New York would smoke. I brought cigars with me, the last time; I will not do that any more. In Italy, as in France, the Government is the only cigar-peddler. Italy has three or four domestic brands: the Minghetti, the Trabuco, the Virginia, and a very coarse one which is a modification of the Virginia. The Minghettis are large and comely, and cost three dollars and sixty cents a hundred; I can smoke a hundred in seven days and enjoy every one of them. The Trabucos suit me, too; I don't remember the price. But one has to learn to like the Virginia, nobody is born friendly to it. It looks like a rat-tail file, but smokes better, some think. It has a straw through it; you pull this out, and it leaves a flue, otherwise there would be no draught, not even as much as there is to a nail. Some prefer a nail at first. However, I like all the French, Swiss, German, and Italian domestic cigars, and have never cared to inquire what they are made of; and nobody would know, anyhow, perhaps. There is even a brand of European smoking-tobacco that I like. It is a brand used by the Italian peasants. It is loose and dry and black, and looks like tea-grounds. When the fire is applied it expands, and climbs up and towers above the pipe, and presently tumbles off inside of one's vest. The tobacco itself is cheap, but it raises the insurance. It is as I remarked in the beginning—the taste for tobacco is a matter of superstition. There are no standards—no real standards. Each man's preference is the only standard for him, the only one which he can accept, the only one which can command him.

Discussion Questions

1. Twain dismisses as superstition the idea that standards regarding tobacco exist. What kinds of evidence does he offer to support his central claim?
2. How does Twain establish his own ethos, or character, in this piece that casts other tobacco users as buffoons? What persona does he present?
3. How does the paragraph on European cigars contribute to the essay? To what degree does this seem like a digression rather than an integral part of the central argument? How does your sense of how an essay should be developed and organized have to stretch in this case?

Writing Activity

1. Write an essay about something common in your life (a sport you play, something you eat or drink, music you listen to) that you believe other people have wrongheaded or superstitious ideas about. Put forward the truth as you see it in your essay.

The Orator

ANTON CHEKHOV

Headnotes/Things to Look For

Anton Chekhov (1860–1904) originally began writing short humorous stories to support his family. He also trained to be a doctor and practiced medicine throughout his life, though he made his living through his literary work. As he matured as an artist, Chekhov's fiction became more serious and layered in its portrayal of Russian society, and he wrote a series of plays that are performed to this day, including The Seagull, Uncle Vanya, Three Sisters, *and* The Cherry Orchard.

Note the sardonic view of Russian society Chekhov delivers in this ostensibly comic story, as the solemn occasion of a funeral is disrupted. As is the case with many writers of his time and place, Chekhov is sensitive to entrenched class distinctions and the institutionalized forms that govern people's behaviors toward each other.

◆

One fine morning the collegiate assessor, Kirill Ivanovitch Babilonov, who had died of the two afflictions so widely spread in our country, a bad wife and alcoholism, was being buried. As the funeral procession set off from the church to the cemetery, one of the deceased's colleagues, called Poplavsky, got into a cab and galloped off to find a friend, one Grigory Petrovitch Zapoikin, a man who though still young had acquired considerable popularity. Zapoikin, as many of my readers are aware, possesses a rare talent for impromptu speechifying at weddings, jubilees, and funerals. He can speak whenever he likes: in his sleep, on an empty stomach, dead drunk or in a high fever. His words flow smoothly and evenly, like water out of a pipe, and in abundance; there are far more moving words in his oratorical dictionary than there are beetles in any restaurant. He always speaks eloquently and at great length, so much so that on some occasions, particularly at merchants' weddings, they have to resort to assistance from the police to stop him.

"I have come for you, old man!" began Poplavsky, finding him at home. "Put on your hat and coat this minute and come along. One of our fellows is dead, we are just sending him off to the other world, so you must do a bit of palavering by way of farewell to him. . . . You are our only hope. If it had been one of the smaller fry it would not have been worth troubling you, but you see it's the secretary . . . a pillar of the office, in a sense. It's awkward for such a whopper to be buried without a speech."

"Oh, the secretary!" yawned Zapoikin. "You mean the drunken one?"

"Yes. There will be pancakes, a lunch . . . you'll get your cab-fare. Come along, dear chap. You spout out some rigmarole like a regular Cicero at the grave and what gratitude you will earn!"

Zapoikin readily agreed. He ruffled up his hair, cast a shade of melancholy over his face, and went out into the street with Poplavsky.

"I know your secretary," he said, as he got into the cab. "A cunning rogue and a beast—the kingdom of heaven be his—such as you don't often come across."

"Come, Grisha, it is not the thing to abuse the dead."

"Of course not, *aut mortuis nihil bene*, but still he was a rascal."

The friends overtook the funeral procession and joined it. The coffin was borne along slowly so that before they reached the cemetery they were able three times to drop into a tavern and imbibe a little to the health of the departed.

In the cemetery came the service by the graveside. The mother-in-law, the wife, and the sister-in-law in obedience to custom shed many tears. When the coffin was being lowered into the grave, the wife even shrieked "Let me go with him! " but did not follow her husband into the grave, probably recollecting her pension. Waiting till everything was quiet again Zapoikin stepped forward, turned his eyes on all present, and began:

"Can I believe my eyes and ears? Is it not a terrible dream this grave, these tear-stained faces, these moans and lamentations? Alas, it is not a dream and our eyes do not deceive us! He whom we have only so lately seen, so full of courage, so youthfully fresh and pure, who so lately before our eyes like an unwearying bee bore his honey to the common hive of the welfare of the state, he who . . . he is turned now to dust, to inanimate mirage. Inexorable death has laid his bony hand upon him at the time when, in spite of his bowed age, he was still full of the bloom of strength and radiant hopes. An irremediable loss! Who will fill his place for us? Good government servants we have many, but Prokofy Osipitch was unique. To the depths of his soul he was devoted to his honest duty; he did not spare his strength but worked late at night, and was disinterested, impervious to bribes. . . . How he despised those who to the detriment of the public interest sought to corrupt him, who by the seductive goods of this life strove to draw him to betray his duty! Yes, before our eyes Prokofy Osipitch would divide his small salary between his poorer colleagues, and you have just heard yourselves the lamentations of the widows and orphans who lived upon his alms. Devoted to good works and his official duty, he gave up the joys of this life and even renounced the happiness of domestic existence; as you are aware, to the end of his days he was a bachelor. And who will replace him as a comrade? I can see now the kindly, shaven face turned to us with a gentle smile, I can hear now his soft friendly voice. Peace to thine ashes, Prokofy Osipitch! Rest, honest, noble toiler!"

Zapoikin continued while his listeners began whispering together. His speech pleased everyone and drew some tears, but a good many things in it seemed strange. In the first place they could not make out why the orator called the deceased Prokofy Osipitch when his name was Kirill Ivanovitch. In the second, everyone knew that the deceased had spent his whole life quarelling with his lawful wife, and so consequently could not be called a bachelor; in the third, he had a thick red beard and had never been known to shave, and so no one could understand why the orator spoke of his shaven face. The listeners were perplexed; they glanced at each other and shrugged their shoulders.

"Prokofy Osipitch," continued the orator, looking with an air of inspiration into the grave, "your face was plain, even hideous, you were morose and austere, but we all know that under that outer husk there beat an honest, friendly heart!"

Soon the listeners began to observe something strange in the orator himself. He gazed at one point, shifted about uneasily and began to shrug his shoulders too. All at once he ceased speaking, and gaping with astonishment, turned to Poplavsky.

"I say! he's alive," he said, staring with horror.

"Who's alive?"

"Why, Prokofy Osipitch, there he stands, by that tombstone!"

"He never died! It's Kirill Ivanovitch who's dead."

"But you told me yourself your secretary was dead."

"Kirill Ivanovitch was our secretary. You've muddled it, you queer fish. Prokofy Osipitch was our secretary before, that's true, but two years ago he was transferred to the second division as head clerk."

"How the devil is one to tell?"

"Why are you stopping? Go on, it's awkward."

Zapoikin turned to the grave, and with the same eloquence continued his interrupted speech. Prokofy Osipitch, an old clerk with a clean-shaven face, was in fact standing by a tombstone. He looked at the orator and frowned angrily.

"Well, you have put your foot into it, haven't you!" laughed his fellow-clerks as they returned from the funeral with Zapoikin. "Burying a man alive!"

"It's unpleasant, young man," grumbled Prokofy Osipitch. "Your speech may be all right for a dead man, but in reference to a living one it is nothing but sarcasm! Upon my soul what have you been saying? Disinterested, incorruptible, won't take bribes! Such things can only be said of the living in sarcasm. And no one asked you, sir, to expatiate on my face. Plain, hideous, so be it, but why exhibit my countenance in that public way! It's insulting."

Discussion Questions

1. How does Chekhov's introduction of the orator Zapoikin set us up to be suspicious of ceremonial speaking?
2. How much of Zapoikin's language could be used for any funeral oration? What comment is Chekhov making about ceremonial discourse through his rendering of the oration?
3. What do Prokofy Osipitch's final words suggest about the social role of funeral orations? What does everyone accept about the form?

Writing Activity

1. Write some standard ceremonial language that could serve as a comment on any person (a teacher, a coach, a politician) at a public occasion saluting their achievements.

Notes on Punctuation
Lewis Thomas

Headnotes/Things to Look For

Lewis Thomas (1913–1993) was born in New York and attended Princeton and then Harvard Medical School. Like Chekhov, he was both a doctor and a writer, specializing in the essay form, ranging over scientific and general topics. In a varied career that saw him serve as Dean of Yale and New York University Medical Schools and

President of the Memorial Sloan-Kettering Institute, he wrote regularly for The New England Journal of Medicine. *His award-winning books include* Lives of a Cell, The Medusa and the Snail, *and* Late Night Thoughts on Listening to Mahler's Ninth Symphony. *Note how Thomas shares his love of even the humblest aspects of language in this essay about the subtle joys of punctuation. In this celebration he finds much to praise as well as a few things to criticize in how people use these ubiquitous marks.*

---------------- ✦ ----------------

There are no precise rules about punctuation (Fowler lays out some general advice (as best he can under the complex circumstances of English prose (he points out, for example, that we possess only four stops (the comma, the semicolon, the colon and the period (the question mark and exclamation point are not, strictly speaking, stops; they are indicators of tone (oddly enough, the Greeks employed the semicolon for their question mark (it produces a strange sensation to read a Greek sentence which is a straightforward question: Why weepest thou; (instead of Why weepest thou? (and, of course, there are parentheses (which are surely a kind of punctuation making this whole matter much more complicated by having to count up the left-handed parentheses in order to be sure of closing with the right number (but if the parentheses were left out, with nothing to work with but the stops we would have considerably more flexibility in the deploying of layers of meaning than if we tried to separate all the clauses by physical barriers (and in the latter case, while we might have more precision and exactitude for our meaning, we would lose the essential flavor of language, which is its wonderful ambiguity)))))))))))).

The commas are the most useful and usable of all the stops. It is highly important to put them in place as you go along. If you try to come back after doing a paragraph and stick them in the various spots that tempt you you will discover that they tend to swarm like minnows in all sorts of crevices whose existence you hadn't realized and before you know it the whole long sentence becomes immobilized and lashed up squirming in commas. Better to use them sparingly, and with affection, precisely when the need for each one arises, nicely, by itself.

I have grown fond of semicolons in recent years. The semicolon tells you that there is still some question about the preceding full sentence; something needs to be added; it reminds you sometimes of the Greek usage. It is almost always a greater pleasure to come across a semicolon than a period. The period tells you that is that; if you didn't get all the meaning you wanted or expected, anyway you got all the writer intended to parcel out and now you have to move along. But with a semicolon there you get a pleasant little feeling of expectancy; there is more to come; to read on; it will get clearer.

Colons are a lot less attractive for several reasons: firstly, they give you the feeling of being rather ordered around, or at least having your nose pointed in a direction you might not be inclined to take if left to yourself, and, secondly, you suspect you're in for one of those sentences that will be labeling the points to be made: firstly, secondly and so forth, with the implication that you haven't sense enough to keep track of a sequence of notions without having them numbered. Also, many writers use this system loosely and incompletely, starting out with number one and number two as though counting off on their fingers but then going on and on without the succession of labels you've been led to expect, leaving you floundering about searching for the ninethly or seventeenthly that ought to be there but isn't.

Exclamation points are the most irritating of all. Look! they say, look at what I just said! How amazing is my thought! It is like being forced to watch someone else's small child jumping up and down crazily in the center of the living room shouting to attract attention. If a sentence really has something of importance to say, something quite remarkable, it doesn't need a mark to point it out. And if it is really, after all, a banal sentence needing more zing, the exclamation point simply emphasizes its banality!

Quotation marks should be used honestly and sparingly, when there is a genuine quotation at hand, and it is necessary to be very rigorous about the words enclosed by the marks. If something is to be quoted, the *exact* words must be used. If part of it must be left out because of space limitations, it is good manners to insert three dots to indicate the omission, but it is unethical to do this if it means connecting two thoughts which the original author did not intend to have tied together. Above all, quotation marks should not be used for ideas that you'd like to disown, things in the air so to speak. Nor should they be put in place around clichés; if you want to use a cliché you must take full responsibility for it yourself and not try to fob it off on anon., or on society. The most objectionable misuse of quotation marks, but one which illustrates the danger of misuse in ordinary prose, is seen in advertising, especially in advertisements for small restaurants, for example "just around the corner," or "a good place to eat." No single, identifiable, citable person ever really said, for the record, "just around the corner," much less "a good place to eat," least likely of all for restaurants of the type that use this type of prose.

The dash is a handy device, informal and essentially playful, telling you that you're about to take off on a different tack but still in some way connected with the present course—only you have to remember that the dash is there, and either put a second dash at the end of the notion to let the reader know that he's back on course, or else end the sentence, as here, with a period.

The greatest danger in punctuation is for poetry. Here it is necessary to be as economical and parsimonious with commas and periods as with the words themselves, and any marks that seem to carry their own subtle meanings, like dashes and little rows of periods, even semicolons and question marks, should be left out altogether rather than inserted to clog up the thing with ambiguity. A single exclamation point in a poem, no matter what else the poem has to say, is enough to destroy the whole work.

The things I like best in T.S. Eliot's poetry, especially in the *Four Quartets*, are the semicolons. You cannot hear them, but they are there, laying out the connections between the images and the ideas. Sometimes you get a glimpse of a semicolon coming, a few lines farther on, and it is like climbing a steep path through woods and seeing a wooden bench just at a bend in the road ahead, a place where you can expect to sit for a moment, catching your breath.

Commas can't do this sort of thing; they can only tell you how the different parts of a complicated thought are to be fitted together, but you can't sit, not even to take a breath, just because of a comma.

Discussion Questions

1. What does Thomas find praiseworthy about punctuation?
2. Why does Thomas rely so heavily on metaphor and simile in his descriptions of the various punctuation marks?
3. How does Thomas dramatize his assertion about the "wonderful ambiguity" of language in the essay?
4. Thomas assigns praise and blame to kinds of punctuation and also to people who use punctuation. What are the blameworthy ways of those who punctuate poorly?

Writing Activity

1. Write a ceremonial essay about some element of everyday life that is generally taken for granted.

Dazed and Bemused

LAURIE ANDERSON

Headnotes/Things to Look For

Laurie Anderson was born in Chicago, Illinois, in 1947. She attended Barnard College and also studied sculpture at Columbia. She came to prominence in the New York art scene of the 1970s as a performance artist, moving on to develop multimedia theatrical experiences combining video, music, and storytelling. Her work has been displayed at many museums in New York and Europe. She has made seven albums of songs, with her biggest hit being "O Superman."

Note the bemused conversational tone of this essay, as well as the digressions and asides, all of which gives the impression of Anderson relating the anecdotes to the reader in a Soho coffeehouse.

———————— ✦ ————————

IS ANYBODY THERE?

The first time I made contact with someone on a Web site was with a guy who said his interests were music and sand. And I said, "Sand?" I have a kind of special interest in sand. When I was on my first and only LSD trip, I went to the beach and I spent 12 hours lying there looking at grains of sand. I had decided to make a collection of the sand, and the idea was to choose six of the most perfect and representative grains—a project that took all day and well into the night. I still have this collection in a small box lined with velvet. And I took some pictures of it with an electron microscope and sent them to this guy at his Web site.

And it took a few days to discover that the person I was talking to was actually a 4-year-old kid and that his interest in sand was going out into his backyard and playing in his sandbox. And it was great—I would never have come up to this guy at a party and said, "Hey, let's talk music and sand."

POLLY-LINGUAL

I've always been fascinated by parrots. The whole idea of talking animals is so deeply creepy! Recently I made an animatronic parrot out of a tough but carvable plastic normally used to design car bodies. He's stuffed with electronics—a servomotor that turns his head and an envelope follower that allows the beak to synchronize with the words (a fanciful addition since parrots don't have lips). The voice is computer generated, so it's quite easy to make him talk: just type into the computer, add processing and you can hear the words immediately.

Out-of-the-box voices have names like Bruce, Agnes and Bubbles (who sounds as if she's drowning in a bathtub). They have a flat, almost Middle Western delivery that adds a melancholy, metallic flavor to my stories. Sometimes when I work with these voices, I have the illusion that I'm in touch with another intelligence, a wacky new life form. This happens only on good days, when all the systems are working. On bad days—when everything crashes and all the voices disappear—I start yelling at my computer, and then I think: "Wait a second. I might as well be talking to my electric pencil sharpener."

Writing the parrot's words was like finding a whole new voice. The computer's functions—shuffle modes, scrambles and trial-and-error methods—taught me a new way to write that culled and clipped words into a mad, jump-cut language, like songwriting, only stranger. So the parrot sits on its perch endlessly expounding and mulling: "I've been seeing dragons again. Yes, it's true. I don't like giving a nude woman a dollar. It's just my policy. So shoot me. That's just the way I see it. Maybe the batteries are running low. Here, let me take this pencil out of my mouth. And John Wayne begat Clint Eastwood begat Bruce Willis begat Brad Pitt. Heavy-duty hombres. Spin doctors of all kinds. O.K. Cut. Action!"

CONTROL FREAKS

I've been thinking about two well-known epic American stories, both about teams of people working in ships. The stories are "Star Trek" and "Moby-Dick"; the ships, the Enterprise and the Pequod. These stories are separated by more than 100 years, and although they have a lot in common—very long voyage, powerful captain, dangerous encounters, wild adventures—they couldn't be more different.

In the original "Star Trek" series, the ship is pretty high tech, and the immaculate workers are endlessly typing commands into their computers and talking into their headsets, presumably affecting the course of the ship somehow. But the person who's really in charge is up on the bridge. And the plot of each episode is virtually the same. Everybody's working away and suddenly the ship goes out of control for some reason or other and the captain starts yelling from the bridge: "I've lost control! I've lost control of the ship!" Losing control is the worst thing that can happen. And the whole plot of the story is how the captain regains control of the ship. It's no coincidence that the whole drama happens in the Control Room.

In "Moby-Dick," the ship is also pretty high tech by 19th-century standards, and there's the hard-working crew and the captain. Except in this ship the captain is completely crazy. What finally happens in "Moby-Dick" is pretty horrendous. The captain goes more or less insane, the ship is snapped in half, most of the crew drowns and the captain is dragged to the bottom of the ocean by the whale he has fanatically hunted. The end.

It's such an incredibly dark story. I mean, you can't imagine telling a story like that now. For example: the Enterprise explodes in a huge accident and all the debris from the wreck gets sucked into a black hole and in the last shot there's a single spaceman turning around, swinging around and around, alone in space. Call me Ishmael. The end.

BAD SOCKET CONNECTION

For the past year, I've been going to a lot of tech conferences, and there are all these computer people there and everyone's really excited about new media. There are seminars on E-cash, search engines and home shopping, and there are lots of demos of cyber-sex. In the demos a man and a woman sit at computers wearing skintight rubber suits wired up with sensors, and they punch in commands that shoot little shocks (zzzhsht!!) to the sensors.

> And she says: Can you feel my heartbeat? Can you feel my heartbeat?
> He says: Hold it! That's command X, then hit option and control at the same time. Wait a minute. Give me a second to figure it out.
> She says: Can you feel my heartbeat? Can you feel my heartbeat?
> He says: I'm getting a weird message on my screen. It just keeps saying I'm losing my connection. Bad socket connection.
> 15 She says: Can you feel my heartbeat? Can you feel my heartbeat?
> He says: Command R?

She says: No, not that one!
He says: Command F1 return.
She says: No, not that one!
20   She says: Shut down. Shut it down now.
He says: I'm trying, but I don't know how.
He says: It just keeps saying I'm losing my connection. Bad
socket connection. Check the power supply on your modem.
I don't know what's happening now. Domain name error.
You know what? I've got to go and get the manual.

BALZAC'S NIGHTMARE

I used to have a great writing room in my loft. It was coated with
several layers of spray-on slate. I could write on the wall, ceiling
and floor and erase things with my socks. Very satisfying. The
room is now a computer room, but I still love to make writing
that's large and physical. When I start a project, whether it's an
opera, a song or a film, I always start by drawing a big chart that
outlines what I want to do. I fill these charts with notes on color,
sketches, words and quotes connected by dotted lines to show
their relationships. I do this by hand rather than in the computer
because it's easier to see connections and direction. Handwriting
suggests what's missing from typing—it suggests the way things
might sound, the way words can turn into pictures and three-
dimensional objects.

One of these charts appears in the imaginary stage set on the
previous pages—"Balzac's Nightmare," so called because one of
the writer's darker mottoes ("Fame is the sun of the dead") lurks
there, along with one of my favorite observations by Gertrude
Stein (the United States is the oldest country in the world because
it's been in the 20th century longest). Words to remember when
working in the cold, speedy techno world.

WHY HUMANS WILL SURVIVE

Last summer I got a call from a media organization inviting me to
come to a very secret event that was being planned by an aero-
space company. They said they were going to launch the first civilian flight to the moon, and they wanted me to come along as a
kind of observer (a "content provider") to write about the experience. I couldn't believe it. I kept saying: "To the moon? To the
moon?" They said they couldn't tell me exactly where or when it

would be because security was very, very tight. They said, "We'll call you back, and we'd appreciate it if you didn't mention this to anyone." I said: "Of course, absolutely. You can count on me."

I hung up the phone and waited about five minutes. Then I called five friends and said, "You won't believe this, but I just got this call and I've been invited to go to the moon! And I told them about how the first civilian flights will be starting in four years and how they're going to orbit the moon in reusable crafts and that they have all these plans to build resorts and retirement colonies on the moon for old people who are losing their mobility. And how great it's going to be for handicapped people who will suddenly be able to do somersaults and free fall. And what the new zero-G sports will be like and the zero-G dance companies. And when I stopped talking, I just heard this silence on the other end of the line. I'm not sure any of my friends believed me. It's like after the big cold war race to the moon was over everybody just sort of forgot the moon was even up there.

Two weeks later they called again and said: "Liftoff is in approximately one month. So we want you to be more or less on alert. Can't tell you more." Click. And I thought, "Gee, shouldn't I be doing some sort of training for this?"

The next call was two days later. They said the flight was proceeding on schedule and that it was going to be a very important simulation. And I said; "What do you mean simulation? You mean we're not going up?" They said that actually this was not going to be an "active" launch and that they hoped there hadn't been any "misunderstanding." We were just going to sit on the ground in a capsule pretending we were going to the moon. But they emphasized that this was a really important scientific project because they wanted to know whether this flight could be considered a vacation. Would it be relaxing? Would people want to go more than once?

Anyway, I finally arrived at the simulated liftoff determined to have fun (or at least to analyze whether other people were having any). They were playing the theme from "2001" on a ghetto blaster, and the eight people chosen for the flight entered the craft, which was made of Sheetrock and plywood and blinking lights. I was part of a ring of observers that surrounded the ship. For four days we monitored the passengers' every move with microphones and cameras.

Every few minutes Mission Control would give them bits of information about where they supposedly were in space, and the flight crew kept giving them little jobs to do that had to be prefaced with the exact time: "O-400 hours. Humidity: nominal; pressure: nominal; thrust: .478." And they had to memorize all these paramilitary commands and rules and repeat specs on things like liquid nitrogen. Every two hours they were given questionnaires. Things like: Do you feel this is a good vacation so far? How do you feel about your fellow passengers? Has your opinion of them changed since the last questionnaire?

And it was all so incredibly claustrophobic. If you can imagine being trapped in a parked station wagon for four days with your family—answering questions every two hours about how much you liked them—that would give you an idea of the excitement level inside the capsule. Twenty minutes would go by and someone would say, "Do you want another Pop Tart?" "No, thanks."

Finally, after four days, the passengers came out of the capsule. The "2001" theme song was playing again. I thought they'd be in a bad mood after talking like automatons and following rules for four straight days. But instead they were all saying things like: "This experience in space has really changed my life. I just see things differently now. Just to be up there in the middle of all those stars. It was awesome. I felt so small. . . ."

And I thought: This is amazing! I'm seeing the incredible power of the human imagination. And this is why humans will survive. We'll survive because we're basically completely insane.

Discussion Questions

1. Anderson sneaks up on her theme, telling a series of stories that form a kind of kaleidoscopic view of how technology influences her life. What purpose does the opening anecdote about her first Web connection with "a guy who said his interests were music and sand" serve?

2. What kind of freedom does technology offer Anderson, as evidenced in her story of the animatronic parrot?

3. What does the last story about the simulated space flight argue about how humans interact with technology?

Writing Activity

1. Put together your own collection of connected anecdotes about your relationship to technology, with the aim of showing its benefits or drawbacks.

Why I Don't Meditate

ANNE LAMOTT

Headnotes/Things to Look For

Anne Lamott is known for her fiction and her autobiographical writing, as well as the writing manual Bird by Bird: Some Instructions on Writing and Life. *Other books include* Operating Instructions: A Journal of My Son's First Year, Traveling Mercies: Some Thoughts on Faith, Plan B: Further Thoughts on Faith, *and* Grace (Eventually): Thoughts on Faith.

Note how Jack Kornfield lurks at the edges of this piece of writing, as Lamott patiently develops her praise of him and the helpfulness of his ideas.

———————— ✦ ————————

I have been reading books on meditation with great enthusiasm since 1975, but have not quite gotten around to becoming a person who meditates. The only times I remember practicing with any regularity were during my drug days when I'd find myself awake at 4 or 5 A.M., which are the hours of the black dogs even under the best of circumstances. I remember lying in bed many nights after all the cocaine was gone, feeling and maybe looking like Bobcat Goldthwaithe, grinding away at my teeth like a horse, lockjawed, weepy, considering the wooden bedpost as a possible teething device, idly wondering what it would feel like to close my hands, slowly, around the sleeping boyfriend's throat. But all of a sudden I would start saying Hail Marys or a mantra, thousands of times in a row, to quiet my feral mind. It always worked, maybe not as effectively as a little something from the Schedule III column, but usually, at some point, I would be able to sleep.

Perhaps a purist would not consider this true meditation. At any rate, right around the time I got sober, I discovered the books of Jack Kornfield, who writes about meditation and compassion. And they were so wonderfully written and wise that I became utterly committed to meditating. To the idea of meditating. Now, while my commitment remains firm, I cannot actually report any real—what is the word?—progress. I still don't meditate. I still just pray like a mother, in the mofo sense of the word. My mind remains a bad neighborhood that I try not to go into alone.

But the last few times I've gone out on a book tour, Jack Kornfield has been waiting for me in various cities when I arrived. Maybe not exactly in the flesh, maybe a little bit more like the face of Jesus in a tortilla, but any port in a storm, right? And he's been a reliable birth coach who keeps showing up even when I am at my most narcissistic and mentally ill.

In a month or so, Sam and I will travel around from city to city by plane, and I will try to get people to like me and buy my books. I'll do readings and Sam will lie on his stomach in bookstores and draw. I'll talk about writing and Jesus and the new book, and discuss my personal problems at length, secretly trying to con my audience into having some sort of awakening—spiritual, creative—so that we can all save the world together, and Sam can grow up and have children and provide me with grandchildren. (Or Sam can grow and be as gay as a box of birds and provide me with someone who laughs at all my jokes and makes me nice snacks.) Sounds like fun, right?

But the problem, the reason I rely so on Jack, is that I do not travel well. Sam does, he thrives. He loves bookstores and hotels, which all have nice floors for drawing, and he loves Spectravision, and snacks from the mini-bar. He even likes flying. I, on the other hand, do not believe in flying, or at any rate, am deeply unclear on the concept. I believe that every plane I get on is doomed, and this is why I like to travel with Sam—so that if and when the plane goes down, we will at least be together, and almost certainly get adjoining seats in heaven—ideally, near the desserts.

Then when we do arrive safely at a bookstore, there are either hardly any people in the audience, at which point my thoughts naturally turn to suicide, or there are so many people, so expectant and so full of love, that it fills me with self-loathing, makes me just anxious as a cat. I start to see myself as a performer or a product, or a performer pitching a product, as if I'm up there at the podium trying to get people to buy a Veg-O-Matic. It's like the Martin Buber line from *I and Thou*: "This is the exalted melancholy of our age, that every Thou in our world must become an it." I become an it, with really, really bad nerves. I seek refuge in shutting down, in trying to hide behind my false self like it's some psychic Guard-All shield.

So this is where Jack has helped me more times than he can possibly be aware. When I first show up at each bookstore, I've usually either stopped breathing or am wheezing away like a dying asthmatic pug. But a number of times, something has nudged me over toward a copy or stash of Jack's books, and they whisper this subversive message to me: Breathe. Pay attention. Be kind. Stop grabbing. And I always end up feeling like I've somehow gotten a grip, or a little grippage, as the French say.

I was in St. Louis once in a bookstore where only ten people had shown up, and of course I was just a little bit disappointed. I peeked around a stack of books at those ten people and imagined mowing them down with an AK-47. I know that makes me sound a little angry, but I had jet lag, the self esteem of a prawn, and to top it off, I had stopped breathing. I sounded just like the English Patient. But it turned out I was standing in front of a shelf full of Jack's books. I opened one and read one sentence, words to the effect that life is so hard, how can we be anything but kind. It was as if God had reached down with God's magic wand, because I looked out at the crowd, which by then had swelled to twelve people—a third of them guilty, beaming employees of the bookstore—and I gave one of the most joyful talks of my life.

I have walked into tables while trying to hide from crowds and rows of empty seats, and knocked over stacks of his books. I was once handed one of his books to use as a tiny desk while autographing something for someone in Seattle. He keeps showing up when I need the message most, when I feel most like Mr. Magoo at the top of an unfinished high-rise, about to step into empty space but finding instead a girder rising up beneath my feet. I show up in crowded bookstores so stoned on myself and adrenaline that I could chase down an airplane, and I read about quietness, peace. I show up to a sea of empty metal chairs, and I read about the fullness of an open heart, and I'm suddenly a sea anemone unfurling her tendrils again, after the danger has passed.

Maybe what I like best about Jack's message is that it's so subversive. The usual message is that there are all kinds of ways for you to fill up, so you'll be strong and nourished and no one can get you; but when you're fortified, fortification by its very nature is braced, and can break. So you're still vulnerable, but now you're anxious and shamed too. You're going to be vulnerable anyway, because you're a small soft little human animal—so the only choice is whether you are most going to resemble Richard Nixon, with his neck jammed down into his shoulders, trying to figure out who to blame, or the sea anemone, tentative and brave, trying to connect, the formless fleshy blob out of which grows the frills, the petals.

It's pretty obvious stuff. And it's wonderful chutzpah not to be afraid of the obvious, to know it instead as a great teacher, to know that right behind the cliché is the original message. So many other people trick it out with draperies and garments and piercing glances; while Jack, in his simplicity and kindness, returns you to yourself; and maybe that's all we have. To know that the simple truth, of love, and the moment, is here to be passed around and around, like a polished stone from the sea, only because it is of itself, and for no other reason. You don't hang words onto it, and you don't need to, because it's got the great beauty and smoothness of having been whacked around for eons. It's beautiful in a muted way, beautiful through feeling, the way it's been smoothed and roughed up and relaxed on the shore, and you pick it up and feel the stasis, the beauty of something lifted out of its ordinary flow, that's gotten its beauty by being tossed about.

I got to meet him finally, just last month, introduced him at one of his readings. He had actually asked the bookstore if it could get me to introduce him, because he cares for me. I couldn't believe it. My heart soared like an eagle. But I showed up feeling self-conscious and anxious anyway. There was a huge crowd. Sam immediately lay on the floor in the back of the bookstore and began to draw. He's simple people. But I went up to the front of the bookstore and in this sort of gritchy, obsequious mood, introduced myself to Jack. You'd have to use the word luminous to describe him. One has the impression also of sandalwood, so smooth and brown, giving off a light, delicious spicy ancient smell. He looked at me with such affection that I might have been a child of his, one he hadn't seen in a while. I thought about all those times in other bookstores, when I was out there trying to get people to buy my book, and out of all that tension and lumpiness something graceful and baroque appeared. And this amazing thing happened: I felt lovely all of a sudden, in a goofy sort of way, exuberant and shy. Clingy scared old me made beautiful, made much more elegant than what's going on—all that self-consciousness and grasping—and I moved from Richard Nixon to a sea anemone, which is something I love. They're so funny and clownish, absurd and lovely, like a roomful of very young girls learning to ballet dance, all those long legs in white tights, or a boy lying on his stomach, drawing on the floor.

Discussion Questions

1. Look carefully at the opening paragraph. How does Lamott introduce herself through her word choice and references to faith and popular culture? What kind of person is she?

2. Writers who address issues of faith run the risk of alienating readers who don't share their beliefs. How does Lamott manage this challenge?
3. How does Lamott describe the substance of Jack Kornfield's teachings? How does her tone shift as the essay develops?

Writing Activity

1. Write about something serious in your life (faith, a family relationship), using humor to keep the reader connected to your exploration of this key element.

Observations on Gender (ceremonial rhetoric too)

Introduction

As noted earlier in the book, Murray Davis theorizes that humor often comes out of transposing elements of two separate systems—of value, of language, of motive—and creating a new logical relationship in which the separate systems form a new whole. The funny comes when the audience figures out the new order, putting together what they know of the two systems the comic has joined in an unexpected union. The laughter acknowledges the ingenuity of both the comic who orchestrates the making of a new reality and the audience savvy enough to get the joke (a variation on Addison's proposal to couch advice in fables).

Gender may be the most fundamental category we're assigned to, trumping religion, nationality, and allegiance to sports teams. With gender comes a comprehensive system, or structure, for understanding and being in the world. The selections in this chapter address the systems of gender, raising the question of whether there can be peace, or a new reality, for members of different and often opposed camps. H. L. Mencken claims that the gulf between the sexes is great, and that the best among us find ways to combine the strengths on both sides of the divide. Helen Rowland describes the challenges faced by bachelor women. Bill Cosby addresses how female and male ways of being can befuddle members of the other tribe, focusing on this conflict in the context of marriage, during which wedding vows can shatter against the actual day-to-day experience of living together.

Another source of gender-based comedy that Bergson would recognize is how gendered behavior can be predicted and thus ridiculed. The rest of the writers in this chapter focus on gender-specific ways of moving through life. Susan Allen Toth writes of going to the movies with different types of men, adjusting to their ways, while Emily Hiestand interacts with a series of men as well in her quest to outfit her car with neon. Marcia Aldrich deals with how hair can define a woman's identity.

From *In Defense of Women*

The Feminine Mind

H. L. MENCKEN

Headnotes/Things to Look For

Henry Louis Mencken (1880–1956) was an important American writer best known for his satirical approach to issues of the day. Influenced by earlier satirists and social critics Jonathan Swift and Mark Twain, Mencken wrote steadily for the Baltimore Sun *and later co-founded the journal* The American Mercury. *His books include* A Mencken Chrestomathy, Notes on Democracy, On Politics: A Carnival of Buncombe, *and* Treatise on Right and Wrong.

Note the tone Mencken uses in describing the group of which he is a member: men. The piece overall indulges in strong general assertions about both men and women, ascribing essential characteristics to both.

——————— ✦ ———————

THE MATERNAL INSTINCT

A man's women folk, whatever their outward show of respect for his merit and authority, always regard him secretly as an ass, and with something akin to pity. His most gaudy sayings and doings seldom deceive them; they see the actual man within, and know him for a shallow and pathetic fellow. In this fact, perhaps, lies one of the best proofs of feminine intelligence, or, as the common phrase makes it, feminine intuition. The mark of that so-called intuition is simply a sharp and accurate perception of reality, an habitual immunity to emotional enchantment, a relentless capacity for distinguishing clearly between the appearance and the substance. The appearance, in the normal family circle, is a hero, a magnifico, a demigod. The substance is a poor mountebank. The proverb that no man is a hero to his valet is obviously of masculine manufacture. It is both insincere and untrue: insincere because it merely masks the egotistic doctrine that he is potentially a hero to every one else, and untrue because a valet, being a fourth-rate man himself, is likely to be the last person in the world to penetrate his master's charlatanry. Who ever heard of a valet who didn't envy his master wholeheartedly? who wouldn't willingly change places with his master? who didn't secretly wish that he was his master? A man's wife labours under no such naïve folly. She may envy her husband, true enough, certain of his more soothing prerogatives and sentimentalities. She may envy him his masculine liberty of movement and occupation, his impenetrable complacancy, his peasant-like delight in petty vices, his capacity for hiding the harsh face of reality behind the cloak of romanticism, his general innocence and childishness. But she never envies him his puerile ego; she never envies him his shoddy and preposterous soul.

This shrewd perception of masculine bombast and make-believe, this acute understanding of man as the eternal tragic comedian, is at the bottom of that compassionate irony which passes under the name of the maternal instinct. A woman wishes to mother a man simply because she sees into his helplessness, his need of an amiable environment, his touching self-delusion. That ironical note is not only daily apparent in real life; it sets the whole tone of feminine fiction. The woman novelist, if she be skilful enough to arise out of mere imitation into genuine self-expression, never takes her heroes quite seriously. From the day of George Sand to the day of Selma Lagerlöf she has always got into her character study a touch of superior aloofness, of ill-concealed derision. I can't recall a single masculine figure created by a woman who is not, at bottom, a booby.

WOMEN'S INTELLIGENCE

THAT IT SHOULD still be necessary, at this late stage of the senility of the human race to argue that women have a fine and fluent intelligence is surely an eloquent proof of the defective observation, incurable prejudice, and general imbecility of their lords and masters. One finds very few professors of the subject, even among admitted feminists, approaching the fact as obvious; practically all of them think it necessary to bring up a vast mass of evidence to establish what should be an axiom. Even the Franco-Englishman, W. L. George, one of the most sharp-witted of the faculty, wastes a whole book upon the demonstration, and then, with a great air of uttering something new, gives it the humourless title of "The Intelligence of Women." The intelligence of women, forsooth! As well devote a laborious time to the sagacity of serpents, pickpockets, or Holy Church!

Women, in truth, are not only intelligent; they have almost a monopoly of certain of the subtler and more utile forms of intelligence. The thing itself, indeed, might be reasonably described as a special feminine character; there is in it, in more than one of its manifestations, a femaleness as palpable as the femaleness of cruelty, masochism or rouge. Men are strong. Men are brave in physical combat. Men have sentiment. Men are romantic, and love what they conceive to be virtue and beauty. Men incline to faith, hope and charity. Men know how to sweat and endure. Men are amiable and fond. But in so far as they show the true fundamentals of intelligence—in so far as they reveal a capacity for discovering the kernel of eternal verity in the husk of delusion and hallucination and a passion for bringing it forth—to that extent, at least, they are feminine, and still nourished by the milk of their mothers. "Human creatures," says George, borrowing from Weininger, "are never entirely male or entirely female; there are no men, there are no women, but only sexual majorities." Find me an obviously intelligent man, a man free from sentimentality and illusion, a man hard to deceive, a man of the first class, and I'll show you a man with a wide streak of woman in him. Bonaparte had it; Goethe had it; Schopenhauer had it; Bismarck and Lincoln had it; in Shakespeare, if the Freudians are to be believed, it amounted to downright homosexuality. The essential traits and qualities of the male, the hallmarks of the unpolluted masculine, are at the same time the hallmarks of the *Schafskopf*. The caveman is all muscles and mush. Without a woman to rule him and think for him, he is a truly lamentable spectacle: a baby with whiskers, a rabbit with the frame of an aurochs, a feeble and preposterous caricature of God.

It would be an easy matter, indeed, to demonstrate that superior talent in man is practically always accompanied by this feminine flavour—that complete masculinity and stupidity are often indistinguishable. Lest I be misunderstood I hasten to add that I do not mean to say that masculinity contributes nothing to the complex of chemico-physiological reactions which produces what we call talent; all I mean to say is that this complex is impossible without the feminine contribution—that it is a product of the interplay of the two elements. In women of genius we see the opposite picture. They are commonly distinctly mannish, and shave as well as shine. Think of George Sand, Catherine the Great, Elizabeth of England, Rosa Bonheur, Teresa Carreño or Cosima Wagner. The truth is that neither sex, without some fertilization by the complementary characters of the other, is capable of the highest reaches of human endeavour. Man, without a saving touch of woman in him, is too doltish, too naïve and romantic, too easily deluded and lulled to sleep by his imagination to be anything above a cavalryman, a theologian or a bank director. And woman, without some trace of that divine innocence which is masculine, is too harshly the realist for those vast projections of the fancy which lie at the heart of what we call genius. Here, as elsewhere in the universe, the best effects are obtained by a mingling of elements. The wholly manly man lacks the wit necessary to give objective form to his soaring and secret dreams, and the wholly womanly woman is apt to be too cynical a creature to dream at all.

Discussion Questions

1. How does Mencken describe the reality that women more accurately perceive than men? What elements of reality do women grasp more clearly, in Mencken's view?

2. What makes a man an "eternal tragic comedian," according to Mencken? In your own reading, have you encountered male characters created by women who are not, in Mencken's term, *boobies*?

3. Mencken ultimately notes the need to combine feminine and masculine qualities to achieve intelligence and even genius. What are the qualities that need to be combined?

Writing Activity

1. Write your own account of feminine and masculine qualities, or choose another set of opposed yet potentially complementary terms to bring into concert (vegetarians and carnivores, jocks and couch potatoes).

Reflections of a Bachelor Girl
HELEN ROWLAND

Headnotes/Things to Look For

Helen Rowland (1875–1950) was, in her time, a well-known humorist specializing in quotable quotes about the vexed relationships between women and men. Her books include The Widow; Reflections of a Bachelor Girl; A Guide to Men: Being Encore Reflections of a Bachelor Girl; If, A Chant for Wives *also* The White Woman's Burden; *and* The Rubaiyat of A Bachelor.

Rowland, like Oscar Wilde, relies on pithy, barbed statements, in this case to expose what she sees as the pitfalls in social interactions between women and men. Note how she shines a light on the reality of marriage separate from the romantic images, perhaps wielding the clear-eyed intellect Mencken ascribes to women.

✦

Kissing a girl, without first telling her that you love her, is as small and mean as letting a salesman take you for a free ride in an automobile when you have no intention of buying it.

Flinging yourself at a man's head is like flinging a bone at a cat; it doesn't fascinate him, it frightens him.

Men say they admire a woman with high ideals and principles; but it's the kind with high heels and dimples that a wife hesitates to introduce to her husband.

Never worry for fear you have broken a man's heart; at the worst it is only sprained and a week's rest will put it in perfect working condition again.

Nothing can exceed the grace and tenderness with which men make love—in novels—except the off-hand commonplaceness with which they do it in real life.

About the only sign of personal individuality that the average woman is allowed to retain after she marries is her toothbrush.

A man seldom discovers that he hasn't married his affinity until his wife begins to get crow's feet around the eyes.

Odd how a man always gets remorse confused with reform; a cold bath, a dose of bromo-selzer, and his wife's forgiveness will make him feel so moral that he will begin to patronize you.

Husbands are like the pictures in the anti-fat advertisements—so different before and after taking.

There are moments when the meanest of women may feel a sisterly sympathy for her husband's first wife.

A woman may have a great deal of difficulty getting married the first time, but after that it's easy, because where one man leads the others will follow like a flock of sheep.

When you see what some girls marry, you realize how they must hate to work for a living.

There is no such thing as a confirmed bachelor in the countries where harems are fashionable.

It isn't tying himself to one woman that a man dreads when he thinks of marrying; it's separating himself from all the others.

It's the men who are least particular about their own morals who are the most particular about a woman's; if Satan should come up here seeking a wife, he would probably demand an angel with gilt wings instead of a nice congenial little devil.

What do they know—about one another that makes every man who kisses a girl warn her so darkly and impressively not to trust any of the others?

Poverty is only a relative affair, after all; it is X minus the things you want.

The woman who is wedded to an art and also to a man pays the full penalty for that kind of bigamy.

Some men are born for marriage, some achieve marriage; but all of them live in the deadly fear that marriage is going to be thrust upon them.

A summer resort is a place where a man will resort to anything from croquet to cocktails for amusement and where a girl will resort to anything from a half-grown boy to an aged paralytic for an escort.

When a man becomes a confirmed old bachelor it is not because he has never met the one woman he could live with, but because he has never met the one woman he couldn't live without.

Don't fancy a man is serious merely because he treats you to French dinners and talks sentiment; wait until he begins to take you to cheap tables d'hôte and talks economy.

It is one of the mockeries of matrimony that the moment two people begin to be awfully courteous to one another round the house it is a sign they are awfully mad.

Discussion Questions

1. Rowland several times highlights the economic aspects of sex and marriage. To what degree have these elements decreased in importance in contemporary relationships? What, if anything, has taken their place?
2. In these brisk assertions Rowland doesn't display a high opinion of men. What does she advance as the keys to male motivation and behavior in their interactions with women?
3. A serious note is sounded when Rowland addresses the difficulty of being a woman "wedded to an art" as well as a man. Are these struggles still evident today? Are men just as prey to the challenges of balancing these dual commitments?

Writing Activity

1. Update Rowland's reflections on bachelorhood based on your own experiences.

Till Talk Do You Part

From *Love and Marriage*

BILL COSBY

Headnotes/Things to Look For

Bill Cosby, born in 1937, is one of America's best-loved comics. He has had great success on a series of television shows, beginning with I Spy *(in which he became one of the first African-Americans featured on a network show) and continuing to* The Bill Cosby Show *and finally* The Cosby Show. *His books include* Fatherhood, Time Flies, Love and Marriage, Childhood, *and* Cosbyology: Essays and Observations from the Doctor of Comedy. *Always concerned with social causes and education, he developed the cartoon series* Fat Albert and the Cosby Kids, *using his comic gifts to teach life lessons.*

Note the way Cosby dramatizes mini-scenes to convey his views of marriage. In his stand-up work, he was known for relying on character and action more than jokes, and the same strategies can be seen in his writing.

---- ✦ ----

In her endless effort to bring her husband out of the cave, the American wife will tell him, "The problem with you is you are not in touch with your feelings." She will tell him this right after he has tried to shotput his son to dramatize some parental point for which mere language lacked clarity. She will tell him this right after he has kicked in the television set as a fitting response to an overtime field goal against his home team. A man can spend an entire morning creatively running amuck; and when he is finished and the foam on his lips has dried, his wife will say, "The problem with you is you are not in touch with your feelings."

Although I'm not a psychologist (my doctorate is in education, my BA in the quarter-mile), it has always seemed to me that I am nicely in touch with my feelings, one of which is an urge to bounce pass the next woman who tells me I am not in touch with my feelings. Of course, what women often mean by this charge is that men don't know how to cry; but crying isn't always an indication of genuine feeling. If it were, then Jimmy Swaggart and Tammy Faye Bakker would be sensitivity's king and queen.

I sometimes think that women may be too involved in revelation, that perhaps a marriage is strained by just four words: not *The children aren't yours* but *How was your day?* It is often too much pressure on a man to ask him to keep giving the six o'clock news, especially when the only thing to report is the weather. What, for example, is a dentist to say when his wife inquires, *How was your day?*

I did six fillings, four root canals, and a small child spat in my eye.

Maybe the best answer a husband can give to *How was your day?* is *I spent it dreading that question.* Or maybe the husband should draw first and ask his *wife, How was your day?* Then, however, he is liable to hear the four grimmest words of all:

I had the children.

• • •

Camille never has to be a district attorney with me, for she has a way to learn what I'm thinking that even allows me to have a good meal.

"If I ever want to find out anything about you," she has said, "I'll invite five of your friends to dinner and just listen in."

By communicating indirectly, sometimes through a basketball team, Camille and I have been able to keep the mystery in our marriage, a quality that the marriage manuals consider important. Of course, these manuals say that communication is important too; and so, the answer seems to be that a couple should communicate mysteriously, each one making sure that the other rarely knows what he is talking about. Every time that Camille and I exchange *That's not what I'm* saying/*Then what's your* point?, we are moving further into foggy paradise.

In this happy pursuit of marital mystery, Camille and I sometimes *almost* have a conversation, but then she thinks better of the idea.

"I want to talk to you," she told me one evening in the kitchen.

"Fine," I said. "Let's do it right after I finish these chili dogs. I don't want to distract my mouth right now."

A few minutes later and a few pounds heavier, I walked into the living room, where she was standing by the fireplace, a stunning portrait of a great lady about to hold forth. I hoped I was equal to the subject. I hoped it was the Cleveland Browns.

"Here I am for the talking," I said. "What was it you wanted?"

"*You* know what I wanted," she replied. "Let's just leave it at that."

And she turned and went up to the bedroom, no doubt for a meeting with Godot.

Because Camille and I have wisely left each other in the dark so often, our marriage has been rich in surprise. It is an atmosphere in which my son can come to me and say, "Dad, I've decided I want to be more involved in politics."

"That's good," I reply.

"So I'm dropping out of college, changing my name to Raul, and joining the Contras."

"Then I guess you'll be wanting some advance allowance."

"Yes, please. Either pesos or traveler's checks."

"You know, this is . . . well, I guess you'd have to call it a surprise. *I* didn't know you wanted to become a Nicaraguan guerrilla. At least not this *semester*."

"Well, *Mom* has known it for months."

"She has?"

"Yes, she even says the Contras are the ideal group for me because I'm always against everything. Dad, if you and Mom did more talking, you'd be ready with a going-away present for me."

My son did not understand, however, that there is a method in the intermittent and semicoherent exchanges of information that Camille and I have: we are trying not to use up the conversation allotted to our marriage. Unaware that this conversational allotment governs every marriage, most young couples do not pace their tongues and suddenly find themselves in three-month lulls.

The next time you're in a restaurant, study some couple that seems to have been married for more than ten years. Watch them exchanging long desperate looks, each of them hoping that the numbing silence will be broken by a good grease fire or a holdup. And each of them is about to be driven to think the unthinkable: *We should have brought the children*.

• • •

Camille and I bring the children. In fact, people have said that we are prisoners of the children because we bring them everywhere we go, from Las Vegas to the South of France. However, I can recall six times in our marriage when we left the children home. *Seven* times if you count the night that Camille walked out on me and I went after her without bothering to get a sitter.

Nevertheless, I have to admit that whenever Camille has suggested that we go off without the children for longer than an hour and a half, I say either, "But it's always more *fun* with the children along" or "Just be patient, dear. In just nine or ten or fifteen years, they'll all be married or in the armed forces and then we'll have the house back. That's our reason to keep *living.*"

However, early one summer in our thirteenth year of marriage, my mother offered to stay with the children for a week so that Camille and I could go on a little vacation alone and recapture the magic of the honeymoon we had always planned to take. For a moment, I had considered having my mother take Camille for a week and letting *me* go off with the children, whose interests were closer to mine; but then I yielded to my yen for adventure and decided to see if Camille and I could make it alone, operating under the handicap of having to talk only to each other.

"Darling," I had said to her, "what would you say if I told you that we're going to take a vacation without the children?"

"I'd say you're a liar," she replied.

"And usually you'd be right, but my mother just offered to stay with them so we can get to know each other again—unless there's someone else you'd rather get to know."

"No, you'll do. But I thought you said it's always more fun with the kids along."

"So it won't be our greatest vacation, but at least it'll be all ours. Just the two of us, dancing away from Fat Albert."

As the moment of our departure approached, Camille and I conceived some rules for this romantic escapade:

- There could be no mention of the children.
- No photographs, tapes of cuteness, or report cards could be taken along.
- No one could become pregnant or in any other way involved with kids.

And so, one afternoon in July, we turned our two girls and our boy over to my mother and then drove out to a charming old inn on eastern Long Island. A few minutes after arriving, as I zipped up the back of Camille's dress before taking her to an elegant dinner, I said, "You look so young and lovely. No one could ever tell that you had two kid . . . um, kidneys. Sorry."

"That's okay," she said. "I miss them too, those precious kidneys. And that spleen."

"Courage," I said, "We can make it."

In the dining room, we found a corner table, where I sat down and began desperately trying to think of things to talk about. So far, I had two: the plight of the dollar and the plight of the whale. I would have to pace myself with them or my mouth would be retired before the soup.

After a silence of no more than five or ten minutes, I tenderly placed my hand on Camille's and said, "Have I ever told you, my darling, that they should let the dollar float?"

"How you *talk*, lover," she demurely replied.

"And speaking of floating, this is a tough time to be a whale, don't you think?"

She smiled helplessly, and then I said, "You look so young and lovely tonight."

"You've said that already, but I don't mind. If my loveliness is the bottom of your barrel, you can go with it for a day or two."

The pressure was getting to me now. How *could* parents keep themselves from talking about their children? I decided that there should be a clinic where addicts could taper off, first looking at photos of their own children, then gradually at someone else's, and finally at slides of vasectomies.

Once our appetizers came, we began to chew our way through a seemingly endless lull. I thought about my oldest daughter often telling me not to talk with a mouthful of food and I congratulated myself on avoiding a demerit from Camille by keeping the thought unexpressed.

"You know, the Owls could go all the way this year," I finally said.

"Some new migration?" she replied.

"The *Temple Owls*. All the way."

"That would be nice. All the way where?"

As a bird-watcher, Camille was no better than Denise. Was *any* woman wise enough to follow my Owls?

After the meal a romantic mood was upon us, so hand in hand we walked down to the beach under a sky full of stars. We went almost to the water's edge, and for four or five minutes nothing was said; but neither of us was trying now, for we both were transported by the awesome beauty of the universe. At last, however, from somewhere deep in my soul, a thought emerged and was given voice.

"Just think," I said. "At this very moment, under these very stars, a little Cosby is wetting the bed." And then I piteously cried, "Oh, honey, I *tried*! You don't *know* how I tried!"

"Don't hate yourself," she said. "I was just about to suggest that we gather some shells for them."

Discussion Questions

1. Cosby makes the case that men avoid talking. If his claim is true, what's left as the basis for marriage or any relationship?
2. What do you make of Cosby's assertion that couples should be careful "not to use up the conversation allotted to" their marriage? What does this suggest about communication between married people?
3. What roles do children play in Cosby's account of his family life?

Writing Activity

1. Write a series of scenes portraying an important relationship in your life, looking to illuminate patterns of behavior that may need correction.

Going to the Movies
SUSAN ALLEN TOTH

Headnotes/Things to Look For

Susan Allen Toth holds degrees from Smith and UC-Berkeley; her doctorate was earned at the University of Minnesota. She has taught English at San Francisco State College and Macalester College. Toth's books include the memoirs Blooming: A Small Town Girlhood *and* Ivy Days: Making My Way Out East. *Her essays have appeared in many journals and magazines.*

Note the episodic structure Toth utilizes in offering this collage of her dating experiences, all of which feature going to the movies.

--- ✦ ---

I

Aaron takes me only to art films. That's what I call them, anyway: strange movies with vague poetic images I don't understand, long dreamy movies about a distant Technicolor past, even longer black-and-white movies about the general meaninglessness of life. We do not go unless at least one reputable critic has found the cinematography superb. We went to *The Devil's Eye*, and Aaron turned to me in the middle and said, "My God, this is *funny*." I do not think he was pleased.

When Aaron and I go to the movies, we drive our cars separately and meet by the box office. Inside the theater he sits tentatively in his seat, ready to move if he can't see well, poised to leave if the film is disappointing. He leans away from me, careful not to touch the bare flesh of his arm against the bare flesh of mine. Sometimes he leans so far I am afraid he may be touching the woman on his other side instead. If the movie is very good, he leans forward too, peering between the heads of the couple in front of us. The light from the screen bounces off his glasses; he gleams with intensity, sitting there on the edge of his seat, watching the screen. Once I tapped him on the arm so I could whisper a comment in his ear. He jumped.

After *Belle de Jour*, Aaron said he wanted to ask me if he could stay overnight. "But I can't," he shook his head mournfully before I had a chance to answer, "because I know I never sleep well in strange beds." Then he apologized for asking. "It's just that after a film like that," he said, "I feel the need to assert myself."

II

Bob takes me only to movies that he thinks have a redeeming social conscience. He doesn't call them films. They tend to be about poverty, war, injustice, political corruption, struggling unions in the 1930s, and the military-industrial complex. Bob doesn't like propaganda movies, though, and he doesn't like to be too depressed either. We stayed away from *The Sorrow and the Pity*; it would be, he said, too much. Besides, he assured me, things are never that hopeless. So most of the movies we see are made in Hollywood. Because they are always very topical, these movies offer what Bob calls "food for thought." When we saw *Coming Home*, Bob's jaw set so firmly with the first half that I knew we would end up at Poppin' Fresh Pies afterward.

When Bob and I go to the movies, we take turns driving so no one owes anyone else anything. We park far away from the theater so we don't have to pay for a space. If it's raining or snowing, Bob offers to let me off at the door, but I can tell he'll feel better if I go with him while he parks, so we share the walk too. Inside the theater Bob will hold my hand when I get scared if I ask him. He puts my hand firmly on his knee and covers it completely with his own hand. His knee never twitches. After a while, when the scary part is past, he loosens his hand slightly and I know that is a signal to take mine away. He sits companionably close, letting his jacket just touch my sweater, but he does not infringe. He thinks I ought to know he is there if I need him.

One night after *The China Syndrome* I asked Bob if he wouldn't like to stay for a second drink, even though it was past midnight. He thought a while about that, considering my offer from all possible angles, but finally he said no. Relationships today, he said, have a tendency to move too quickly.

III

Sam likes movies that are entertaining. By that he means movies that Will Jones of the *Minneapolis Tribune* loved and either *Time* or *Newsweek* rather liked; also movies that do not have sappy love stories, are not musicals, do not have subtitles, and will not force him to think. He does not go to movies to think. He liked *California Suite* and *The Seduction of Joe Tynan*, though the plots, he said, could have been zippier. He saw it all coming too far in advance, and that took the fun out. He doesn't like to know what is going to happen. "I just want my brain to be tickled," he says. It is very hard for me to pick out movies for Sam.

When Sam takes me to the movies, he pays for everything. He thinks that's what a man ought to do. But I buy my own popcorn, because he doesn't approve of it; the grease might smear his flannel slacks. Inside the theater, Sam makes himself comfortable. He takes off his jacket, puts one arm around me, and all during the movie he plays with my hand, stroking my palm, beating a small tattoo on my wrist. Although he watches the movie intently, his body operates on instinct. Once I inclined my head and kissed him lightly just behind his ear. He beat a faster tattoo on my wrist, quick and musical, but he didn't look away from the screen.

When Sam takes me home from the movies, he stands outside my door and kisses me long and hard. He would like to come in, he says regretfully, but his steady girlfriend in Duluth wouldn't like it. When the *Tribune* gives a movie four stars, he has to save it to see with her. Otherwise her feelings might be hurt.

IV

I go to some movies by myself. On rainy Sunday afternoons I often sneak into a revival house or a college auditorium for old Technicolor musicals, *Kiss Me Kate, Seven Brides for Seven Brothers, Calamity Jane*, even, once, *The Sound of Music*. Wearing saggy jeans so I can prop my feet on the seat in front, I sit toward the rear where no one will see me. I eat large handfuls of popcorn with double butter. Once the movie starts, I feel completely at home. Howard Keel and I are old friends; I grin back at him on the screen, admiring all his teeth. I know the sound tracks by heart. Sometimes when I get really carried away I hum along with Kathryn Grayson, remembering how I once thought I would fill out a formal like that. Skirts whirl, feet tap, acrobatic young men perform impossible feats, and then the camera dissolves into a dream sequence I know I can comfortably follow. It is not, thank God, Bergman.

If I can't find an old musical, I settle for Hepburn and Tracy, vintage Grant or Gable, on adventurous days Claudette Colbert or James Stewart. Before I buy my ticket I make sure it will all end happily. If necessary, I ask the girl at the box office. I have never seen *Stella Dallas* or *Intermezzo*. Over the years I have developed other peccadilloes: I will, for example, see anything that is redeemed by Thelma Ritter. At the end of *Daddy Long Legs* I wait happily for the scene where Fred Clark, no longer angry, at last pours Thelma a convivial drink. They smile at each other, I smile at them, I feel they are smiling at me. In the movies I go to by myself, the men and women always like each other.

Discussion Questions

1. How would you describe the types represented by Aaron, Bob, and Sam? What aspects of their behavior make them comic figures?
2. How do the vignettes lay out a continuum of relationships in which Toth participates? Are any of the relationships happy ones?
3. What's different about the final vignette in terms of how Toth relates to the movies she goes to see on her own? How would you describe her relationship to the movies?

Writing Activity

1. Write a series of vignettes describing an action that you repeat with different people, or at different times of the year, or at different times in your life.

Neon Effects

EMILY HIESTAND

Headnotes/Things to Look For

Emily Hiestand, who publishes in a range of genres including non-fiction and poetry, has won many writing awards, including The Whiting Writers Award, The Pushcart Prize, *the National Magazine Award, the National Poetry Series prize, and* The Nation/Discovery Award. *Her work has appeared in* The Atlantic Monthly, The New Yorker, The Nation, Salon, *and literary journals including* The Georgia Review *and* Partisan Review. *She is also a successful photographer and communications consultant.*

Note how Hiestand develops a picture of the neon culture, incorporating gender expectations and interactions into the story she tells.

———————— ✦ ————————

At times all I need is a brief glimpse, an opening in the
midst of an incongruous landscape, a glint of lights in the
fog, the dialogue of two passersby . . . and I think that,
setting out from there, I will put together, piece by piece,
the perfect city, made of fragments . . . of signals . . .

—ITALO CALVINO, INVISIBLE CITIES

"DO YOU WANT to know what I think?" Tommy asks, mildly and
not rhetorically but offering his customer the small window
of free will, the chance to *not know* what already burdens
Tommy's superior automotive mind.

What Tommy Hoo thinks has rarely been apparent in the
eight years that he and Steve Yuen and their pals at Nai Nan Ko
Auto Service have cared for my Subaru three-door coupe. No,
normally one must urge Tommy and Steve to say what they think,
posing brutally direct questions: "Do I need a new battery before
winter or not?" "Is the gurgle in the transmission trouble or not?"
Even when Tommy and Steve do answer, they convey a sense that
the jury is still out on the beloved Western idea "cause and effect."
They have a bone-deep respect for the contingency of all things,

and have never before actually volunteered a definitive opinion. It is an unprecedented moment in our relationship.

"Do you want to know what I think?"

"Yes, yes," I murmur.

Encouraged, my mechanic declares, firmly and unambiguously, "Don't put it on your car."

What I want to put on my car came as a gift from my husband, Peter, who was with me the palmy summer night that I saw a medium-size UFO floating down Brighton Avenue, hovering on a cushion of clear blue light that came billowing from underneath the craft—an airy, etherealizing light, shedding a serene glow over the asphalt road and its scurrying film of detritus. Some of us have been half-hoping for this all our lives, those of us who as children crept out after bedtime on summer nights, who stood in our backyards barefoot in the mowed grass to look up at the implacable dark glittering. And we have been well prepared for the moment in the close of darkened movie theatres; the special effects teams of Spielberg and Lucas have taught us, shown us, how to experience an encounter. We grow quiet, we suspend yet more disbelief, we feel a naïve awe and a shiver of fear as the Mother Ship appears, huge and resplendent with lights beyond our ken, and again when the fragile, more-advanced-than-us beings step out into our atmosphere. But we think it will happen far away—if it happens at all—in a remote desert, on some lonely country road, to someone else. We are not prepared for this astonishment to visit our own city street, to glide publicly past the Quickie Suds and Redbone's Bar-B-Que. Now Peter has pulled up close to the hovercraft and I can see inside its glowing body. There, not abducted, are two teenage boys such as our own planet produces.

"It's a Camaro," Peter says.

It is. A late model silver Camaro to which the boys have Done Something—something that washed over me, as Philip Larkin said of jazz, the way love should, "like an enormous yes."

And now Tommy has said, "Don't put it on your car," pronouncing where Tommy has never before pronounced.

• • •

"It" is two neon tubes which mount on the underside of a car and create a ravishing fusion of color and light whenever you flick a switch on the dashboard. The effect—"The Ultimate Effect" it says on the package—is produced by an underbody lighting kit that consists of the neon tubes, mounting hardware, and a fat wad of wiring.

This kit is one of the thousands of devices collectively known as "automotive aftermarket products": sound systems, sunroofs, drinkholders, mudflaps, seat covers, carpeting, coats for nose grills, and ice machines. (And, I like to think, bud vases.) One nice thing about the genre of aftermarket products is that it opens up what might have otherwise seemed closed and finite. Implicit in every aftermarket product is the idea that a vehicle is never a *fait accompli*; rather, its manufacturer has merely stopped fabrication at a reasonable point and has delivered a work-in-progress—a canvas.

The present canvas has the contour of a lithe sedan, but within that contour lies a hatchback that gives the sleek sedan the carrying capacity of a pickup truck. The rear window is a marvel of the glassmaker's art, an immense, gently curving expanse that arcs snugly over the chassis like the canopy of an F-16 over its Blue Angel. I have come with this car and the kit to Tommy and Steve because I trust them, and because their shop is so nearby that I can walk over whenever Tommy calls to say "You *cah* is ready," in his crisp, then soft, muscular speech that accents unexpected syllables, often with a faint gust of air—the sounds and emphases of Chinese overlaying English and giving it a gently pneumatic texture.

It helps to be able to *walk* to the garage of an auto mechanic whose wall is covered with letters of praise and satisfaction. It is one of the village-scale civilities that can be found in the urban world, a place that can be an impersonal tale, not least because of the automobile itself, the ways it reconfigures lives, flattens the depth of space, blurs time. So I don't want to go to another mechanic across town. I want to work with Tommy and Steve on this. When we talked over the telephone, Tommy had said, "No, we don't do that." And then he paused and asked, "Is it a *pinstripe?*" and, as always, his tone conveyed that we were only beginning, together, to enter into another automotive mystery.

Seeing the opening, I replied, "Oh no, it's not a pinstripe, it's just a couple of neon tubes mounted on the undercarriage. I could almost do it myself." (An outrageous lie if taken literally, but Tommy took my meaning: that the operation would be child's play for his shop.) "But there *is* some wiring to hook up, and I wouldn't want to mess with the electrical system."

"No, we don't do that."

I didn't say anything, and then Tommy said, "Why don't you bring over. We will take look."

• • •

One look at the kit, however, and Tommy and Steve are dead against it, and the reason is rust. "Rust," they intone together, as clerics of old must have said "Grim Reaper"—capitals implied in bitter homage. Here is the problem: to install the Ultimate Effect, a row of holes must be drilled on the undercarriage of the car, and this, my clerics believe, is an open invitation to the corroding enemy. Moreover, on this car the rocker panels offer the only site on which to mount tubes, which fact gives us reason to say "rocker panels" several times (and me to remember a charged scene in *The French Connection*), but it must not be a good thing because the faces of Tommy and Steve remain glum.

The men also point out that the kit instructions say: IF YOUR AREA EXPERIENCES SNOW AND ICY CONDITIONS, YOU MUST REMOVE THE SYSTEM BEFORE THE WINTER SEASON. Needless to say, New England experiences these conditions, yet it would seem simple enough to remove neon tubes each November and re-mount them in April (dark when Persephone descends, illuminated when she rises). But Tommy notes that no quick-release clamp system is provided with the kit, and points out that he is not inclined to jury-rig one.

"Half-hour to take off, half-hour to install. Each time," he says funereally.

The two mechanics and I stand and look at one another politely, the current automotive mystery now fully declared. After another moment Tommy says softly, kindly, "Miss *Hies*tan', this will not add to the *value* of *you cah.*"

After a long moment peering at each other as across a gulf, I venture an explanation.

"It's for fun," I say.

"For fun," Nai Nan Ko's mechanics repeat slowly, skeptically. And then, nimbly, before my very eyes, they begin to absorb the new concept.

"For fun," they say to each other. And now they are smiling and trying very hard not to smile, nearly blushing and bashful, and unable to look at me directly. We have unexpectedly stepped over into some new and intimate territory.

• • •

Upon reflection, one knows why these men did not consider fun at the first. Commonly I appear, as all their customers do, in a stoic, braced attitude awaiting the estimate, or later in miserly ponderings: Can the brake repair be put off a few weeks? (No.) Would a less expensive battery be okay? (No.) Fun has not come up during our eight years of dealings, not once. And now optional tubes that cost a bundle to install, tubes that tempt fate, that add no value, do not strike Tommy and Steve as barrels of it.

In the new silence that steals over us as we stand about the neon kit, I mention that it is a gift from my husband, that I will have to talk with him about the rust problem. At this piece of information, the situation transforms. Immediately, Tommy and Steve are smiling at me directly and sympathetically, relieved to be able to believe that I am on a wifely errand of humoring. In a near jolly mood, Steve stows the kit in the trunk of my car, and when last I see the two mechanics they are huddled, brooding happily under the raised hood of a banged-up Civic.

I am also left to brood. Here is dull old duality, posing its barbaric polarity: radiant swoon or structural integrity. Shrinking from the horrible choice, it occurs to me that someone must know how to do this, that the fine mechanics of Nai Nan Ko may simply not know the tricks that New England's custom shops have devised to deal with neon and rust, neon and winter, even as MIT's particle physicists do not necessarily know how to keep a cotton-candy machine from jamming. Sure enough, Herb, at the Auto Mall in Revere, knew all about neon effects.

"Four tubes or two? For two tubes, lady, that will be three hours, a hundred and fifty to install." And he is emphatic about rust, roaring out "No problem!" One of America's mantras and a phrase that wants a whole essay for itself.*

"None at all?" I persist. "Won't the holes allow water to seep in, especially during the winter when the tubes are out?"

"Well, sure," Herb replies peevishly, "a little water is going to get in, but it's not going to rot out right away, maybe in the *future* or sometime. Hold on a minute, lady. Eddie!" Herb calls into his

---

*Glancingly, one can say of "No problem!" that its subtext is often a radical laissez-faire-ism, the speaker's Mr. Magoo-esque state of mind, which triggers a semantic backfire, making you think, this guy may not only *not* solve any existing problem, he may cause an entirely new one. The term is also used now in situations where previously a speaker would have been expected to say "You're welcome." And this second usage creates a curious sensation, introducing into the exchange of simple courtesies the idea of some problem, albeit one that is, for the moment, absent.

shop. "That guy with the black Saturn gets his CD-changer installed in the trunk." Then back to me. "Where were we?"

"About the underbody rusting," I prompt, but greatly savoring the sound of Herb's Future—a place where rust *does* occur but whose temporal locus is so indeterminate as to make precautions about it absurd.

"See," says Herb, "I use a non-acid silicon sealant and we prime the holes with a primer."

Pressing the harried Herb one more degree, I ask if he has devised a quick-release system for the tubes for winter removal.

"Naah," Herb replies. "I've never taken one off. They just leave 'em on."

"Really?" I ask. "But these instructions say that ice and snow destroys the neon tubes."

"Yeah, maybe," says Herb. "But I've never taken them off for anybody. *Nobody* takes them off in the winter." As an afterthought, he adds, "And that's when they get wrecked."

And that's when they get wrecked. In a tone that means, Winter is the time, lady, when neon tubes on cars are *supposed* to get wrecked, Ecclesiastically speaking.

"Anything else?" Herb asks.

• • •

About the time that our ground begins to relax into spring, Annie, the tango dancer, tells me about Bigelow Coachworks. Annie has a leonine shock of gold hair, a closet full of swirly skirts, and a collection of vintage Fiestaware. She dances the slow Argentine-style tango and I felt sure that her word about neon customizers would be trustworthy. The first thing I notice about Bigelow Coachworks (other than it being named coachworks) is that the shop is immaculate. Not one oil-soaked rag. Inside the office there is a counter and a young woman behind it whose strawberry blond hair has been teased and sprayed into what used to be called a beehive. For neon, the young woman says, I must talk with Jim Jr.

No sooner have I said the word "neon" than Jim Jr., who has the palest kind of amber eyes, has plunged into the issues: First, the switch and ways it can be wired—into the headlights or parking lights, or independently onto the dash. The independent switch is a problem, Jim says, because you can forget to turn it off and drain your battery. Next, do I want two tubes or four? Two is plenty in Jim Jr.'s opinion; in fact, having no rear-mounted tube avoids the messy matter of plastic cases melted by the exhaust pipe. Now the mounting. Am I aware that the tubes aren't really made for New England winters? And do I know that the kits don't come with dismounting hardware? Do I know that Jim has engineered custom clamps that stay in place and make it easy to pop the tubes in and out with the seasons? As for rust, a touch of silicon on each screw will suffice.

It is a virtuoso romp, all the nuts and bolts of the neon sublime known and mastered by Jim, who has installed some fifteen systems, including, he says with a shy smile, the one on his own truck. My man. Jim Jr. levels with me about the thirty-six-inch tubes.

"These are going to give a *lame* effect," he says, examining the kit. "There isn't enough *juice* here for the effect we want."

Fortunately, the fifty-four-inch tubes for the effect we do want can be had right up the street, at Ellis The Rim Man's Auto Parts store, a temple to the aftermarket product where a beefy salesman shows me the selection (all made by the Rodriguez brothers) and then says, in the tone of a man who wants to have a clear conscience,

"You know, it's really dying out."

"Dying?"

"I think the kids just got tired of being harassed by the police." The salesman now pauses, glances at the two young salesclerks at the counter, and clues me in: "It's only boys who buy this stuff—you know, ethnics, Hispanic boys."

As the present contradiction occurs to him, he studies me evenly.

When the young men at the counter see what I am buying, one of them asks politely, "Is this for your son?"

My son, I think, not the least insulted, only feeling the sudden sensation of having one, and being the kind of mother who would get a top-of-the-line neon kit for him.

"No, it's for me," I say, smiling.

"Al-*right*," the boys say, and shoot me the hubba-hubba look. Now they want to talk neon.

"*Si, si*," of course they have it on their *caros*. Enrique has green and José has aqua. They have neon *inside* their cars too— under the dash, on their gear shift knobs. The store has a demonstration model. José gets it out, plugs it in; we stand around it to ogle the colored coils zooming around inside the clear plastic handle.

What do Enrique and José like about having neon on their cars? What *don't* they like! It's way *chevere*, way cool, it's like being inside a nightclub! Man, it lights up your whole body and everything you go by, and makes things look really, really bright. When José and Enrique hear that I saw my first neon car near the store, they cry out in unison.

"That was *us!*"

"You drive a silver Camaro?"

"Oh, no" they cry again, just as pleased. "Oh, no, that *wasn't* us, that was Alberto. That's Alberto's spaceship!"

Now they want to tell me something way-way *chevere:* the festival is coming. That's where we can see all the best neon cars and also the low-riders slow-dancing their cars down the road, each spotless vehicle also booming with salsa.

"So neon hasn't died out?"

"No way," gapes Enrique, incredulous at the thought. Wait and see! Much lighting-up in the streets before summer is over.

The boys hold the door as I exit the showroom—carrying a long cardboard box of glass, transformer, and rare gas under my arm. They step out with me onto the broad sidewalk of our city's Commonwealth Avenue. It is about nine at night, July, prime time, and while we are standing there a boy that Enrique knows comes billowing by in a Cougar with some brand-new magenta light to spill. He creeps almost to a stop.

"*Hola!*" he calls.

"*Hola!*" the boys call back. "*Que lindo se ve.* How nice it looks. *Que bufiao! Miraeso.* Look at that. *Ooouuu, la luz.*"

Discussion Questions

1. Like Toth, Hiestand sets up her essay as a series of interactions. How does Hiestand describe her relationship with Tommy and Steve, her long-time mechanics? How does the relationship shift when Hiestand reveals her motive for installing neon on her car?

2. How does Hiestand's relationship with the second mechanic, Herb, differ from the relationship with Tommy and Steve?

3. In the final section of the essay, when Hiestand encounters first Jim and then José and Enrique, how does she add cultural differences to the gender dynamics of the story?

Writing Activity

1. Describe your experience with an activity or hobby that is generally associated with one gender or some other particular group.

Hair

MARCIA ALDRICH

Headnotes/Things to Look For

Marcia Aldrich is a member of the faculty at Michigan State University, where she teaches creative writing and has also directed the creative writing program. Her books include Girl Rearing: Memoir of a Girlhood Gone Astray, *a collection of linked essays, and* Impromptu Mourner. *Her work has appeared in* The Best American Essays *and many literary journals including* The Seneca Review, The Best of Brevity, *and* Nerve.

Note how Aldrich describes a focus on hair particular to women of a certain time and socioeconomic class, although she also demonstrates that the daughters of such women must craft their own relationships with their hair.

✦

I've been around and seen the Taj Mahal and the Grand Canyon and Marilyn Monroe's footprints outside Grauman's Chinese Theater, but I've never seen my mother wash her own hair. After my mother married, she never washed her own hair again. As a girl and an unmarried woman—yes—but, in my lifetime, she never washed her hair with her own two hands. Upon matrimony, she began weekly treks to the beauty salon where Julie washed and styled her hair. Her appointment on Fridays at two o'clock was never cancelled or rescheduled; it was the bedrock of her week, around which she pivoted and planned. These two hours were indispensable to my mother's routine, to her sense of herself and what, as a woman, she should concern herself with—not to mention their being her primary source of information about all sorts of things she wouldn't otherwise come to know. With Julie my mother discussed momentous decisions concerning hair color and the advancement of age and what could be done about it, hair length and its effect upon maturity, when to perm and when not to perm, the need to proceed with caution when a woman desperately wanted a major change in her life like dumping her husband or sending back her newborn baby and the only change she could effect was a change in her hair. That was what Julie called a "dangerous time" in a woman's life. When my mother spoke to Julie, she spoke in conspiratorial, almost confessional, tones I had never heard before. Her voice was usually tense, on guard, the laughter forced, but with Julie it dropped much lower, the timbre darker than the upper-register shrills sounded at home. And most remarkably, she listened to everything Julie said. As a child I was puzzled by the way my mother's sense of self-worth and mood seemed dependent upon how she thought her hair looked, how the search for the perfect hairstyle never ended. Just as Mother seemed to like her latest color and cut, she began to agitate for a new look. The cut seemed to have become a melancholy testimony, in my mother's eyes, to time's inexorable passage. Her hair never stood in and of itself; it was always moored to a complex set of needs and desires her hair couldn't in itself satisfy. She wanted her hair to illuminate the relationship between herself and the idea of motion while appearing still, for example. My mother wanted her hair to be fashioned into an event with a complicated narrative past. However, the more my mother attempted to impose a hairstyle pulled from an idealized image of herself, the more the hairstyle seemed to be at odds with my mother. The more the hairstyle became substantial, the more the woman underneath was obscured. She'd riffle through women's magazines and stare for long dreamy hours at a particular woman's coiffure. Then she'd ask my father in an artificially casual voice: "How do you think I'd look with really short hair?" or "Would blonde become me?" My father never committed himself to an opinion. He had learned from long experience that no response he made could turn out well; anything he said would be used against him, if not in the immediate circumstances, down the line, for my mother never forgot anything anyone ever said about her hair. My father's refusal to engage the "hair question" irritated her.

So too, I was puzzled to see that unmarried women washed their own hair, and married women, in my mother's circle at least, by some unwritten dictum never touched their own hair. I began studying before and after photographs of my mother's friends. These photographs were all the same. In the pre-married mode, their hair was soft and unformed. After the wedding, the women's hairstyles bore the stamp of property, looked constructed from grooming talents not their own, hairstyles I'd call produced, requiring constant upkeep and technique to sustain the considerable loft and rigidity—in short, the antithesis of anything I might naively call natural. This was hair no one touched, crushed, or ran fingers through. One poked and prodded various hair masses back into formation. This hair presented obstacles to embrace, the scent of the hair spray alone warded off man, child, and pests.

I never saw my father stroke my mother's head. Children whimpered when my mother came home fresh from the salon with a potent do. Just when a woman's life was supposed to be opening out into daily affection, *the* sanctioned affection of husband and children, the women of my mother's circle encased themselves in a helmet of hair not unlike Medusa's.

In so-called middle age, my mother's hair never moved, never blew, never fell in her face: her hair became a museum piece. When she went to bed, she wore a blue net, and when she took short showers, short because, after all, she wasn't washing her hair and she was seldom dirty, she wore a blue plastic cap for the sake of preservation. From one appointment to the next, the only change her hair could be said to undergo was to become crestfallen. Taking extended vacations presented problems sufficiently troublesome to rule out countries where she feared no beauty parlors existed. In the beginning, my parents took overnighters, then week jaunts, and thereby avoided the whole hair dilemma. Extending their vacations to two weeks was eventually managed by my mother applying more hair spray and sleeping sitting up. But after the two week mark had been reached, she was forced to either return home or venture into an unfamiliar salon and subject herself to scrutiny, the kind of scrutiny that leaves no woman unscathed. Then she faced Julie's disapproval, for no matter how expensive and expert the salon, my mother's hair was to be lamented. Speaking just for myself, I had difficulty distinguishing Julie's cunning from the stranger's. In these years my mother's hair looked curled, teased, and sprayed into a waved tossed monument with holes poked through for glasses. She believed the damage done to her hair was tangible proof she had been somewhere, like stickers on her suitcases.

My older sisters have worked out their hair positions differently. My oldest sister's solution has been to fix upon one hairstyle and never change it. She wants to be thought of in a singular fashion. She may vary the length from long to longer, but that is the extent of her alteration. Once, after having her first baby, the "dangerous time" for women, she recklessly cut her hair to just below the ear. She immediately regretted the decision and began growing it back as she walked home from the salon, vowing not to repeat the mistake. Her signature is dark, straight hair pulled heavily off her face in a large silver clip, found at any Woolworth's. When one clip breaks, she buys another just like it. My mother hates the timelessness of my sister's hair. She equates it with a refusal to face growing old. My mother says. "It's immature to wear your hair the same way all your life." My sister replies,

"It's immature to never stop thinking about your hair. If this hairstyle was good enough when I was twenty, it's good enough when I'm forty, if not better."

"But what about change?" my mother asks.

"Change is overrated," my sister says flipping her long hair over her shoulder definitively. "I feel my hair."

My other sister was born with thin, lifeless, nondescript hair: a cross she has had to bear. Even in the baby pictures, the limp strands plastered on her forehead in question marks wear her down. Shame and self-effacement are especially plain in the pictures where she posed with our eldest sister, whose dark hair dominates the frame. She's spent her life attempting to disguise the real state of her hair. Some years she'd focus on style, pulling it back in ponytails so that from the front no one could see there wasn't much hair in the back. She tried artless, even messy styles—as if she had just tied it up any old way before taking a bath or bunched it to look deliberately snarled. There were the weird years punctuated by styles that looked as if she had taken sugar water and lemon juice and squeezed them onto her wet hair and then let them crystallize. The worst style was when she took her hair and piled it on the top of her head in a cone shape and then crimped the ponytail into a zigzag. Personally, I thought she had gone too far. No single approach solved the hair problem, and so now, in maturity, she combines the various phases of attack in hope something will work. She frosts both the grey strands and the pale brown, and then perms for added body and thickness. She's forced to keep her hair short because chemicals do tend to destroy. My mother admires my sister's determination to transform herself, and never more than in my sister's latest assault upon middle age. No one has known for many years nor does anyone remember what the untreated color or texture of either my mother's or my sister's hair might be.

As the youngest by twelve years, there was little to distract Mother's considerable attention from the problem of my hair. I had cowlicks, a remarkable number of them, which like little arrows shot across my scalp. They refused to be trained, to lie down quietly in the same direction as the rest of my hair. One at the front insisted on sticking straight up while two on either side of my ears jutted out seeking sun. The lack of uniformity, the fact that my hair had a mind of its own, infuriated my mother and she saw to it that Julie cut my hair as short as possible in order to curtail its wanton expression. Sitting in the swivel chair before the mirror while Julie snipped, I felt invisible, as if I was unattached to my hair.

Just when I started to menstruate, my mother decided the battle plan needed a change, and presto, the Page boy replaced the pixie. Having not outgrown the thicket of cowlicks, Mother bought a spectrum of brightly colored stretch bands to hold my hair back off my face. Then she attached thin pink plastic curlers with snap on lids to the ends of my hair to make them flip up or under, depending on her mood. The stretch bands pressed my hair flat until the very bottom, at which point the ends formed a tunnel with ridges from the roller caps—a point of emphasis, she called it. Coupled with the aquamarine eyeglasses, newly acquired, I looked like an overgrown insect that had none of its kind to bond with.

The women in my family divide into two general groups: those who fasten upon one style, become identified with a look, and are impervious to change, weathering the years steadfastly, and those who, for a variety of reasons, are in the business of transforming themselves. In my sister's case, the quest for perfect hair originates in a need to mask her own appearance; in my mother's case, she wants to achieve a beauty of person unavailable in her own life story. Some women seek transformation, not out of dissatisfaction with themselves, but because hair change is a means of moving along in their lives. These women create portraits of themselves that won't last forever, a new hairstyle will write over the last.

Since my mother dictated my hair, I never took a stand on the hair issue. In maturity, I'm incapable of assuming a coherent or consistent philosophy. I have wayward hair: it's always becoming something else. The moment it arrives at a recognizable style, it begins to undo itself, it grows, the sun colors it, it waves. When one hair pin goes in, another seems to come out. Sometimes I think I should follow my oldest sister—she claims to never give more than a passing thought to her hair and can't see what all the angst is about. She asks, "Don't women have better things to think about than their hair?"

I bite back: "But don't you think hair should reflect who you are?"

"To be honest, I've never thought about it. I don't think so. Cut your hair the same way, and lose your self in something else. You're distracted from the real action."

I want to do what my sister says, but when I walk out into shoplined streets, I automatically study women's hair and always with the same question: How did they arrive at their hair? Lately, I've been feeling more and more like my mother. I hadn't known how to resolve the dilemma until I found Rhonda. I don't know if I found Rhonda or made her up. She is not a normally trained hairdresser: she has a different set of eyes, unaffected. One day while out driving around to no place in particular, at the bottom of a hill, I found: "Rhonda's Hair Salon—Don't Look Back" written on a life-size cardboard image of Rhonda. Her shop was on the top of this steep orchard planted hill, on a plateau with a great view that opened out and went on forever. I parked my car at the bottom and walked up. Zigzagging all the way up the hill, leaning against or sticking out from behind the apple trees were more life-sized cardboard likenesses of Rhonda. Except for the explosive sunbursts in her hair, no two signs were the same. At the bottom, she wore long red hair falling below her knees and covering her entire body like a shawl. As I climbed the hill, Rhonda's hair gradually became shorter and shorter, and each length was cut differently, until when I reached the top, her head was shaved and glistening in the sun. I found Rhonda herself out under one of the apple trees wearing running shoes. Her hair was long and red and looked as if it had never been cut. She told me she had no aspirations to be a hairdresser, "she just fell into it." "I see hair," she continued, "as an extension of the head and therefore I try to do hair with a lot of thought." Inside there were no mirrors, no swivel chairs, no machines of torture with their accompanying stink. She said, "Nothing is permanent, nothing is forever. Don't feel hampered or hemmed in by the shape of your face or the shape of your past. Hair is vital, sustains mistakes, can be born again. You don't have to marry it. Now tip back and put your head into my hands."

Discussion Questions

1. Why does Aldrich begin this essay on hair with references to the Taj Mahal, the Grand Canyon, and Marilyn Monroe's footprints? How does this opening begin to establish the importance of the actual topic?

2. In your own experience, are certain behaviors related to hair still as ritualized and gender-specific as what Aldrich describes?

3. Aldrich consistently uses language—"stamp of property," "museum piece"—that objectifies hair, as if it exists separately from the person. Why does she do this? Toward the end of the essay, how does Aldrich shift the terms of the argument, exploring the "philosophy" of hair?

Writing Activity

1. Write the history of your own understanding of your hair or another body part, exploring how you learned to think about its meaning.

Imitation Is the Sincerest Form of Comedy

Introduction

Parody gives comic pleasure by precisely reproducing and then in most cases exaggerating the features of a genre or a writing style we recognize. Humorists can aim for affectionate parody with a ceremonial element of praise, or their purpose can be to develop a critical parody with a deliberative element warning us away from the mocked behavior. Parody almost always mimics the style and organizational structure of its target, but much of the humor in this comic form comes from applying the style and structure to different, seemingly inappropriate content. We saw examples of this strategy in Ian Frazier's "Coyote v. Acme" and "Laws Concerning Food and Drink" and Madeleine Begun Kane's "A Pre-Musical Agreement" in Chapter 4. This method also puts into practice Davis's sense of the comic element of transposed systems, bringing the textual conventions of a recognizable genre to bear on unexpected though familiar subject matter.

Ambrose Bierce commandeers the familiar format of the dictionary to offer cynical definitions of a range of words. Joseph Dennie borrows the strategies of literary scholars to make a case for the high quality of a children's rhyme, while Benjamin Franklin makes a scientific proposal about a basic (and base) element of human experience. Jon Stewart imagines an archeological find unearthing a very different account of a supper for Jesus and his disciples, and Louis Phillips brings Aristotle's taxonomizing habit of mind to bear on baseball. Finally, Dave Barry lampoons grammar handbooks, and Paul Davidson imagines a newfangled blog by an old-style comedy team.

In considering parody, we might note that we all learn to write through imitation—from laboriously shaping the letters of the alphabet as children to crafting essays, theses, dissertations, and perhaps books later on. Parody takes control away from the already-existing model—who hasn't resented the need to reproduce a form to prove to a teacher or boss that one can do it? Parody invests the writer with rhetorical authority, with power over the form, with the freedom to explode the model through exaggeration and transposition, taking it on wings of comic invention to places where the form never dreamed of venturing on its own.

From *The Devil's Dictionary*
AMBROSE BIERCE

Headnotes/Things to Look For

Ambrose Bierce (1842–1914), like Twain and Mencken, began his writing career as a journalist. After serving in the Union Army during the Civil War, he made his way to San Francisco, contributing to and editing several newspapers and magazines, eventually joining the staff of The San Francisco Examiner. *He wrote poetry and verse, but he is best known for his short stories, including "An Occurrence at Owl Creek Bridge."*

Aligning himself with the other curmudgeons included in this book, Bierce skewers the conventional sense of words by revealing the true operations of courts and political bodies in these definitions (returning us to the forensic and deliberative arenas of earlier chapters).

---- ✦ ----

Accomplice, n. One associated with another in a crime, having guilty knowledge and complicity, as an attorney who defends a criminal, knowing him guilty. This view of the attorney's position in the matter has not hitherto commanded the assent of attorneys, no one having offered them a fee for assenting.

Accuse, v.t. To affirm another's guilt or unworth; most commonly as a justification of ourselves for having wronged him.

Amnesty, n. The state's magnanimity to those offenders whom it would be too expensive to punish.

Arrest, v.t. Formally to detain one accused of unusualness.

Conservative, n. A statesman who is enamored to existing evils, as distinguished from the Liberal, who wishes to replace them with others.

Consul, n. In American politics, a person who having failed to secure an office from the people is given one by the Administration on condition that he leave the country.

CourtFool, n. The plaintiff.

Defame, v.t. To lie about another. To tell the truth about another.

Diplomacy, n. The patriotic art of lying for one's country.

Decalogue, n. A series of commandments, ten in number—just enough to permit an intelligent selection for observance, but not enough to embarrass the choice. Following is the revised edition of the Decalogue, calculated for this meridian.

Thou shalt no God but me adore:
'Twere too expensive to have more.

No images nor idols make
For Robert Ingersoll to break.

Take not God's name in vain; select
A time when it will have effect.

Work not on Sabbath days at all,
But go to see the teams play ball.

Honor thy parents. That creates
For life insurance lower rates.

Kill not, abet not those who kill;
Thou shalt not pay thy butcher's bill.

Kiss not thy neighbor's wife, unless
Thine own thy neighbor doth caress.

Don't steal; thou'lt never thus compete
Successfully in business. Cheat.

Bear not false witness—that is low—
But "hear 'tis rumored so and so."

Covet thou naught that thou hast not
By hook or crook, or somehow, got.

Discussion, n. A method of confirming others in their errors.

Elector, n. One who enjoys the sacred privilege of voting for the man of another man's choice.

Executive, n. An officer of the Government, whose duty it is to enforce the wishes of the legislative power until such time as the judicial department shall be pleased to pronounce them invalid and of no effect.

Habeas Corpus. A writ by which a man may be taken out of jail when confined for the wrong crime.

Hangman, n. An officer of the law charged with duties of the highest dignity and utmost gravity, and held in hereditary disesteem by a populace having a criminal ancestry. In some of the American States his functions are now performed by an electrician, as in New Jersey, where executions by electricity have recently been ordered—the first instance known to this lexicographer of anybody questioning the expediency of hanging Jerseymen.

Harangue, n. A speech by an opponent, who is known as an harrangue-outang.

Homicide, n. The slaying of one human being by another. There are four kinds of homocide: felonious, excusable, justifiable, and praiseworthy, but it makes no great difference to the person slain whether he fell by one kind or another—the classification is for advantage of the lawyers.

Inadmissible, adj. Not competent to be considered. Said of certain kinds of testimony which juries are supposed to be unfit to be entrusted with, and which judges, therefore, rule out, even of proceedings before themselves alone. Hearsay evidence is inadmissible because the person quoted was unsworn and is not before the court for examination; yet most momentous actions, military, political, commercial and of every other kind, are daily undertaken on hearsay evidence. These is no religion in the world that has any other basis than hearsay evidence. Revelation is hearsay evidence: that the Scriptures are the word of God we have only the testimony of men long dead whose identity is not clearly established and who are not known to have been sworn in any sense. Under the rules of evidence as they now exist in this country, no single assertion in the Bible has in its support any evidence admissible in a court of law. It cannot be proved that the battle of Blenheim ever was fought, that there was such a person as Julius Caesar, such an empire as Assyria.

But as records of courts of justice are admissible, it can easily be proved that powerful and malevolent magicians once existed and were a scourge to mankind. The evidence (including confession) upon which certain women were convicted of witchcraft and executed was without a flaw; it is still unimpeachable. The judges' decisions based on it were sound in logic and in law. Nothing in any existing court was ever more thoroughly proved than the charges of witchcraft and sorcery for which so many suffered death. If there were no witches, human testimony and human reason are alike destitute of value.

Incumbent, n. A person of the liveliest interest to the outcumbents.

Justice, n. A commodity which in a more or less adulterated condition the State sells to the citizen as a reward for his allegiance, taxes and personal service.

Lawful, adj. Compatible with the will of a judge having jurisdiction.

Lawyer, n. One skilled in circumvention of the law.

Litigant, n. A person about to give up his skin for the hope of retaining his bones.

Litigation, n. A machine which you go into as a pig and come out of as a sausage.

Logic, n. The art of thinking and reasoning in strict accordance with the limitations and incapacities of the human misunderstanding. The basic of logic is the syllogism, consisting of a major and a minor premise and a conclusion—thus:
Major Premise: Sixty men can do a piece of work sixty times as quickly as one man.
Minor Premise: One man can dig a posthole in sixty seconds; therefore—
Conclusion: Sixty men can dig a posthole in one second. This may be called the syllogism arithmetical, in which, by combining logic and mathematics, we obtain a double certainty and are twice blessed.

Marriage, n. The state or condition of a community consisting of a master, a mistress and two slaves, making in all, two.

Misdemeanor, n. An infraction of the law having less dignity than a felony and constituting no claim to admittance into the best criminal society.

Oath, n. In law, a solemn appeal to the Deity, made binding upon the conscience by a penalty for perjury.

Opposition, n. In politics the party that prevents the Government from running amuck by hamstringing it.

The King of Ghargaroo, who had been abroad to study the science of government, appointed one hundred of his fattest subjects as members of a parliament to make laws for the collection of revenue. Forty of these he named the Party of Opposition and had his Prime Minister carefully instruct them in their duty of opposing every royal measure. Nevertheless, the first one that was submitted passed unanimously. Greatly displeased, the King vetoed it, informing the Opposition that if they did that again they would pay for their obstinacy with their heads. The entire forty promptly disemboweled themselves.

"What shall we do now?" the King asked. "Liberal institutions cannot be maintained without a party of Opposition."

"Splendor of the universe," replied the Prime Minister, "it is true these dogs of darkness have no longer their credentials, but all is not lost. Leave the matter to this worm of the dust."

So the Minister had the bodies of his Majesty's Opposition embalmed and stuffed with straw, put back into the seats of power and nailed there. Forty votes were recorded against every bill and the nation prospered. But one day a bill imposing a tax on warts was defeated—the members of the Government party had not been nailed to their seats! This so enraged the King that the Prime Minister was put to death, the parliament was dissolved with a battery of artillery, and government of the people, by the people, for the people perished from Ghargaroo.

Politics, n. A strife of interests masquerading as a contest of principles. The conduct of public affairs for private advantage.

Precedent, n. In Law, a previous decision, rule or practice which, in the absence of a definite statute, has whatever force and authority a Judge may choose to give it, thereby greatly simplifying his task of doing as he pleases. As there are precedents for every-thing, he has only to ignore those that make against his interest and accentuate those in the line of his desire. Invention of the precedent elevates the trial-at-law from the low estate of a for-tuitous ordeal to the noble attitude of a dirigible arbitrament.

Presidency, n. The greased pig in the field game of American politics.

President, n. The leading figure in a small group of men of whom—and of whom only—it is positively known that immense numbers of their countrymen did not want any of them for President.

Proof, n. Evidence having a shade more of plausibility than of unlikelihood. The testimony of two credible witnesses as opposed to that of only one.

Quorum, n. A sufficient number of members of a deliberative body to have their own way and their own way of having it. In the United States Senate a quorum consists of the chairman of the Committee on Finance and a messenger from the White House; in the House of Representatives, of the Speaker and the devil.

Radicalism, n. The conservatism of to-morrow injected into the affairs of to-day.

Republic, n. A nation in which, the thing governing and the thing governed being the same, there is only a permitted authority to enforce an optional obedience. In a republic, the founda-tion of public order is the ever lessening habit of submission inherited from ancestors who, being truly governed, submit-ted because they had to. There are as many kinds of republics as there are graduations between the despotism whence they came and the anarchy whither they lead.

Senate, n. A body of elderly gentlemen charged with high duties and misdemeanors.

Tariff, n. A scale of taxes on imports, designed to protect the domestic producer against the greed of his consumer.

Technicality, n. In an English court a man named Home was tried for slander in having accused his neighbor of murder. His exact words were: "Sir Thomas Holt hath taken a cleaver and stricken his cook upon the head, so that one side of the head fell upon one shoulder and the other side upon the other shoulder." The defendant was acquitted by instruction of the court, the learned judges holding that the words did not charge murder, for they did not affirm the death of the cook, that being only an inference.

Vote, n. The instrument and symbol of a freeman's power to make a fool of himself and a wreck of his country.

Discussion Questions

1. How would you describe Bierce's sense of the legal system and its workings? What role does the pursuit of justice play?

2. How does Bierce present the motivations of politicians, whether liberal or conservative?

3. Along with distrusting the legal and political systems, Bierce is suspicious as well of the worth of logic. How does he use the form of the syllogism to call logic into question?

Writing Activity

1. Write a parody of a Wikipedia entry, bringing to light the true nature of your subject.

Jack and Gill: A Scholarly Commentary

JOSEPH DENNIE

Headnotes/Things to Look For

Joseph Dennie (1768–1812) graduated from Harvard and considered a law career before turning to writing. With his partner Royall Tyler he began by writing satirical essays for newspapers, but he made his reputation with a series of essays entitled The Lay Preacher; or, Short Sermons for Idle Readers.

Note the consistency of Dennie's scholarly tone as he takes us line by line through this familiar but underappreciated epic poem. He establishes his thesis before commencing the close reading, establishing that previous critics have missed the simple grandeur of this concise masterpiece.

✦

Among critical writers, it is a common remark that the fashion of the times has often given a temporary reputation to performances of very little merit, and neglected those much more deserving of applause. I shall endeavor to introduce to the nation a work, which, though of considerable elegance, has been strangely overlooked by the generality of the world. It has, of late, fallen into disrepute, chiefly from the simplicity of its style, which in this age of luxurious refinement, is deemed only a secondary beauty, and from its being the favorite of the young.

I must acknowledge that at first I doubted in what class of poetry it should be arranged. Its extreme shortness, and its uncommon metre, seemed to degrade it into a ballad, but its interesting subject, its unity of plan, and above all, its having a beginning, middle, and an end, decide its claim to the epic rank.

The opening is singularly beautiful:

JACK AND GILL

The first duty of the poet is to introduce his subject, and there is no part of poetry more difficult. Here our author is very happy: for instead of telling us, as an ordinary writer would have done, who were the ancestors of Jack and Gill, that the grandfather of Jack was a respectable farmer, that his mother kept a tavern at the sign of the Blue Bear; and that Gill's father was a Justice of the Peace, he introduces them to us at once in their proper persons.

I cannot help accounting it, too, as a circumstance honorable to the genius of the poet, that he does not in his opening call upon the Muse. This is an error into which Homer, and almost all the epic writers after him, have fallen; since by thus stating their case to the Muse, and desiring her to come to their assistance, they necessarily presuppose that she was absent, whereas there can be no surer sign of inspiration than for a muse to come unasked.

The personages being now seen, their situation is next to be discovered. Of this we are immediately informed in the subsequent line, when we are told:

JACK AND GILL
WENT UP A HILL

Here the imagery is distinct, yet the description concise. The poet meant to inform us that two persons were going up a hill. Had the poet told us how the two heroes went up, whether in a cart or a wagon, and entered into the particulars which the subject involves, they would have been tedious, because superfluous.

These considerations may furnish us with the means of deciding a controversy, arising from a variation in the manuscripts; some of which have it *a* hill, and others *the* hill. As the description is in no other part local, I incline to the former reading. It has, indeed, been suggested that the hill here mentioned was Parnassus, and that the two persons are two poets, who, having overloaded Pegasus, the poor jaded creature was obliged to stop at the foot of the hill, whilst they ascended for water to recruit him. This interpretation, it is true, derives some countenance from the consideration that Jack and Gill were, in reality, as will appear in the course of the poem, going to draw water, and that there was on Parnassus such a place as Hippocrene, that is, a *horsepond*, at the top; but, on the whole, I think the text, as I have adopted it, to be the better reading.

Having ascertained the names and conditions of the parties, the reader naturally becomes inquisitive into their employment, and wishes to know whether their occupation is worthy of them.

JACK AND GILL
WENT UP A HILL
TO FETCH A BUCKET OF WATER

Here we behold the plan gradually unfolding. We now discover their object, which we were before left to conjecture. Our acute author, instead of introducing a host of gods and goddesses, who might have impeded the journey of his heroes, by the intervention of the bucket, which is, as it ought to be, simple and conducive to the progress of the poem, has considerably improved on the ancient plan.

It has been objected that the employment of Jack and Gill is not sufficiently dignified for an epic poem; but, in answer to this, it must be remarked that it was the opinion of Socrates, and many other philosophers, that beauty should be estimated by utility, and surely the purpose of the heroes must have been beneficial. They ascended the rugged mountain to draw water, and drawing water is certainly more conducive to human happiness than drawing blood, as do the boasted heroes of the *Iliad*, or roving on the ocean and invading other men's property, as did the pious Aeneas.

Yes, they went to draw water. It might have been drawn for the purpose of culinary consumption; it might have been to quench the thirst of the harmless animals who relied upon them for support; it might have been to feed a sterile soil, and to revive the drooping plants, which they raised by their labors. Is not our author more judicious than Appollonius, who chooses for the heroes of his Argonautics a set of rascals, undertaking to steal a sheep skin? Do we not find the amiable Rebecca busy at the well? Does not one of the maidens in the *Odyssey* delight us by her diligence in the same situation?

But the descriptive part is now finished, and the author hastens to the catastrophe. At what part of the mountain the well was situated, what was the reason of the sad misfortune, or how the prudence of Jack foresook him, we are not informed, but so, alas! it happened:

JACK FELL DOWN—

Unfortunate Jack, at the moment when he was nimbly, for aught we know, going up the hill, perhaps at the moment when his toils were to cease, he made an heedless step, his centre of gravity fell beyond his base, and he tumbled. Buoyed by hope, we suppose his affliction not quite remediless, that his fall is an accident to which the wayfarers of this life are daily liable, and we anticipate his immediate rise to resume his labors. But:

JACK FELL DOWN
AND BROKE HIS CROWN—

Nothing now remains but to deplore the fate of the unhappy Jack. The mention of the *crown* has much perplexed the commentators. The learned Microphilus, in the 513th page of his *"Cursory Remarks"* on the poem, thinks he can find in it some allusion to the story of Alfred, who, he says, is known to have lived, during his concealment, in a mountainous country, and as he watched the cakes on the fire, might have been sent to bring water. But Microphilus' acute annotator, Vandergruten, has detected the fallacy of such a supposition, though he falls into an equal error in remarking that Jack might have carried a crown or a half crown-piece in his hand, which was fractured in the fall. My learned readers will doubtless agree with me in conjecturing that, as the crown is often used metaphorically for the head, and as that part is, or without any disparagement to the unfortunate sufferer, might have been, the heaviest, it was really his pericranium that sustained the damage.

Having seen the fate of Jack, we are anxious to know that of his companion. Alas!

AND GILL CAME TUMBLING AFTER

Here the distress thickens on us. Unable to support the loss of his friend, he followed him, determined to share his disaster, and resolved that, as they had gone up together, they should not be separated as they came down.

In the midst of our afflictions, let us not, however, be unmindful of the poet's merit, which, on this occasion, is conspicuous. He evidently seems to have in view the excellent observation of Adam Smith, that our sympathy arises not from a view of the passion, but of the situation that excites it. Instead of unnecessary lamentation, he gives us the real state of the case; avoiding at the same time that minuteness of detail, which is so common among pathetic poets, and which, by dividing a passion and tearing it to rags, as Shakespeare says, destroys its force.

Of the bucket, we are told nothing, but it is probable that it fell with its supporters.

Let us conclude with a review of the poem's most prominent beauties. The subject is the *fall of man*. The heroes are men who did not commit a single fault, and whose misfortunes are to be imputed, not to indiscretion, but to destiny. The poet prudently clipped the wings of imagination, and repressed the extravagance of metaphorical decoration. All is simple, plain, consistent.

That part, too, without which poetry is useless sound, the moral, has not escaped the view of the poet. When we behold two young men, who but a short moment before stood up in all the pride of health, falling down a hill, how must we lament the instability of all things.

Discussion Questions

1. How does Dennie make virtues out of what other critics have considered flaws in "Jack and Gill"? How does he keep up a running conversation with his benighted peers?
2. The business of the literary critic is to illuminate the subject in ways the solitary untrained reader may not be able to do. How does Dennie's commentary reveal what's not immediately apparent in the poem?
3. How does Dennie's reading lead inexorably to his final pronouncement regarding the scope and true meaning of the poem?

Writing Activity

1. Write your own analysis of an underappreciated work of art—an advertisement, a song lyric, a text message.

On Perfumes

A Letter to the Royal Academy of Brussels

BENJAMIN FRANKLIN

Headnotes/Things to Look For

Benjamin Franklin (1706–1790), along with being recognized as one of the Founding Fathers of the United States, distinguished himself in many other areas as well; he was a writer and publisher, a practicing politician who also theorized about politics, a scientist and inventor who did groundbreaking work with electricity, and a diplomat who helped make the American Revolution possible through his cultivation of French support.

Franklin here takes on the Royal Academy of Brussels, posing a scientific problem the solution of which he argues would provide true utility to humankind. Note how Franklin handles the opposition of philosophical and physical inquiry, making a case for solving an everyday problem.

---- ◆ ----

Gentlemen:

I have perused your late mathematical prize question, proposed in lieu of one in natural philosophy for the ensuing year, viz: *"Une figure quelconque donnée, on demande d'y inscrire le plus grand nombre de fois possible une autre figure plus petite quelconque, qui est aussi donnée."*

I was glad to find by these following words, *"L'Académie a jugé que cette découverte, en étendant les bornes de nos connoissances, ne seroit pas sans utilité,"* that you esteem *utility* an essential point in your inquiries, which has not always been the case with all academies; and I conclude therefore that you have given this question instead of a philosophical, or, as the learned express it, a *physical* one, because you could not at the time think of a physical one that promised greater *utility*.

Permit me then humbly to propose one of that sort for your consideration, and through you, if you approve it, for the serious inquiry of learned physicians, chemists, etc., of this enlightened age.

It is universally well known that, in digesting our common food, there is created or produced in the bowels of human creatures a great quantity of wind.

That the permitting this air to escape and mix with the atmosphere is usually offensive to the company, from the fetid smell that accompanies it.

That all well-bred people therefore, to avoid giving such offense, forcibly restrain the efforts of nature to discharge that wind.

That so retained contrary to nature, it not only gives frequently great present pain, but occasions future diseases such as habitual cholics, ruptures, tympanies, etc., often destructive of the constitution, and sometimes of life itself.

Were it not for the odiously offensive smell accompanying such escapes, polite people would probably be under no more restraint in discharging such wind in company than they are in spitting or in blowing their noses.

My prize question therefore should be: To discover some drug, wholesome and not disagreeable, to be mixed with our common food, or sauces, that shall render the natural discharges of wind from our bodies not only inoffensive, but agreeable as perfumes.

That this is not a chimerical project and altogether impossible, may appear from these considerations. That we already have some knowledge of means capable of *varying* that smell. He that dines on stale flesh, especially with much addition of onions, shall be able to afford a stink that no company can tolerate; while he that has lived for some time on vegetables only, shall have that breath so pure as to be insensible to the most delicate noses; and if he can manage so as to avoid the report, he may anywhere give vent to his griefs, unnoticed. But as there are many to whom an entire vegetable diet would be inconvenient, and as a little quicklime thrown into a jakes will correct the amazing quantity of fetid air arising from the vast mass of putrid matter contained in such places, and render it rather pleasing to the smell, who knows but that a little powder of lime (or some other thing equivalent), taken in our food, perhaps a glass of limewater drunk at dinner, may have the same effect on the air produced in and issuing from our bowels? This is worth the experiment. Certain it is also that we have the power of changing by slight means the smell of another discharge, that of our water. A few stems of asparagus eaten shall give our urine a disagreeable odor; and a pill of turpentine no bigger than a pea shall bestow on it the pleasing smell of violets. And why should it be thought more impossible in nature to find means of making perfume of our wind than of our water?

For the encouragement of this inquiry (from the immortal honor to be reasonably expected by the inventor), let it be considered of how small importance to mankind, or to how small a part of mankind have been useful those discoveries in science that have heretofore made philosophers famous. Are there twenty men in Europe this day the happier, or even the easier, for any knowledge they have picked out of Aristotle? What comfort can the vortices of Descartes give to a man who has whirlwinds in his bowels! The knowledge of Newton's mutual *attraction* of the particles of matter, can it afford ease to him who is racked by their mutual *repulsion*, and the cruel distensions it occasions? The pleasure arising to a few philosophers, from seeing, a few times in their lives, the threads of light untwisted, and separated by the Newtonian prism into seven colors, can it be compared with the ease and comfort every man living might feel seven times a day, by discharging freely the wind from his bowels? Especially if it be converted into a perfume; for the pleasure of one sense being little inferior to those of another, instead of pleasing the *sight*, he might delight the *smell* of those about him, and make numbers happy, which to a benevolent mind must afford infinite satisfaction. The generous soul, who now endeavors to find out whether the friends he entertains like best claret or Burgundy, champagne or Madeira, would then inquire also whether they chose musk or lily, rose or bergamot, and provide accordingly. And surely such a liberty of *ex-pressing one's scent-iments, and pleasing one another*, is of infinitely more importance to human happiness than that liberty of the *press*, or of *abusing one another*, which the English are so ready to fight and die for.

In short, this invention, if completed, would be, as *Bacon* expresses it, *bringing philosophy home to men's business and bosoms*. And I cannot but conclude that in comparison therewith for *universal* and *continual utility*, the science of the philosophers abovementioned, even with the addition, gentlemen, of your *"figure quelconque,"* and the figures inscribed in it, are, all together, scarcely worth a Fart-hing.

Discussion Questions

1. How does Franklin use scientific form and diction to set up the problem he wishes to solve? What features of scientific language does he adapt to his own use?

2. How does Franklin answer the charge that the problem he poses cannot be solved?

3. Franklin takes pains to show that alleviating physical discomfort does a greater service to people than more conventional scientific and philosophical inquiry. To what degree is he serious in this argument? What point is he making about science?

Writing Activity

1. Write a grant proposal aimed at solving an everyday problem that might not initially be considered important enough to warrant formal scientific inquiry.

The Last Supper, or The Dead Waiter

Jon Stewart

Headnotes/Things to Look For

Jon Stewart, born in New York City in 1962, has been host of The Daily Show *since 1999, garnering a large following as the "most trusted name in fake news." He attended the College of William and Mary in Virginia, where he majored in psychology and played on the soccer team. Earlier television work included roles on* The Larry Sanders Show, Spin City, *and* NewsRadio, *and he has also hosted the Academy Awards, the Grammys, and* Saturday Night Live. *His books are* Naked Pictures of Famous People *and* The Daily Show with Jon Stewart Presents America (The Book): A Citizen's Guide to Democracy Inaction.

Note how Stewart sets up an academic frame for this parody of biblical scholarship, citing Shecter's dissertation and the excavations in the Sinai Peninsula.

◆

The lack of information and interpretation concerning the life and times of Jesus Christ has, for years, frustrated scholars, theologians and lovers of information and interpretation. To date, the only notable published material on the subject is Franz Shecter's thorough yet ambiguous dissertation, "That Guy from the Thing." So little is known of Jesus because, as Shecter asserts, "He died a long time ago."

This virtual blackout has recently been lifted, in light of an astonishing discovery in the Sinai Peninsula. A German tourist in Israel, searching for the keys to his luggage, stumbled upon an ancient city buried beneath two thousand years of desert sand and a Starbucks. A month's excavation later, this man, still wearing the same pants and shirt he originally traveled in, found what is to date the only written account pertaining to the existence of Jesus Christ. The manuscript contains explicit reference to a dinner party Jesus had with twelve male friends. It is an eyewitness account penned by Avram the Waiter, who served the Christ party at the then-popular Jerusalem eatery, Jerry's. The conventional wisdom concerning the manuscript was that it proved Shecter's Crucifixion hypothesis of a "bachelor party gone awry." Although when Shecter reread the document, this time with his glasses on, grave doubts arose. Now you can decide for yourself as the ancient memoir has finally been translated from its original Spanglish.

THE MANUSCRIPT OF "AVRAM THE WAITER"

So much for things being slow during Passover. It was April of 33 and as usual Jerry's was jammed. Jerry's was the "in" spot of the moment. Ever since Pilate started coming here the place has been packed with gawkers and wannabes. Personally, I could care less. You're a person; I'm a person. Doesn't matter if you're Augustus or Barabbas. You treat me with respect, you get good service. Anyway, I'm at the end of an eight-hour double, slopping kishke to drunken centurions, and in walks Jesus with his flock of hangers-on. "Here comes trouble," I say to Moishe the barback. We'd all seen Jesus and his little bunch of frat boys around town and believe me, *not impressed.* The Greeks invented a lot of great things—namely naked wrestling—but fraternities, or any other platonic male organization for that matter, weren't one of them.

So Luke, he's the skinny one with the greasy hair—oops, that's all of them—Luke says to me with a snotty attitude, "Table for thirteen . . . I believe it's under *Christ.*" So I check the book. "Well,

I can't find your reservation and besides, it looks like there's only eight of you here," I say to him. I'm telling him the truth, by the way, not just being pissy. They didn't have a reservation and even if they did, I can't seat them if the whole party hasn't shown. Sorry, but it's not my rule. "They're coming. They'll be here. They got a little hung up. Holiday traffic," Luke says. You're kidding! Hung up in traffic? Well, that changes everything . . . please. Anyway, the guy's just checking out the scene, not even looking me in the eye. So all I say is, and Moishe will back me up on this, "You're welcome to hang out in the bar and wait for them . . . But I'm afraid—" and boom, he's on me. "Wait in the bar? You want *us* to wait in the bar. We're not waiting in the bar, little man." The way he was carrying on you'd have thought I asked him to bathe. (P.S. If Jesus is right and there is an afterlife, I hope they've got soap.)

"Let me ask you something. What year is it?" Luke says. I know what he's going for but I play dumb. "What do you mean?" I ask innocently. You should have seen me, all wide-eyed and sheepish. Elijah caught my performance and said he was going to throw me a graduation party because it was obvious I no longer needed acting classes. "33 A.D.," Luke says. I just let it hang there. "*Anno Domini?* . . . Year of *the Lord*," he says, giving the head nod over in Christ's direction. "You got me?" he says. So I turn to him real cool and go, "Well last time *I* checked *my* calendar it was still 3706." And then I snap my fingers and go back to marrying ketchups. Luke's jaw about hit the floor. Moishe turns and says, "Bathsheba one, Luke zero." It was really funny, but I wasn't just being a bitch. A lot of the folks at Jerry's did still use the Hebrew calendar. And besides, with that attitude those boys weren't getting any special treatment from me. Jesus slips his tunic over his head just like the rest of us; I don't care who his father is.

I do have to admit I was a little scared. Some of these apostles are pretty rough trade, the blue-collar Nazareth crowd. And I think the others work out. They were pissed. Luke was yelling at me, saying if they don't get their table right away, Jesus is going to turn all our Château Lafite-Rothschild into low-grade zinfandel. "Do it!" I say. It's not like it's my wine.

Jesus' boys are in a bit of a frenzy, giving me the third degree. "What's your name?" "We want to talk to the manager!" "Fine," I say, "talk to the manager. Get me fired." I'm an artisan/poet. I'm putting up a night of spoken word in three weeks. I don't need to take shit from cult members. I should have gotten the Etruscan bouncer, Vito the Unreasonable. He'd have thrown them out on their apostles. So just as I'm about to hurl some sea salt in Peter's face, Jesus pipes up. "Boys," he says. "Please. The wise builder doesn't build on sand, but the foolish builder can't build on rock." I had no idea what he was talking about, but suddenly, the angry mob's all kittens and puppies. It's "Right, Rabbi." "Sorry, Rabbi." "Couldn't have put it better myself, Teacher." Please! They're so affected. Jesus could've said, "Hey, look at me, I've got a banana up my ass!" and they would've acted like they just heard the word of God.

Finally, everybody shows up. It's nine o'clock. It's my last table, and the kitchen wants to close. So lucky me has to try and wrangle their order. It ain't easy. Matthew "has" to sit next to Jesus but John is having none of it, because his birthday's Monday and Jesus promised. Simon's blowing into his hand and pretending he farted. Mark and James are pouting because I carded them. Thomas wants a Caesar salad but doesn't believe it when I tell him you can hardly taste the anchovies in the dressing. Paul says he's lactose intolerant and claims if there's sour cream in his borscht, it's coming out of my tip. Judas sits glowering because no one will split an appetizer with him, and the rest of them just giggle at my ASK ME ABOUT OUR KUGEL! button. The way they all behaved, I should have made them order off the children's menu.

If my ex-roommate hadn't just screwed me on last month's rent, believe me, I would've walked. I needed the shekels, but obviously none of these guys had ever waited tables. One of them actually snapped his fingers at me for a water refill. Not even to drink. He wanted to wash Jesus' feet! That's right, feet! Right at the table! It was enough to make Caligula nauseous. The only bev they ordered, one glass of house red. They all *split* it. Hello! Misers, party of thirteen.

At this point I think they saw I was getting pissed and realized I would be handling their food. If you think that kind of thing doesn't happen in good restaurants all the time, you're kidding yourself. We had a bartender, Isaac, who had a special drink recipe for rude customers. I'll give you a hint: The magic ingredient is yak piss. You think I'm lying? He's a Bedouin and believe me those people could give a shit.

After I got them settled down, everyone ordered the lamb, except John, who'd had lamb for lunch. You'd have thought we were feeding the lions the way they attacked that thing. I hope Jesus is planning some commandments on table manners.

Anyway, we got through dinner but you can be sure I had Carlos prepare a fatty cut, even though they asked for lean.

As far as Jesus goes, we'd all heard about the miracles he performs, but he actually seemed pretty normal. I've had friends who get a little success and immediately turn into assholes, but he was cool about it. My friend's sister caught him when he did two nights in Thebes. She said it was OK. He bent some spoons and guessed that one guy in the audience was thinking about changing jobs, but she said he was better when he was still with the Lepers. Jesus definitely did no miracles at this dinner, although one of the waiters who got his autograph said it cleared up his sinuses.

No real pearls of wisdom either. Once, right before dessert, Jesus said to no one in particular, "Why do people park on a driveway and drive on a parkway?" It was *kind of* funny. Truthfully. Jesus spent most of the time asking people whether or not a beard would make him look smarter. There was a bit of a scuffle when Paul liked the idea but Judas thought it was trendy. I say cut the hair. Please. You're not a musician and it's very B.C.

Personally, when I found out one of those guys had betrayed Jesus, it didn't surprise me a bit. You can ask David son of Phil. I told him that night, " I would *not* trust these guys if I were Jesus." It's so obvious they're not really his friends. They're just hanging around him because he's famous. You should have seen them scatter when I brought the bill. "Can you cover me, Jesus?" "I'll get you next time, Jesus," "I gotta go drain the staff, Jesus!" I don't know how Jesus puts up with it. Poor guy probably had to walk on water just to get some peace and quiet.

Not that it kept me up nights. Let's face it. Messiahs come and go. Just last week I had a creep on table five who claimed that if I followed him, I would enjoy eternal joy in a place called Utah. He said I could have as many wives as I wanted but not caffeine. Get real. Me? Choose women over coffee? Please. Still, I *was* sorry to hear what happened to Jesus. He was a good tipper.

Editor's note: After this piece was published it was brought to our attention that Avram's manuscript is not the only document pertaining to the life and times of Jesus Christ. A work titled "The New Testament" was sent to our offices along with a large number of other pertinent volumes. We regret this oversight. Also, upon great scholarly review, Avram's manuscript was found to be written in Magic Marker, an implement not discovered until the early nineteen hundred and fifties. Again, our regrets.

Discussion Questions

1. How does Stewart introduce and then balance the incongruity of the two systems featured in the essay, old Jerusalem and a contemporary dining establishment?
2. How is this manuscript of "Avram the Waiter" a commentary on the relationship between Jews and Gentiles?
3. Why might a believer object to the characterizations of Jesus and his disciples in this essay? What strategies does Stewart use that might be considered sacrilegious or at the least inappropriate?

Writing Activity

1. Write an account of an historical event involving famous people, transposing the usual facts and behaviors with an incongruous dimension.

Aristotle's 'On Baseball'
LOUIS PHILLIPS

Headnotes/Things to Look For

Louis Phillips is a poet, playwright, and short-story writer whose books include A Dream of Countries Where No One Dare Live *and* The Bus to the Moon.

Phillips claims to be translating a treatise by Aristotle, beginning with the premise that baseball is Greek. Note how this sets up the transposition that will guide the parody of Aristotle's analytical methods.

✦

Baseball is Greek, in being national, heroic, and broken up in the rivalries of city-states.

ON BASEBALL

Our subject is the art of baseball in general and the theories of hitting, catching, and pitching in particular, the specific effect of each genre, and the way to play the game so that the sport be pleasing to the eye and soul of the spectator. Let us start, as is proper, with basic principles.

Baseball As Imitation

Dithyrambic baseball, as it was originally named, is the imitation of something, perhaps Tragedy. Perhaps not. In such matters it is difficult to be definitive.

As I have written elsewhere, Comedy is the imitation of inferior men who are not altogether vicious. Thus, the owners of teams are Comedic; the players, with their dreams of immortality and another season in the sun, Tragic.

Derivation of the Word

The term *baseball* comes from two obscured roots—*baseios*, meaning low, and *ballein*, referring to a type of whale. Hence, the low song of a whale. Or the song of a low whale. How this derivation came about has yet to be determined. Homer maintains that in the early years of the games, when the games were dedicated to the god Poseidon, a whale was sacrificed at the conclusion of each home stand. Unfortunately, the above may well be a folk etymology. After all, everybody knows that Homer frequently preferred a colorful story to the truth.

What scholars do agree upon, especially Danaus and Chaeremon (in spite of his mixed meters), is that baseball was originally called *baseode*, or Amusement (song) for the lowborn.

Whatever the origin of the term, we do know the word was born hundreds of years before *Tragos ode* or Tragedy.

Definition of the Term

Baseball is the good action which is complete and of a certain length (usually nine innings) by means of players who are made pleasing for each of their respective positions; it relies in its various elements not on acting, nor on narrative, but upon skill exhibited within a natural setting; through Pity and Fear, the completed game achieves the cleansing of these emotions. It involves the fall of a team from one level (either of play or of positions in the standings) to a lower level.

The Earliest Use of the Term

The earliest mention of baseball is, of course, to be found in Book VI of Homer's *Odyssey*, where the Princess Nausica tosses a ball. The following passage is of great interest to all scholars of the game and needs, of course, since we are Greek, no translation: "And presently, when Nausica and her maiden servants had finished their lunch, they removed the scarves from their heads and other headdresses and began playing with a ball. Nausica of the white led them in song."

This passage is of especial interest because it shows that at its inception women were not banned from the game (or *agon*) as they are now.

The Six Elements or Aspects of Dithyrambic Baseball

Every baseball game contains six necessary elements (or seven, if your team is managed by a barbarian) that make the game what it is: Agents, Contracts, Character, Diction, Spectacle, and Music. Most exhibitions of the game involve these elements in much the same manner.

Prophecy and Individual Games

Dithyrambic baseball might well have become more popular in Greece in particular and in Europe, but there is no longer any doubt that its popularity has been dampened by the omnipresence of Tiresias and other prophets addicted to bird prophecy. How disturbing it is to the common mind to have a baseball contest interrupted by the sight of an eagle flying over the stadiums of Athens and dropping a snake into the lap of the judges. It is even more disturbing to see a prophet tear open a pig or a chicken and spill its entrails across the bleachers—all in the hope of looking for a sign.

Indeed, as Agathon has observed in his monumental *Encyclopedia of Dithyrambic Baseball*, numerous contests have no sooner gotten underway when Tiresias, blind umpire that he was, would announce the final score. Disgruntled fans would then get up and leave, abandoning the hometown IX for some Dionysian revelry. Who dare blame them? The essence of baseball is the same as the essence of rhetoric—suspense. When suspense is removed from a baseball *agon*, because of vain bubbling of prophets, the game loses all its savor. Indeed, what spectator among us desires to know ahead of time whether or not Oedipus shall hit for the cycle?

It has also been well documented that the Athens Metropolitans lost something in the neighborhood of 580,000 drachmas each and every year they played. No wonder ship owners of certain families near Tampa looked elsewhere to make their fortune.

Until blind prophets are banned from attending the baseball *agon*, the game will certainly suffer a lack of dramatic tension.

The Three Essential Parts

Dithyrambic baseball, as a whole, consists of three parts: the Pitch, the Catch, and the Hit. (I know I have written earlier about the six elements or aspects of the game, but elements are not parts or if they are parts they are very subtle ones.)

We shall consider each one in turn.

The Pitch is sometimes physical, ofttimes purely linguistic. For example, Androtion, formerly of the A's and now a noted politician, would, after each *agon* or contest, post himself at one of the major exits to the stadium and sell tip sheets to the various chariot races going on about town. He also hawked razors. A number of commentators deplored the pitcher's actions and predicted (correctly) that such pitching would bring forth the mercenary side of players.

The Catch. An old saying goes: like the Pitch, the Catch. What it means is difficult to explain. Allow us to begin with the notion that the Catch possesses a twofold nature. There is the physical Catch, defined as the act of a fielder (in or out) plucking a battered ball from thin air. And then there is the other kind of Catch, the legal kind which players refer to when perusing the fine print in their contracts. For example, if a player (such as the aforementioned and deplored Androtion) is induced for a substantial bonus to sign a contract with the Spartans so that the Spartans can trade him to Crete for players (or agonists) to be named later, then the player and/or his agent may rightfully refer to the above play as a Catch.

The Hit. After each game, players have been seen approaching young ladies in the stands and "Hitting" on them. Sometimes, while trying to convince a female fan to join him in a night of debauchery, the player strikes out. Sometimes he gets to first base. This is what players mean most of the time when they talk about Hitting (see Scoring).

Three Additional Elements

Three additional elements of a game may be considered without undue comment. The[y] are Peripety, Discovery, and Suffering. These parts belong properly to the spectators. Especially Suffering.

Three Kinds of Games to be Avoided

There are some forms of the *agon* that should be avoided at all cost:

1. A good team must not be seen passing from happiness to misery because of the misguided actions of its owner.
2. A bad player must not be seen passing from misery to happiness because of a bad bounce or pure chance. Players must act consistent with their skills.
3. An extremely bad *agon* should not be prolonged more than necessary.

Of Baseball and Thought

Thought, most rightly, should be considered in my treatise on Rhetoric, but since Thought occupies a central position in the meaning of the game, we shall mention it here.

Baseball is considered to be boring by the nonthinking. But those who think find the game exciting. This is what is frequently referred to as Athena's Paradox. Athena's Paradox also applies to the rites of Aphrodite.

Indeed, we should also point out that, although everyone on a baseball team thinks, not all members think at the same time. That is why errors occur and why managers have been deemed, by Zeus, as necessary.

As I have said, all members of a baseball team, at some time during a season, think, but for some reason, only the catcher is allowed to adorn himself with the tools of ignorance. This is also a paradox, for the catcher is frequently the most learned player on the field. Some have even been known to take part in the Lenaca in the month of Gamelion. But the comic playwrights deserve what they get.

Antisthenes, the philosopher and protégé of Socrates, insists that excessive squatting (as performed by the catcher) causes the nerves and brains to settle low in the body. Antisthenes is, alas, a cynic.

Baseball and Ritual Murder

Anyone who has set foot inside the bleacher section of a well-contested *agon* has no doubt heard the cry go up:

Kakist' apoloith' ho brabeus

Most evilly may perish the Umpire. This well-known imprecation has sent chills up and down the spines of novices to the game. Were umpires actually slaughtered? Yes. After whales were abandoned, umpires were brought in to provide atonement and ritual cleansing. Fortunately, however, because of unionization of the craft of well-seeing and considered judgment, that practice has been rendered unlawful, except in some foreign countries.

But the cry goes on, thus showing us how slowly the rhetoric of the game changes and how eternal baseball truly is.

Discussion Questions

1. Aristotle's rhetorical categories have helped us organize the readings in this book. What does Phillips find comical in Aristotle's way of approaching the world?

2. What knowledge and lore specific to baseball does Phillips draw on in developing this account?

3. What knowledge and texts from classical Athens does Phillips draw on to create a context for understanding the origins of baseball? How does he bring the two systems into conversation with each other?

Writing Activity

1. Write an Aristotelian treatise on a contemporary sport or other cultural activity or event.

What Is and Ain't Grammatical
DAVE BARRY

Headnotes/Things to Look For

Dave Barry, a Pulitzer Prize–winning columnist, was born in Armonk, New York, in 1947. He wrote for The Miami Herald *from 1983 to 2005, also writing a number of books, including collections of his columns, fiction, and a range of nonfiction charting his course through family life. He occasionally tours with the Rock Bottom Remainders, a group of literary types who want to play loud. His life was the basis of the situation comedy* Dave's World.

Note how Barry takes dead aim at grammarians who expect people to know too much beyond the two rules accepted by Americans.

─────────── ✦ ───────────

I cannot overemphasize the importance of good grammar. What a crock. I could easily overemphasize the importance of good grammar. For example, I could say: "Bad grammar is the leading cause of slow, painful death in North America," or "Without good grammar, the United States would have lost World War II."

The truth is that grammar is not the most important thing in the world. The Super Bowl is the most important thing in the world. But grammar is still important. For example, suppose you are being interviewed for a job as an airplane pilot, and your prospective employer asks you if you have any experience, and you answer: "Well, I ain't never actually flied no actual airplanes or nothing, but I got several pilot-style hats and several friends who I like to talk about airplanes with."

If you answer this way, the prospective employer will immediately realize that you have ended your sentence with a preposition. (What you should have said, of course, is "several friends with who I like to talk about airplanes.") So you will not get the job, because airline pilots have to use good grammar when they get on the intercom and explain to the passengers that, because of high winds, the plane is going to take off several hours late and land in Pierre, South Dakota, instead of Los Angeles.

We did not always have grammar. In medieval England, people said whatever they wanted, without regard to rules, and as a result they sounded like morons. Take the poet Geoffrey Chaucer, who couldn't even spell his first name right. He wrote a large poem called *Canterbury Tales*, in which people from various professions—knight, monk, miller, reever, riveter, eeler, diver, stevedore, spinnaker, etc.—drone on and on like this:

In a somer sesun when sofie was the sunne
I kylled a younge birde ande I ate it on a bunne.

When Chaucer's poem was published, everybody read it and said: "My God, we need some grammar around here." So they formed a Grammar Commission, which developed the parts of speech, the main ones being nouns, verbs, predicants, conjectures, particles, proverbs, adjoiners, coordinates, and rebuttals.

Then the commission made up hundreds and hundreds of grammar rules, all of which were strictly enforced.

When the colonists came to America, they rebelled against British grammar. They openly used words like "ain't" and "finalize," and when they wrote the Declaration of Independence they deliberately misspelled many words. Thanks to their courage, today we Americans have only two rules of grammar:

RULE I. THE WORD "ME" IS ALWAYS INCORRECT

Most of us learn this rule as children, from our mothers. We say things like: "Mom, can Bobby and me roll the camping trailer over Mrs. Johnson's cat?" And our mothers say: "Remember your grammar, dear. You mean: 'Can Bobby and *I* roll the camping trailer over Mrs. Johnson's cat?' Of course you can, but be home by dinnertime."

The only exception to this rule is in formal business writing, where instead of "I" you must use "the undersigned." For example, this business letter is incorrect:

"Dear Hunky-Dory Canned Fruit Company: A couple days ago my wife bought a can of your cling peaches and served them to my mother who has a weak heart and she damn near died when she bit into a live grub. If I ever find out where you live, I am gonna whomp you on the head with a ax handle."

This should be corrected as follows:

". . . If the undersigned ever finds out where you live, the undersigned is gonna whomp you on the head with an handle."

RULE 2. YOU'RE NOT ALLOWED TO SPLIT INFINITIVES

An infinitive is the word "to" and whatever comes right behind it, such as "to a tee," "to the best of my ability," "tomato," etc. Splitting an infinitive is putting something between the "to" and the other words. For example, this is incorrect:

"Hey man, you got any, you know, spare change you could give to, like, me?"

The correct version is:

". . . spare change you could, like, give to me?"

• • •

The advantage of American English is that, because there are so few rules, practically anybody can learn to speak it in just a few minutes. The disadvantage is that Americans generally sound like jerks, whereas the British sound really smart, especially to Americans. That's why Americans are so fond of those British dramas they're always showing on public television, the ones introduced by Alistair Cooke. Americans *love* people who talk like Alistair Cooke. He could introduce old episodes of "Hawaii Five-O" and Americans would think they were extremely enlightening.

So the trick is to use American grammar, which is simple, but talk with a British accent, which is impressive. This technique is taught at all your really snotty private schools, where the kids learn to sound like Elliot Richardson. Remember Elliot? He sounded extremely British, and as a result he got to be Attorney General, Secretary of State, Chief Justice of the Supreme Court and Vice President *at the same time*.

You can do it, too. Practice in your home, then approach someone on the street and say: "Tally-ho, old chap. I would consider it a great honour if you would favour me with some spare change." You're bound to get quick results.

Discussion Questions

1. What's Barry's attitude toward grammar? Considering his long and successful career as a writer, how do you think his attitude toward language and its uses might contrast with what he offers here about grammar?

2. Why does Barry choose the example of the airline pilot to make a point about the role grammar plays in interviews and job performance?

3. How does Barry use historical references to give us a short history of why and how English came to have grammar?

Writing Activity

1. Write your own account of what grammar is good for, including the rules you believe are most helpful.

http://www.abbottandcostello. com/blog/

Subject: Our Newest Blog Comedy Routine

PAUL DAVIDSON

Headnotes/Things to Look For

Paul Davidson is a screenwriter and television producer as well as a writer whose work has appeared in Wired *and* mental floss. *In addition, he is a contributor to National Public Radio's* All Things Considered. *His books include* Consumer Joe: Harassing Corporate America, One Letter at a Time *and* The Lost Blogs. *His own blog is entitled* Words for My Enjoyment.

Note how Davidson brings a classic comedy team, Abbott and Costello, into the blogosphere, echoing their famous routine, "Who's on First."

———————— ✦ ————————

Hey folks, Abbott here! Wanted to thank all our great fans for supporting us over the years by giving you the first look at our new comedy sketch! We think you'll like it. But if you don't, don't send me any thoughts to abbott@acprods.com.

ABBOTT: *So, technology is pretty amazin', isn't it, Costello?*
COSTELLO: *You know it, boss.*
ABBOTT: *The way people can share their thoughts from their own personal diaries . . .*
COSTELLO: *I don't wanna read any of your personal thoughts. That scares me.*
ABBOTT: *Oh, relax! The thing is, you gotta get a whole buncha things goin' before you can just start writin'.*
COSTELLO: *Oh yeah? I didn't know that. Like what?*
ABBOTT: *Well, you need an I.P. address.*
COSTELLO: *I don't know about you, but I know where I pee and I don't need any stinkin' address to fig'r that out!*

ABBOTT: *No, Costello—not your home address . . . You gotta let people know that URL!*

COSTELLO: *First of all, I'm not the one askin' you to tell people where you pee—and second of all, I'm not the one who's ill! You are ill! Not me!*

ABBOTT: *Costello . . .*

COSTELLO: *What.*

ABBOTT: *I didn't say you were sick. URL!*

COSTELLO: *What, like mentally ill?*

ABBOTT: *No, Costello, not mentally ill.*

COSTELLO: *You're telling me that in order to share my own thoughts with the public . . .*

ABBOTT: *Go on . . .*

COSTELLO: *I gotta . . . give out my "I pee address" and give 'em the ol' . . .*

ABBOTT: *URL thing.*

COSTELLO: *And I'm sacrificin' my own career and doing this for what reason?*

ABBOTT: *To get comments.*

COSTELLO: *To get comments?*

ABBOTT: *Yes. If you let people know your I.P. address and that URL . . . People will come and leave comments.*

COSTELLO: *And tell me that I'm a deranged lunatic, most likely for telling them that I pee.*

ABBOTT: *Whether or not you tell 'em you're a deranged lunatic is your own business, Costello . . . I'm not gonna tell you how to live your life!*

COSTELLO: *But you are!*

ABBOTT: *I'm just telling you how to get people to read what you have to say. To get you a whole bunch of hits.*

COSTELLO: *(Flinches here) Who's gonna hit me?*

ABBOTT: *Not hit you . . . Hits.*

COSTELLO: *So, more than one person is gonna hit me?*

ABBOTT: *Well, if you're lucky—hundreds and thousands.*

COSTELLO: *What!?!?*

ABBOTT: *It's a good thing, Costello.*

COSTELLO: *I don't know what kind of world you're livin' in, buddy boy, but I don't consider having people come to my I pee address and watch me and tell me I'm ill and leave me comments and hit me . . . to be a good thing.*

ABBOTT: *Well, it's better than spam.*

COSTELLO: *I like Spam.*

ABBOTT: *You don't have Spam.*

COSTELLO: *Well, I've had Spam.*

ABBOTT: *Once you have spam, you always have spam.*

COSTELLO: *I had Spam last Christmas, then didn't have Spam until Easter.*

ABBOTT: *You had spam in December, then no spam until April!? That's not possible.*

COSTELLO: *Ask my mother!*

ABBOTT: *What does your mother know about spam!?*

COSTELLO: *That's her business! She makes sure everyone in my family gets Spam!*

ABBOTT: *Well, Costello—I can't say I was ever more disappointed in your mother than at this very moment.*

COSTELLO: *That's not very nice.*

ABBOTT: (Deep sigh here) *Here's the thing, Costello. If you don't want hits . . .*

COSTELLO: *No, I don't want hits!*

ABBOTT: *And you won't give out your I.P. address or let people know that URL . . .*

COSTELLO: *I refuse! I ain't no sicko!*

ABBOTT: *Then the only other way is to give out links to others . . .*

COSTELLO: *First Spam, now sausage links! You hungry or something?*

ABBOTT: *I'm not talking food, Costello, I'm talking links.*

COSTELLO: *Well, I don't know what country you live in my friend, but where I come from—links ARE food.*

ABBOTT: *I guess, figuratively, that's sorta true.*

COSTELLO: *You betcha bipper!*

ABBOTT: *Well then, Costello—I'm not gonna tell you how or where to give out those links. You do what you wanna do.*

COSTELLO: *I will! And I ain't givin' nobody nothing, just to come and read what I gotta say. They can come if they want, or they don't hafta. But I ain't getting hit, givin' out food, or tellin' them that I'm sick or even telling them that you are ill!*

ABBOTT: *Well, I'm sure they don't care if you're sick or not . . . But they do wanna know that URL.*

COSTELLO: *Which I'm not!*

ABBOTT: Not, what?

COSTELLO: *Ill!*

ABBOTT: *I never said you were ill.*

COSTELLO: *You did, just then!*

ABBOTT: *You're scaring me, Costello.*

COSTELLO: *Agggggghhhh!!! I think I'm havin' a heart attack!*
ABBOTT: *So, then you ARE ill!*

(Costello faints. Abbott picks him up and drags him offstage.)

Discussion Questions

1. Comedy teams often depend on the clash between different conceptual frames to generate conflict and ultimately humor. What are the different frames that Abbott and Costello bring to this interaction?
2. How effectively does this kind of comic dialogue work on the page, in contrast to having live performers act it out?

Writing Activity

1. Find Abbott and Costello's "Who's on First" routine in written form or ideally in video form. Write an essay analyzing how Davidson borrows from the structure of the skit to generate this blog.

A Short Bibliography on Comic Rhetoric

Ajaye, Franklin, *Comic Insights: The Art of Stand-Up Comedy* (Silman-James Press, 2002)

Allen, Steve, *How to Be Funny: Discovering the Comic You* (Prometheus Books, 1998)

Allen, Steve, *Make 'Em Laugh* (Prometheus Books, 1993)

Berger, Arthur Asa, *The Genius of the Jewish Joke* (Jason Aronson, Inc., 1997)

Cohen, Ted, *Jokes: Philosophical Thoughts on Joking Matters*, (University of Chicago Press, 1999)

Dougherty, Barry, *How to Do It Standing Up: The Friars Club Guide to Being a Comic, a Cut-Up, a Card, or a Clown* (Black Dog & Leventhal Publishers, 2002)

Halpern, Charn, Del Close, and Kim "Howard" Johnson, *Truth in Comedy: The Manual of Improvisation* (Meriwether Publishing Ltd, 1994)

Helitzer, Melvin, *Comedy Writing Secrets* (Writer's Digest Books, 1987)

Hendra, Tony, *Going Too Far* (Dolphin Doubleday, 1987)

Kachuba, John, editor, *How to Write Funny* (Writer's Digest Books, 2001)

Macks, Jon, *How to Be Funny: The One and Only Practical Guide for Every Occasion, Situation, and Disaster (no kidding)* (Simon & Schuster, 2003)

Mankoff, Robert, *The Naked Cartoonist: A New Way to Enhance Your Creativity* (Black Dog & Leventhat, 2002)

Nachman, Gerald, *Seriously Funny: The Rebel Comedians of the 1950s and 1960s* (Pantheon Books, 2003)

Paulos, John Allen, *I Think, Therefore I Laugh: The Flip Side of Philosophy* (Columbia University Press, 2000)

Provine, Robert, *Laughter: A Scientific Investigation* (Penguin 2000)

Sankey, Jay, *Zen and the Art of Stand-Up Comedy* (Routledge, 1998)
Sweet, Jeffrey, *Something Wonderful Right Away: An Oral History of The Second City and The Compass Players* (Limelight, 1978)

COMIC RHETORIC ANTHOLOGIES

Barreca, Regina, *The Signet Book of American Humor (revised edition)* (New American Library, 2004)
Jones, Richard Glyn, *This Fish Is Loaded! The Book of Bizarre and Surreal Humour* (Citadel Press, 1991)
Lesser, Raymond and Susan Wolpert, *The Best of the Best American Humor* (Three Rivers Press, 2002)
Novak, William and Moshe Waldoks, *The Big Book of New American Humor* (Harper Perennial, 1990)
Remnick, David and Henry Finder, *Fierce Pajamas: An Anthology of Humor Writing from* The New Yorker (Random House, 2001)
Richler, Mordecai, *The Best of Modern American Humor* (Knopf, 1983)
Rosen, Michael, *May Contain Nuts: A Very Loose Canon of American Humor* (Perennial Currents/HarperCollins, 2004)
Rosen, Michael, *Mirth of a Nation: The Best Contemporary Humor* (Perennial/HarperCollins, 2000)
Rosen, Michael, *More Mirth of a Nation: The Best Contemporary Humor* (Perennial/HarperCollins, 2002)
Sarrantonio, Al, *The National Lampoon Treasury of Humor* (Fireside/Simon and Schuster, 1991)
Sarrantonio, Al, *Treasury of Great Humor* (Wings Books, 1987)
Shalit, Gene, *Laughing Matters: A Celebration of American Humor* (Ballantine, 1987)
Warren, Roz, *Women's Glib: A Collection of Women's Humor* (The Crossing Press, 1991)
Warren, Roz, *Women's Glibber: State-of-the-Art Women's Humor* (The Crossing Press, 1992)

CHAPTER 1

From LAUGHTER: An Essay on the Meaning of the Comic by Henri Bergson, translated by Cloudesley Brereton and Fred Rothwell, 1911.

Excerpt from WHAT'S SO FUNNY?: The Comic Conception of Culture and Society by Murray S. Davis, pp. 11–27. © 1993 by The University of Chicago. Reprinted by permission.

"Tickling the Naked Ape," from ONLY JOKING by Jimmy Carr and Lucy Greeves, copyright © 2006 by Jimmy Carr & Go Tiger Ltd. Used by permission of Gotham Books, an imprint of Penguin Group (USA) Inc. In Canada, reprinted by permission of the Peters Fraser and Dunlop Group Limited on behalf of: Jimmy Carr.

"Relaxing the Rules of Reason" by Robin Hemley from HOW TO WRITE FUNNY: ADD HUMOR TO EVERY KIND OF WRITING, pp. 5–16. Copyright Robin Hemley. Reprinted with permission.

CHAPTER 2

"Stooping to Conquer" by Elizabeth Kolbert. Originally published in THE NEW YORKER, April 19 & 26, 2004, pp. 116–122. Reprinted with permission.

"Ridicule: An Instrument in the War on Terrorism" by J. Michael Waller from THE INSTITUTE OF WORLD POLITICS PAPERS & STUDIES, Public Diplomacy White Paper No. 7. Reprinted by permission of J. Michael Waller.

"Light Bulb Jokes: Charting an Era" by Daniel Harris. First appeared in THE NEW YORK TIMES MAGAZINE, March 23, 1997. Reprinted with permission.

CHAPTER 3

CHAPTER 4

CHAPTER 5

CHAPTER 6

CHAPTER 7